ALSO BY JAMES A. WARREN

God, War, and Providence: The Epic Struggle of Roger Williams and the Narragansett Indians Against the Puritans of New England

Giap: The General Who Defeated America in Vietnam

American Spartans: The U.S. Marines: A Combat History from Iwo Jima to Iraq

The Lions of Iwo Jima: The Story of Combat Team 28 and the Bloodiest Battle in Marine Corps History, coauthored with Major General Fred Haynes (USMC-RET)

YEAR OF THE HAWK

America's Descent into Vietnam, 1965

JAMES A. WARREN

SCRIBNER

New York   London   Toronto   Sydney   New Delhi

Scribner
An Imprint of Simon & Schuster, Inc.
1230 Avenue of the Americas
New York, NY 10020

First Scribner hardcover edition November 2021

SCRIBNER and design are registered trademarks of The Gale Group, Inc., used under license by Simon & Schuster, Inc., the publisher of this work.

For information about special discounts for bulk purchases, please contact Simon & Schuster Special Sales at 1-866-506-1949 or business@simonandschuster.com.

The Simon & Schuster Speakers Bureau can bring authors to your live event. For more information or to book an event, contact the Simon & Schuster Speakers Bureau at 1-866-248-3049 or visit our website at www.simonspeakers.com.

Interior design by Wendy Blum

Printed in Italy

1 3 5 7 9 10 8 6 4 2

Library of Congress Cataloging-in-Publication Data has been applied for.

ISBN 978-1-9821-2294-2
ISBN 978-1-9821-2296-6 (ebook)

This book is for all the Americans and Vietnamese
who fought in the Vietnam War.

CONTENTS

Part III: Looking Back

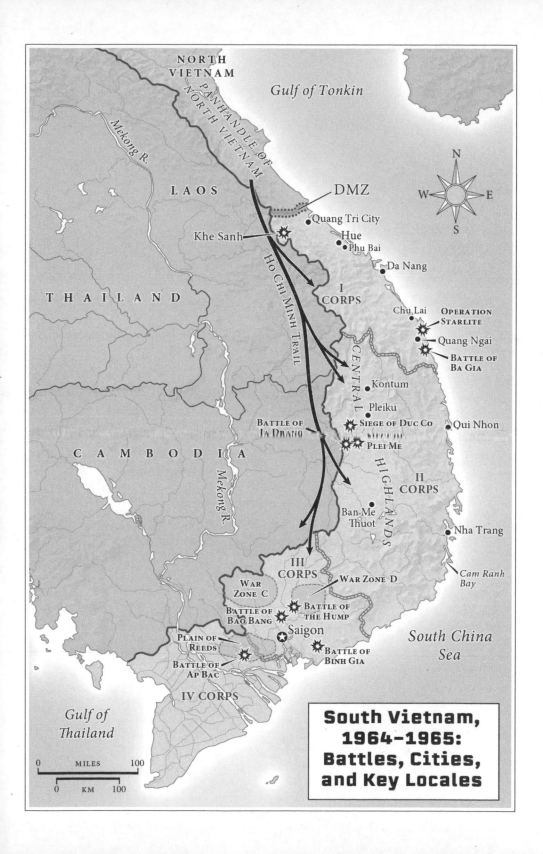

NORTH VIETNAM

Gulf of Tonkin

Mekong R.

LAOS

PANHANDLE OF NORTH VIETNAM

DMZ

Quang Tri City

Khe Sanh

Hue

Phu Bai

Da Nang

THAILAND

I CORPS

Ho Chi Minh Trail

Chu Lai

OPERATION STARLITE

CENTRAL

Quang Ngai

BATTLE OF BA GIA

Kontum

Pleiku

BATTLE OF IA DRANG

SIEGE OF DUC CO

PLEI ME

Qui Nhon

CAMBODIA

Mekong R.

HIGHLANDS

II CORPS

Ban Me Thuot

Nha Trang

III CORPS

Cam Ranh Bay

WAR ZONE C

WAR ZONE D

BATTLE OF THE HUMP

South China Sea

BATTLE OF BAO BANG

Saigon

Plain of Reeds

BATTLE OF AP BAC

BATTLE OF BINH GIA

IV CORPS

Gulf of Thailand

0 MILES 100

0 KM 100

N W E S

South Vietnam, 1964–1965: Battles, Cities, and Key Locales

YEAR
OF THE
HAWK

INTRODUCTION:
AMERICA IN 1965

In 1965, the United States of America was widely regarded as the most powerful and prosperous nation on earth. As the undisputed leader of the "Free World," the country was in the forefront of expanding the boundaries of democracy and liberty abroad. Its military power was the major bulwark against communist expansionism in Europe and Asia. The US economy, along with Americans' increasingly consumer-driven way of life, was the envy of much of the rest of the world. Indeed, the American economy that year set new records in terms of gross national product, total sales of goods, numbers of people employed, and total income. The inflation rate rose slightly to a very manageable 1.59 percent. A loaf of bread cost twenty-one cents, gasoline was thirty cents a gallon, and the average home cost $13,500—only a bit more than twice the average yearly income of $6,400.

Millions of the nation's World War II veterans and their families had already escaped the congested cities for the crabgrass frontier, the suburbs, where they lived lives of material abundance that would have astonished their parents. Millions more Americans planned to do the same, and soon. High school graduates in America were flooding into four-year colleges in unprecedented numbers, and a rising percentage of those students were women.

In 1965, there were 194 million Americans. The big movies of the year were *The Sound of Music*, a heartwarming story about a real-life children's singing group and their governess in Austria just before World War II, and *Thunderball*, a spy movie about stolen atomic bombs starring Sean Connery as the suave British secret agent James Bond. Teenagers in America were nuts about two new arrivals on department store shelves: Super Balls and skateboards. Young men were beginning to wear their hair longer than their parents liked.

The latest women's fashion craze was the miniskirt, a welcome development in the eyes of straight young men.

The American people, it's fair to say, were by and large an optimistic and confident bunch. Their republic had been tested in the annealing fires of a civil war, two world wars, a devastating depression, and most recently by the assassination of a beloved president and war hero, John F. Kennedy. The country, in short, seemed by almost any measure to be at the forefront of history. There were challenges ahead, to be sure, but the future looked bright.

That wise and judicious Puritan, Governor John Winthrop of Massachusetts, where John Kennedy had grown up, had spoken of America as early as 1630 as a "city upon a hill," a beacon of hope and light to the troubled souls of the Old World. The idea that America was somehow different, closer to God's vision of what a human society should look like than any other nation, still held firm. The notion that America was special in the eyes of God, and the eyes of ordinary human beings as well, undergirded the efforts of President Lyndon Baines Johnson's ambitious program of legislation called "the Great Society." The purpose of the program, to put it simply, was to close the gap between American ideals and the realities of American life as it was lived among the poor and disadvantaged by granting them access to better housing, jobs, health care, and schooling.

Yet beneath all the optimism and the prosperity, there were unmistakable signs of racial and social turbulence, and revolutionary change. The most important and obvious struggle grew out of Black Americans' concerted effort to obtain voting rights, equal justice under law, and access to the American dream. The effort to strip away the legal basis of segregation in the South, and integrate Blacks into a largely white society was enthusiastically embraced by an increasingly influential bastion of liberal democratic reformers—clergy, academics, students, and politicians. But millions of ordinary Americans—in the North as well as the South—saw such radical change as a threat to their own notions of propriety and good social order. They resisted change, often strenuously. Violence, often shockingly brutal violence inflicted by police as well as civilians against nonviolent protesters, was increasingly common at civil rights demonstrations. The understandable rage of the Black community in the face of this resistance manifested itself in many ways. The Reverend Martin Luther King Jr. continued to preach nonviolence to his legions of followers. Not everyone was so patient. In

August, in the Black section of Los Angeles, Watts, violence and chaos reigned for five days of riots. After it was all over, thirty-four people had been killed and $40 million worth of property destroyed.

Amid all this racial tension, there were subtle signs of an emerging "counterculture" on college campuses and in urban areas, where mostly white, middle-class students were drawn to the work of antiestablishment writers like the beat poets and novelists Ken Kesey and Jack Kerouac. These artists expressed an interest in Eastern mysticism, spiritual spontaneity, and unconventional lifestyles. Young people were drawn as well to rock and roll musicians like Elvis Presley, the Beatles, and the Rolling Stones, and to experimenting with pot and other drugs. These young Americans were increasingly critical of the complacency and materialism of mainstream consumer culture. They wanted something different, something better, something more fulfilling, though they were not yet sure exactly what it was.

As 1965 began, President Johnson and his chief advisers were increasingly preoccupied with a foreign policy crisis in a relatively small and obscure Southeast Asian nation, adjacent to the People's Republic of China. It was called Vietnam. Few Americans could have found Vietnam on a world map in early 1965, but Washington had committed itself a decade earlier to preventing a powerful communist insurgency in South Vietnam from crushing the beleaguered pro-American administration in Saigon, and uniting South Vietnam with North Vietnam under a single communist-led government.

By the end of February 1965, Lyndon Johnson had decided the only way to preserve South Vietnam's independence was to commit United States ground forces to fight against the insurgency in the South, and to conduct an air war against the North Vietnamese, who both supported and directed that insurgency. Johnson's was one of the most fateful decisions in the entire history of America, with immense implications for the future of the country, and for its vision of itself. Only six weeks after the first American ground troops arrived in Vietnam, more than twenty thousand Americans, mostly college students, gathered together for "The March on Washington to End the War in Vietnam." It was the largest antiwar demonstration in American history up until that time. There would soon be other, larger protests, as well as a veritable torrent of criticism over the Johnson administration's policies and strategies in Southeast Asia from a wide range of foreign and military policy experts. Within two years, America would find itself swept up in the vortex of a social revolution, and the Vietnam War would be at the heart of it all.

A Brief Note to the Reader

After well over a year of conducting research for a book on the Vietnam War full-time, I came to two conclusions, more or less simultaneously. The first was that a detailed exploration of the crucial decisions, strategies, and politico-military campaigns at the beginning of the American war—from late 1964 through to the early days of 1966—would reveal in a powerful way the peculiar dynamics and pathologies of the entire war, and thus illuminate one of the most amazing events in twentieth-century history: the defeat of a superpower with the world's most capable military by a revolutionary communist movement that mobilized large segments of the Vietnamese peasantry behind its cause.

The second conclusion was that the rolling barrage of events and forces at work in the war during this relatively brief time frame would best be explored not through a single, straightforward chronological narrative, but by dividing the story into three parts. Accordingly, Part I of *Year of the Hawk* focuses intensively on the crucial historical background and the "big picture" decisions and strategies developed by the adversaries from late 1964 until the end of July 1965, by which point North Vietnam and the United States had fully committed themselves to going to war with their own regular armies. The second part of the book explores the ramifications of those decisions and strategies in the key theaters of the conflict: on the ground, in the air, and in the realm of politics, on both the American and Vietnamese home fronts. Part III offers an assessment and some reflections on the meaning of the story told in Parts I and II.

PROLOGUE
STRANGE LANDING,
STRANGE WAR

0600 hours, March 8, 1965. *Four thousand yards off the coast of the city of Danang, Republic of Vietnam*

Suddenly, American marines and sailors of Amphibious Task Force 76 heard the harsh bark of an order they had been eagerly awaiting for days as they crisscrossed the South China Sea: "Land the landing force!"

Sailors scurried to their battle stations. Amphibious boat coxswains scrambled down into the well decks to man their landing craft. Feeling both anticipation and dread, marines in full combat gear lined up at their assigned positions to board the craft that would take them ashore. At long last, they were going to war. . . .

Well, not quite. The weather was sullen, overcast, and drizzling. The sea was angry. Eight-foot swells stalled the landing for well over an hour.

Around 0830, the sea swells calmed, and the 3rd Battalion of the 9th Marines—the vanguard of the 9th Marine Expeditionary Brigade under Brigadier General Frederick Karch—began to motor toward the beach in four discrete waves of amphibious tractors and landing craft from their starting point, or line of departure, several thousand yards offshore. At 0902, the first wave of olive drab–clad infantrymen reached the shoreline without incident; by 0918, all four waves of combat-ready marines were ashore in good order. The unit's tanks and artillery soon crossed the beach as well.

The first American ground troops had arrived in Vietnam, but they were hardly the first Americans to join the fight against a powerful insurgency in that country. US military advisers had deployed to the jewel in the crown of France's empire, Vietnam, in 1950. Their mission was to help the French and their Vietnamese allies fight against the forces of an independence movement led by the Communist Party of Vietnam, known as the Vietminh. Much to the shock of the entire Western world, the French had lost their war in 1954, and the communists had established dominion over all of Vietnam north of the 17th parallel, more or less bisecting the narrow, S-shaped country in half, and setting up their government in the French-built city of Hanoi.

This victory was an extraordinary accomplishment: for the first time in modern history a small, underdeveloped agricultural nation had defeated its erstwhile colonial master. Now, in March 1965, the Americans were trying to prevent the communists from extending their domain over all of Vietnam south of the 17th parallel, which meant, of course, defending another great French-designed city, Saigon, as well as the rich and fertile Mekong Delta.

United States Military Assistance Command, Vietnam (MACV for short), the top American military headquarters in the country, estimated that six thousand communist guerrillas were within striking distance of Red Beach, where the marines had come ashore. Yet not a single rifle or mortar round greeted America's sea soldiers. But the mayor of Danang, South Vietnam's second-largest city, was there to welcome the marines with a short, upbeat speech. So was "the Warlord of the North," General Nguyen Thanh Thi, a tough, no-nonsense soldier who had fought the Vietminh with the French and now commanded all South Vietnamese forces in the five provinces that comprised the Republic of Vietnam's northernmost military region.

Dozens of university students in a carefree mood were also on hand, much to the surprise of the Americans. A cluster of smiling young women approached General Karch and his command group and presented them with bright leis of local flowers. Karch had received a very different reception twenty years earlier, when he had landed on a tiny spit of volcanic rock in the western Pacific called Iwo Jima. So far, Vietnam was a strange war. It would soon get much stranger.

After these pleasantries, 3/9's marines formed up into platoons and companies on the beach for the motor march to the bustling Danang Air Base a few miles to the southeast. There, American and South Vietnamese fighter-bombers were already actively engaged in operations against communist North Vietnam (aka the Democratic Republic of Vietnam, or the DRV) and the powerful insurgency it supported in the South, bent on seizing control of South Vietnam before US forces could arrive in strength.

Around 0945, the motorized column carrying 3/9 began the short trek to the airbase. Vietnamese children lined the road, holding up signs in English and Vietnamese welcoming the Americans. That afternoon, leading elements of a second battalion of the 9th Marine Expeditionary Brigade (MEB), the 1st Battalion of the 3rd Marine Regiment, flew into the airbase at Danang. A few VC rifle rounds found their mark, penetrating the wing of one of the C-130 transports just before it touched ground. Otherwise the landing was uneventful.

Much to their chagrin, the marines had not been sent to Vietnam to take the fight to the enemy. The Joint Chiefs of Staff's landing order made that abundantly clear: "The U.S. Marine Force will not, repeat not, engage in day-to-day actions against the Viet Cong."[1] That mission, for the time being anyway, remained in the hands of General Thi's forces. Neither General William C. Westmoreland, MACV commander, nor President Johnson was prepared to commit American combat troops to offensive operations in Southeast Asia. Not yet, at least. The political and strategic implications of that decision would be enormous, for once US combat forces were in the thick of the fighting, there could be no going back. Key decision makers in Washington fully expected that American combat forces would soon be conducting such operations, but they were determined to hide their thinking from both Congress and the American people. Johnson feared that the country would not support his ambitious "Great Society" domestic reform program if the country entered a major ground war, so he presented the landing of the marines not as the first step in a new American war, but as a temporary measure to help the South Vietnamese. Technically, America was still "assisting" in the fighting.

The marines' mission was to defend the Danang Air Base, full stop. Westmoreland had every reason to believe it might well come under a major Vietcong attack. A month earlier, a daring Vietcong raid on the American airbase at Pleiku in the Central Highlands had killed nine Americans, wounded a hundred others, and damaged or destroyed more than twenty aircraft. In Saigon, political intrigue and chaos reigned, as various factions, political and military, Buddhist and Catholic, vied for power and influence. The capital was roiling in such disarray and intrigue that some observers questioned whether anyone was truly running the government. No one, not even the American ambassador in Saigon, General Maxwell Taylor, was really sure who was in charge, so prevalent were coups and internal government reshuffles. The Vietcong had stepped up the number and intensity of their attacks across the country. At the same time, the communists' political operatives, called cadres, were enjoying unprecedented success in extending their shadow government—the highly resilient political infrastructure of the National Liberation Front (NLF)—across large swaths of the countryside. The Front was the successor organization to the Vietminh front that had defeated the French. It controlled both the political and military forces of the insurgency in South Vietnam.

Thus, fatalism, a sense of resignation, had begun to take hold within the political and military elite of South Vietnam. LBJ's senior national security adviser, a brilliant former Harvard dean named McGeorge Bundy, had toured Vietnam in early February on a special fact-finding mission, and reported back to the president: "The situation is deteriorating, and without new U.S. action, defeat appears inevitable. . . . There is still time, but not much."[2]

PART I

BACKSTORY, CRUCIAL DECISIONS, AND STRATEGIES

CHAPTER 1

VIETNAM'S STRUGGLE AGAINST FRENCH COLONIALISM

World War II dealt a fatal blow to European colonialism by awakening passionate yearnings among the peoples of Asia and Africa to shape their own destinies, free from foreign domination. Americans and their allies envisaged the war against the Axis powers as a titanic struggle of freedom and light against the forces of oppression and darkness. By signing the Atlantic Charter in 1941, Franklin Roosevelt and Winston Churchill committed their nations to shaping a postwar world according to the principles of self-determination, the rule of law, and respect for human rights. All peoples of the world, the charter declared, had a right to govern their own affairs free from outside interference. The implicit message was that European empires would be dismantled after the war, yet it was nonetheless widely believed in the West that the path to independence in each colony should be a deliberate one, guided by the helping hand of the colonial power.

In the immediate aftermath of World War II, however, the colonial powers showed considerable reluctance to relinquish their control over countries they had long exploited for natural resources, cheap labor, and trade. British, Dutch, and French efforts to retain control of their imperial possessions were bound to clash with the rising political expectations of the colonized peoples. They clashed dramatically in the ancient Indo-Chinese nation of Vietnam, which had been colonized by France in the second half of the nineteenth century. French statesmen took the view that the restoration of their Indochina empire was necessary to restore French honor after its humiliating defeat at the hands of the Germans, and entirely appropriate, given France's status as both a great civilization and a world power. Vietnam was the epicenter of a French empire that comprised a significant portion of North Africa and all of Indochina—Laos, Cambodia, and Vietnam.

Politically active Vietnamese thought otherwise. By 1945, a political front organization led by a visionary nationalist who adopted the name Ho Chi Minh—"He Who Enlightens" in Vietnamese—had successfully mobilized several million people in a quest to challenge France's inevitable effort to reassert dominance over the entire country as soon as its Japanese occupiers surrendered to the Allies. The struggle between France, the colonial masters of all of Vietnam since the 1880s, and the Vietnamese nationalists turned out to be extraordinarily complex, protracted, and violent. The First Indochina War, known as the Anti-French Resistance War by the Vietnamese, was fought between 1946 and 1954. It resulted in the partition of Vietnam into a communist state north of the 17th parallel, the Democratic Republic of Vietnam governed by Ho Chi Minh's political front, and a pro-Western South Vietnam, the Republic of Vietnam. Well before the First Indochina War ended, the conflict developed serious Cold War ramifications, leading slowly but surely to America's war in Indochina in the 1960s and early 1970s.

Vietnam, and the Vietnamese

Vietnam is one of the oldest nations on earth. Its people have a long and tumultuous history of resistance to foreign domination. Anthropologists tell us that the Viets, a people of Mongolian origin, first settled in the "cradle of Vietnamese civilization," the Red River Valley, sometime around 700 BCE. Recorded Vietnamese history begins in 208 BCE, when Trieu Da, a rebel Chinese general, established an independent kingdom that stretched from the mountains of contemporary northern Vietnam down to the contemporary city of Danang. It was called Dai Viet.

In 111 BCE, China conquered Dai Viet, and the Chinese ruled over the Vietnamese for almost a thousand years, introducing them to the plow, rice cultivation, and draft animals, as well as Confucian ideas of enlightened government and social ethics. The Viets adapted the Chinese language for official purposes, and Chinese remained the idiom for the Vietnamese ruling and administrative class up through the nineteenth century. The ethnically distinct Vietnamese adopted many Chinese institutions and ideas as their own, but they proved stubbornly resistant to assimilation. The family and the village have always been the main social institutions of the Vietnamese. Rural Vietnamese people have an ancient tradition of running their own local affairs—a tradition borne out in the well-known saying that "the emperor's rule halts at the village gate." During the time of China's rule, the Vietnamese developed a unique spiritual identity, a richly textured blend of indigenous ancestor worship, Buddhism, which came to Vietnam in the fifth century via Silk Road traders, and Confucianism. Nearly a thousand years of Chinese domination sharpened their sense of being a distinct people with their own history, culture, and set of myths.

The Trung sisters, two of Vietnam's most revered patriots, led the first of many revolts against Chinese authority, vanquishing their conquerors in 40 CE, and briefly establishing an independent kingdom under their rule. When the Trungs were defeated by another Chinese army just three years later, they committed suicide rather than submit once again to domination by their powerful neighbors to the north. Many other insurrections followed. "Resistance broke out often when the Chinese court pursued assimilationist policies or tried to impose direct rule instead of remembering the advantages of accommodation, flexibility, and indirect rule," writes Christopher Goscha, a leading historian of the Vietnamese people.[1]

Finally, in 939 CE, the Vietnamese won back their independence by luring a Chinese fleet into a river laden with iron-tipped spikes, destroying or stranding most of the ships. Over the next millennia, the Vietnamese were divided into several polities ruled by regional warlords. The warlord families vied to extend their power over one another, but nonetheless managed to unite their forces to fend off yet another series of Chinese incursions, as well as no less than three invasions by the Mongol Kublai Khan's armies in the thirteenth century.

In 1406, Ming dynasty armies, the most powerful in Asia, briefly reestablished Chinese hegemony over the Vietnamese. Emperor Le Loi, another legendary hero who looms large in the Vietnamese past, forged the guerrilla forces of a coterie of warlords into a powerful army and drove the Chinese out of Vietnam in 1427, this time for good, but the Vietnamese borrowed the Ming dynasty's highly efficient system of government administration, as well as its military organization and technology, to build a more formidable Vietnamese state.

Given the Vietnamese people's resistance to the Chinese and the Mongols across more than one thousand years, it is hardly surprising that war occupies a crucial place in their collective consciousness today, as it has for centuries. The Vietnamese think of themselves as an indomitable people, who again and again have employed guile, patience, and guerrilla warfare to defeat enemies much more powerful than themselves. Having defeated the forces of no less than four empires—the Chinese, the Mongols, the French, and the Americans—they have good reason to think so. Not for nothing have the Vietnamese been called the "Prussians of Southeast Asia."

By 1800, Vietnam had developed into one of the most dynamic societies in all of Asia. The Vietnamese people had completed their "Great March South"— the Vietnamese version of America's manifest destiny—pushing down into the narrow neck of land south of the Red River Delta, along the South China Sea, and then into the Mekong Delta as far south as the Ca Mau Peninsula, conquering the ancient kingdoms of Champa and Angkor. In 1802, Vietnam was at last unified into one polity by Emperor Gia Long of the Nguyen dynasty, and its territory for the first time took on the S-like shape the country possesses today.

But even a unified Vietnam in the nineteenth century was no match for an industrialized Western power like France, bent on expanding its imperial presence in both Asia and Africa. Religion and commerce went hand in hand, as they so often did in the age of European colonization. The French established a Catholic diocese on the central coast of Vietnam in 1846, and began an energetic program of missionary work. When the local population rejected Catholicism and began to persecute priests and converts, the French launched a methodical but ruthless campaign of conquest under the guise of "civilizing and Christianizing" the locals. It was called *mission civilisatrice*.

Gradually, France established control over Vietnam's three geographical regions of Cochinchina, including the highly populated, fertile Mekong Delta in the south; Annam in the narrow center; and Tonkin, including the bustling Red River Delta, in the north. By 1880, with the help of a small class of wealthy

Vietnamese landowners, France ruled over all of Vietnam with an iron hand, stripping the country of rubber, tin, and rice for the benefit of the mother country.

The French might have governed Vietnam indirectly, working through Vietnamese people and institutions, as the British would do in India. Instead, they imposed direct rule of the harshest sort. Workers on large rubber plantations and in coal mines lived in wretched conditions as virtual slaves, and were paid a pittance. Peasants were stripped of their land and forced to pay as much as 60 percent of their crops as rent. While rice production quadrupled between 1880 and 1930, per capita consumption among the peasantry declined precipitously. A British visitor to Vietnam remarked that the French in Indochina adopted an attitude toward the natives "identical with that of any of the old slave-owning aristocracies. It is one of utter contempt, without which effective exploitation would probably be impossible."[2]

The Vietnamese stubbornly resisted. As early as 1862, the French commander of Cochinchina reported, "We have enormous difficulties in enforcing our authority. . . . Rebel bands disturb the country everywhere. They appear from nowhere in large numbers, destroy everything and then disappear into nowhere."[3]

Eighty percent of Vietnamese had some degree of literacy before French colonization; by 1939 only 15 percent of the country's children were in school at all. The Vietnamese intelligentsia, most of whom had attended French schools designed primarily to educate the children of the French civil service, were deeply frustrated by their lack of opportunity for advancement. Political expression by Vietnamese was for all intents and purposes banned.

Vietnamese Nationalism, Ho Chi Minh, and World War II

The Imperial Court at Hue, seat of the Vietnamese emperor, was divided as to how to respond to French repression and domination. Some officials favored heading to the hills to conduct a guerrilla warfare campaign. Others thought it best to try to work within the French system to implement political and economic reform. Little progress was made in the first two decades of the twentieth century, in part because Vietnamese reformers couldn't agree on an avenue of approach to the problem.

In the 1930s, many disgruntled members of the small, educated class of Vietnamese became radicalized, joining underground independence movements. These groups disagreed on many things, but they were united in the belief that the "reform from within" approach was an exercise in futility. The most successful of the nationalist organizations was the Indochinese Communist Party, which was founded in 1930. The French secret police in Vietnam, the Sûreté, devoted a great deal of effort to getting intelligence on the group's members and repressing its activities because it clearly posed the greatest threat to the status quo. The party staged several rebellions and demonstrations, all of which were put down with brute force. Each incident of repression only inspired greater resistance. Political prisoners filled the jails, with no recourse to justice.

World War II broke out in 1939. After France surrendered to Germany in June 1940, the Japanese established control over most of Southeast Asia, including Vietnam. This development, in and of itself, challenged long-accepted ideas of European superiority and delegitimized France's position within Vietnam in the eyes of most of the population. Despite their slogan of "Asia for the Asians," the Japanese were utterly indifferent to the Vietnamese's desire for independence. While they occupied the urban centers and plundered the country's natural resources for their war effort, they were content to let a weak and demoralized Vichy French administration maintain law and order in the countryside—or attempt to do so.

Using highly effective communist mobilization and organizational techniques, Ho Chi Minh and a coterie of his followers established a broad political front movement of various parties and social associations, in a cave near the village of Pac Bo, deep in the mountains of northern Vietnam, in May 1941. It was called Viet Nam Doc Lap Dong Minh Hoi—the League for the Independence of Vietnam, or Vietminh, for short. Ho's objective was to gather up as many different nationalist groups and parties as possible under clandestine communist leadership, mobilize and politicize the peasantry that constituted about 90 percent of Vietnam's population, and wrest the nation from its Japanese and French occupiers.

The Vietminh proved to be as resilient and effective as any nationalist movement in the colonized world at that time. The striking success of the organization in establishing itself as the leading voice of Vietnamese nationalism was due in large part to the extraordinary charisma and political savvy of Uncle Ho, as he was called affectionately by a steadily mushrooming number of adherents. Ho correctly anticipated the trajectory of the world war in Asia, and developed with the help of his chief lieutenants, Vo Nguyen Giap and Truong Chinh, an ingenious politico-military strategy to take advantage of rapidly changing circumstances. Today, Ho Chi Minh is widely regarded as one of the towering political figures in twentieth-century history.

Just who was this man?

He was born Nguyen Tat Thanh in 1890 and grew up in Nghe An Province in north-central Vietnam, long a hotbed of resistance to French rule. The son of a poor Confucian scholar, Ho immersed himself in the classical Chinese texts with the intention of joining the civil service. After studying for two years at the prestigious Quoc Hoc school at Hue, he was expelled for lending support to peasant demonstrations against high taxes and forced labor. Before he was twenty, Ho had found his calling as a political organizer and patriot, with an unyielding commitment to liberating his country from the shackles of French oppression.

Between 1911 and 1941, Ho lived in exile from his country, wandering the world. He ventured by turns to Paris, London, Brooklyn, Moscow, and several cities in China, supporting himself as a laborer, pastry chef, photo retoucher, and, finally, as a highly successful agent of communist revolution. All the while, he deepened his knowledge of radical anticolonial politics and built up a vast network of contacts among Vietnamese expatriates, as well as prominent socialists and communists in Asia and Europe. He also read deeply in French and American history, and learned a great deal about democratic ideals and politics. After founding an association of Vietnamese nationalists in Paris, the first of perhaps a dozen organizations he was to found and deftly manipulate to achieve his own ends, he presented a petition to the Allies at Versailles in 1919, calling for self-determination for the Vietnamese people. The great powers ignored the petition, but he became a hero to Asian patriots of many stripes for his passionate commitment to liberation movements in colonial societies.

In the summer of 1920, Ho had an epiphany while reading Lenin's "Theses on the National and Colonial Questions" in his Paris apartment. Lenin argued

that, contrary to traditional Marxism, capitalist-imperialist power in agrarian nations could only be overthrown by organizing and educating the peasantry, and
linking their struggle with that of the worldwide proletariat. "What emotion,
enthusiasm, clear-sightedness and confidence this pamphlet instilled in me!" he
recalled years afterward. "I was overjoyed to tears. Though sitting alone in my
room, I shouted aloud as if addressing a large crowd: 'Dear martyrs, compatriots!
This is what we need! This is the path to liberation!'"[4]

After attending a school for revolutionaries in Moscow, Ho was involved
in various kinds of organizing for the Party. He helped found the Indochinese
Communist Party in 1930, and went on to organize and train a group of patriotic
Vietnamese exiles in Canton, China. Ho was imprisoned briefly by both the
British in Hong Kong and the Chinese for subversive political activities. Despite
Ho's physical absence from his country, he remained a pivotal figure in the ICP
leadership throughout the decade.

Not long after the Japanese seized control over Vietnam in 1940, Ho crossed
from China into northern Vietnam for the first time in thirty years and founded
the Vietminh. Now fifty years old, Ho seamlessly integrated communist political
and organizational doctrine with his own brand of nationalism and revolutionary
ethics, drawing on the Confucian values of thrift, modesty, patience, respect for
learning, and discipline. Ho's asceticism contrasted sharply with the arrogance
and corruption that swirled around the French colonial administration. While
rival Vietnamese nationalist leaders quarreled constantly over platforms and
minute questions of ideology and method, Ho displayed a rare gift for mediating
conflicts within his own party, and for establishing temporary alliances with
rivals to accomplish short-term Vietminh goals.

Alone among Vietnamese nationalist parties, the Vietminh recognized the
latent power of the peasantry, and sought to marshal that strength in the fight
for independence. Ho has often been described as an organizational genius by
serious students of history for a good reason. He was. Ho had an almost mystical
ability to instill confidence and commitment in others. One revolutionary who
met Ho before World War II spoke for many when he remarked that this wisp
of a man possessed an "imperturbable dignity that enveloped him as though it
were a garment. He conveyed a sense of inner strength and generosity of spirit
that impacted upon me with the force of a blow."[5]

Although Ho Chi Minh was a Moscow-trained revolutionary, he was no rigid ideologue. In a long career as revolutionary statesman, he exhibited remarkable pragmatism and flexibility. Quite a number of hard-core communists in the Soviet Union and China suspected the Vietnamese revolutionary was a nationalist first and a communist second. Today, this is a view widely shared among Western historians and biographers. One of the many tragedies of the American war in Southeast Asia is that American Cold War statesmen, with very few exceptions, thought Ho and his Vietnamese revolution were ultimately under the control of the Chinese, the Russians, or both. Ho proved ready and willing to work cooperatively with powers hostile to communism, including France and the United States, to achieve his dream of Vietnamese independence. "Ho's desire to unify all Vietnamese patriots into one movement," writes historian Sophie Quinn-Judge, "was far stronger than his attachment to Communist dogma; he preferred peaceful political transformation to revolutionary violence."[6]

This frail-looking, modest man with bright, piercing eyes was invariably kitted out in a plain khaki uniform and sandals. He loved to talk to ordinary Vietnamese people, especially children. His air of gentleness and good humor was an indispensable asset to the Independence movement. It won millions of followers in Vietnam, and millions of sympathizers in the world at large. But Uncle Ho's gentle personal demeanor belied his utter ruthlessness when it came to achieving the revolution's political and military objectives. Like his close lieutenants, Ho was more than willing to sacrifice the lives of millions of his countrymen for the great cause. He also condoned widespread torture and assassination in the pursuit of revolutionary objectives, but never explicitly. Giap, the commander in chief of the Vietminh's army, was much more direct and candid when it came to the use of revolutionary violence. "Every minute, hundreds of thousands of people die upon this earth," he said. "The life or death of a hundred, a thousand, tens of thousands of human beings, even our compatriots, means little."[7]

During the Japanese occupation, from 1940 to 1945, the power vacuum in the countryside presented the Vietminh with a golden opportunity to build a revolutionary political infrastructure among the peasantry, and a guerrilla army to defend and expand the shadow political apparatus. In May 1945, American agents serving with the OSS arrived at Ho's base camp deep in a cave near Pac

Bo, just two miles from the Chinese border. They agreed to exchange small arms and ammunition for intelligence on Japanese forces and downed American flyers. Ho would cleverly exploit this informal "alliance" with the powerful Americans to recruit numerous guerrilla bands and rival political operatives into the Vietminh in the crucial months ahead. Just days after the Japanese surrendered to the Allies in August 1945, the Vietminh army, a small but potent force of five thousand troops that General Giap had trained rigorously deep in the hinterlands of northern Vietnam, was able to seize power in Hanoi and in many district and provincial capitals.

This was the famous "August Revolution" still celebrated in Vietnam today. Before a jubilant crowd of tens of thousands in Hanoi's Ba Dinh Square, Ho declared Vietnamese independence on September 2, 1945, quoting the opening lines in America's Declaration of Independence in the process. A handful of American army officers joined Giap in the reviewing stand, and a Vietminh band even played "The Star-Spangled Banner." It was a classic Ho maneuver. He was trying to lay a foundation for obtaining American support for the revolution he led. Ho also sought to mask the Vietminh's commitment to world communism to the Americans, to other Vietnamese, and to the world at large. He stressed that the organization was first and foremost a vehicle for Vietnamese independence and "democratic" reforms, not communist revolution in its conventional meaning, and thus worthy of American support.

Postwar Friction with France, and the Intrusion of the Cold War

In October 1945, two months after the Japanese surrendered, a powerful French Expeditionary Force Corps (FEC) of twenty-five thousand troops landed in Saigon, determined to reassert French control over all of Indochina. The French governor-general, Georges Thierry d'Argenlieu, was a deeply conservative former priest who seemed to be living in an earlier century. He was disdainful of the Vietminh upstarts, and refused to recognize their authority. It soon became clear that the French were prepared to grant the Vietnamese a "modicum of self-government," writes historian Fredrik Logevall, but only to a local "administration willing to cooperate with the French on French terms."[8] Independence in any truly meaningful sense of the term was not a live option.

Ho continued to look to the United States for support for months after the end of World War II, knowing that President Roosevelt, at least, had been determined to resist France's return to power in Indochina on the grounds that French rule had left the people there in considerably worse shape than they had been before they were colonized. FDR had wanted Vietnam to be governed by an international trusteeship as it prepared for full independence.

But Roosevelt died in April 1945. His successor, Harry Truman, increasingly alarmed by the Soviets' determination to dominate Eastern and Central Europe, needed France's support for an American-led anti-Soviet alliance in Europe. So he did not challenge France's plan to retain its Indochina colonies. Ho Chi Minh wrote several letters to Truman. Truman never wrote back, perhaps because, as Secretary of State George C. Marshall wrote, the United States at this critical early stage of the Cold War simply could not "afford to assume that Ho is anything but Moscow directed."[9]

After a year of tortuous negotiations, power sharing, and several violent clashes between Vietminh and French forces, only one thing was clear: the Vietminh and the French had irreconcilable ideas about Vietnam's future. Full-scale war broke out between the two adversaries in December 1946.

Although officially remaining neutral in the early years of the conflict between France and its colony, Washington did affirm France's right to return to Vietnam, and even provided indirect military support to its war there. (The US provided military aid for France's forces in Europe, but France redirected that aid to Indochina.)

The Vietminh's Protracted War Strategy

The Vietminh leadership had thought long and hard about how a poor, agricultural country with a peasant army might fight and win a war against an industrialized, Western democracy like France. Ho and Giap opted to fight the war according to fellow communist Mao Zedong's three-stage model of protracted warfare, albeit with certain refinements in light of local traditions and conditions, devised mainly by General Giap. In stage one, the Vietminh would be on the strategic defensive. Base areas would be built both as training grounds for a conventional army and sanctuaries for guerrilla forces; mobilization by thousands of political cadres would lay the groundwork for mass recruiting and the development of intelligence networks and a shadow government in the countryside. Meanwhile, guerrilla units could harass French installations and lines of communications.

In stage two, the equilibrium stage, the French would reach their peak military strength, and consolidate their hold on the cities and towns. Simultaneously, the Vietminh would gradually shift from the defensive to the offensive on both the political and military fronts. The communists would begin to deploy their regular army in conjunction with guerrilla operations against French columns and isolated garrisons in powerful hit-and-run attacks. The French people, deeply ambivalent about the war from the outset, would begin to lose heart as the struggle dragged on inconclusively.

In stage three, the "counteroffensive," regular Vietminh divisions of ten thousand men would engage in conventional campaigns, while widespread guerrilla attacks forced the FEC to remain widely dispersed to defend government centers and military installations—and thus vulnerable to attack. By this point, after several years of intense political mobilization, the countryside would be largely under Vietminh control. The FEC would be demoralized. Ultimately, military setbacks and the political power of the masses in the countryside would force the French government to withdraw from Vietnam entirely. Ho, Giap, and the other senior Vietminh leaders were convinced that external factors, especially the growing strength of Mao's army in China, the rise of anti-colonial sentiment worldwide, and the likely effect of prolonged warfare on the French public's will to continue the fight, would determine the outcome of the conflict.

The First Indochina War

The grueling and bitter First Indochina War (1946–1954) followed the three-stage path envisaged by the communist revolutionaries, for the most part. For the first four years of the war, the conflict took the form of a low-intensity insurgency as the Vietminh concentrated on political mobilization of the villages, military training in the remote northern mountains, and small-unit guerrilla raids on remote French installations. Deep in the Viet Bac—the Vietminh forces' primary base area centered on Cao Bang Province near the Chinese border—Giap built up a highly disciplined and spartan light infantry army of sixty thousand men in six divisions.

The Soviets' acquisition of the atomic bomb in August 1949 and Mao's ascent to power just two months later in China expanded and intensified the global Cold War, and internationalized the conflict in Vietnam. Taken together, these events "appeared to shift the global balance of power against the United States, and . . . created the impression that communism was on the move, and the West increasingly on the defensive."[10] Soon, an obscure, alcoholic senator from Wisconsin named Joe McCarthy was drumming up fears among the American people that communist agents in the US government had "lost" China, and that monolithic world communism was on the verge of vast conquests because of subversion from within, particularly within the US State Department. The Truman administration was "soft" on communism and infested with communist spies, said McCarthy. More catastrophic Cold War setbacks were just around the corner, unless America took drastic action, and fast. One result of McCarthyism was a purge of the State Department's "old hands" on the Asian desk, leaving Washington perilously thin on expertise in matters relating to both China and Southeast Asia.

The Truman administration decided in March of 1950 to provide both military and economic aid to the French in their war against the Vietminh. Truman justified this support under the new American national security doctrine widely known as containment. The doctrine had gained an influential following within the government in 1946, as Stalin's "iron curtain" descended on Eastern Europe. Its primary exponent was a brilliant Sovietologist in the State Department who wrote in clear, sculpted prose, George F. Kennan.

In the July 1947 issue of the leading international affairs journal, *Foreign Affairs*, Kennan traced the origins of the Soviet Union's deep-seated insecurity and expansionism to Russia's czarist history: the Russians had gradually taken over neighboring states in order to diminish opportunities for invasion by Western powers. Stalin could justify both his domestic repression and his domination of Eastern Europe as a necessary response to Western efforts to encircle the Soviet state. Security for Moscow came in the form of territorial expansion into Eastern

Europe, and elsewhere. The Kremlin's political action, he wrote, "is a fluid stream which moves constantly, wherever it is permitted to move, toward a given goal. Its main concern is that it has filled every nook and cranny available to it in the basin of world power."[11] Thus, American foreign policy should be centered on "the adroit and vigilant application of counter-force at a series of constantly shifting geographical and political points, corresponding to the shifts and maneuvers of Soviet policy."[12] The United States and its allies, said Kennan, must use whatever tools available—diplomatic, economic, military, spiritual—to contain the spread of communism in strategically important places around the globe.

The decision to back France's war against the Vietminh with money and military advisers grew out of a sweeping reassessment of national security policy in light of recent communist advances. The new policy was encapsulated in National Security Council Memorandum 68, a top-secret policy document approved on April 7, 1950, by President Truman. NSC-68 significantly militarized American foreign policy. It called for tripling the defense budget and vast increases in aid to allies in order to meet the menacing challenge of communist expansion in Asia as well as Europe. The sense of foreboding and crisis that permeated the thinking of American policy makers at the time is evident in both the substance and tone of the memo: "The assault on free institutions is worldwide now . . . and a defeat for free institutions anywhere is a defeat everywhere."[13]

Kennan had advocated the use of *military* means to contain communist expansion only in places where the United States had a vital interest. Vietnam, as Kennan saw it, did not fit the bill. In and of itself, Vietnam had no strategic importance, and taking a military stand there, he felt, might well constrict progress in coming to a workable modus operandi with the Soviet Union and China. Unfortunately, the Truman administration was caught up in the general sense of fear that gripped the entire nation, and Truman's secretary of state, Dean Acheson, marginalized Kennan's views within the State Department. George Kennan soon left government and went on to become one of the nation's most articulate critics of a containment policy that he, more than anyone else, had devised.

Two months after NSC-68 was signed, another crisis emerged in the Cold War that would exert a strong influence on the way Truman and his successors dealt with Vietnam. On June 25, 1950, communist North Korea invaded South Korea with a powerful, heavily armored force, captured Seoul, and came within a hair's breadth of driving the unprepared American and South Korean forces off the peninsula. The consensus in the West at the time was that Stalin had green-lighted the invasion. (He had not.) A UN task force led by General Douglas MacArthur, consisting primarily of the US 1st Marine Division, made an exceedingly risky amphibious landing behind the communist lines at Inchon in September, and crushed the North Koreans. It was one of the most dramatic reversals in the history of warfare. By early November, two UN armies pushed deep into North Korea toward China, one on each side of the Taebaek Mountains that formed the spine of the Korean peninsula. As the UN armies pushed north deeper and deeper into North Korea, three hundred thousand Chinese "volunteers" crossed the border with North Korea and attacked UN forces, sending them reeling back south. Hard fighting continued in Korea until July 1953, when an armistice restored the border between the two Koreas where it had been before the North Korean invasion.

By the time the Chinese joined the fray in Korea in November 1950, Beijing had been providing substantial military aid and advice to the Vietminh for several months. A Chinese Military Advisory Group consisting of some of the best officers in the People's Liberation Army began to work with Giap to expand and modernize his army. Since Indonesia, Malaya, and Burma were also in the grips of communist-inspired insurgencies at that time, the idea took hold in American foreign policy circles that the Chinese were deeply committed to orchestrating communist revolutions in Asia whenever and wherever they could do so. This belief hardened in the age of McCarthyism, and lingered on as an unshakable article of faith for a great many influential people in the US foreign policy establishment through the mid-1960s. We now know that Chinese rhetoric was a great deal more militant than Chinese policy, but the American foreign policy establishment tended to believe the talk, in large measure because of the shock of the PRC's entrance into the Korean War.

Giap Goes on the Offensive

Equipped with heavy weapons, motor transport, and thousands of tons of war matériel from Communist China, Giap went on the offensive against French forces. In the fall of 1950, his army wiped out several French columns along

Route Coloniale 4, deep in northern Vietnam, and forced the evacuation of a string of French forts there. This spectacular and unexpected victory made worldwide headlines. As Bernard Fall, the leading Western authority on modern Vietnam at the time put it, "When the smoke cleared, the French had suffered their greatest colonial defeat since Montcalm at Quebec. They had lost 6,000 troops, 13 artillery pieces and 125 mortars, 450 trucks and three armored platoons, 940 machine guns . . . and more than 8,000 rifles. Their abandoned stocks alone sufficed for the equipment of a whole additional Viet-Minh division."[14] But the shift to stage three operations turned out to be premature, as the Vietminh were badly defeated in a series of conventional battles in 1951. So they simply reverted to stage two operations, and stepped up their (already extensive) indoctrination efforts of both the population and the army to rebuild strength and confidence.

In late 1952 and 1953, the Vietminh again took the offensive, this time against French forces in Laos, and against isolated French outposts outside the Red River Delta in Tonkin. Here Giap established himself as a master strategist and logistician, as the French were routed in the Battle of Hoa Binh, and unable to halt a Vietminh drive deep into Laos that threatened its capital. French morale in the field and at home plummeted, and growing numbers of politicians on the left of the political spectrum in Paris began to call for France to pull out of *la sale guerre*—the dirty war.

As the conflict entered its final year, Giap, who had learned his trade exclusively from books and in the bush, had shown audacity and flexibility, as well as a striking ability to control the momentum of a war France's best generals had anticipated winning over the course of a year or two. In the fall of 1953, in the mountains of northwest Vietnam near a strategic road junction leading to both China and Laos, the French established a fortified airbase manned by fifteen thousand troops, including elite paratrooper and Foreign Legion units. The base was called Dien Bien Phu.

The FEC command hoped to lure Giap's main force divisions into a set-piece battle there and, by destroying the bulk of his army with superior artillery and airpower, bring an end to the war. The senior leadership of the Vietminh decided to accept the challenge. By the time the last of Giap's divisions had marched into the hills surrounding Dien Bien Phu in early March 1954, his army had completed one of the most impressive logistical accomplishments in the history of military logistics. It had positioned five divisions of infantry and more than 150 heavy artillery pieces in the mountains ringing the French fortress and cut off all roads leading to the valley. The French garrison would have to be re-supplied and reinforced exclusively by air. Giap and his engineers had mobilized more than a hundred thousand peasants from the countryside, many of them women, to construct a vast logistical network from southern China to the main People's Army of Vietnam (PAVN) bases in central Tonkin, and then on to the very edge of the valley of Dien Bien Phu. And they had done all this while under periodic bombardment by French airpower.

Giap's weaponry included lethal 105 mm cannons, many of them captured from the United States by China during the Korean War, and came down from southern China via truck as far as Na Nham, six miles from the rim of the valley. Moving these four-thousand-pound guns from Na Nham to their casemates in the rocky hills surrounding the French base proved to be a feat of human endurance seldom rivaled in modern war. The guns had to be hauled over newly cut mountain trails. Vietminh officer Tran Do recalled that "on ascents, hundreds of men dragged the guns on long ropes, with a winch on the crest to prevent them from slipping. The descents were much tougher, the guns so much heavier, the tracks twisting and turning. Gun crews steered and chocked their pieces, while infantry manned the ropes and winches. It became the work of a whole torchlit night to move a gun five hundred or a thousand yards" by one-hundred-man teams using oxen, block and tackles, and ropes.[15]

From March 13 until May 7, the Vietminh conducted a relentless series of assaults on the French, inflicting—and taking—horrendous casualties in the process. One by one, the eight major strongpoints of the French fortress were obliterated. The monsoon rains came to the valley in April, flooding the dilapidated French tunnels and bunkers. The FEC was low on ammunition, fighting on half rations, and hanging on by a thread. The end came on May 7, when a Vietminh assault team overwhelmed the last French defenders, burst into the command bunker, and took the French commander prisoner. All resistance ceased. French casualties totaled 1,600 dead and 4,800 wounded. The Vietminh lost almost 8,000 killed and 15,000 wounded. Of the 8,000 FEC prisoners of war taken after the battle, fewer than half would return to France alive.

An American Dilemma
and the Geneva Accords

Until the very last days of this terrible battle, Paris held out hope that the United States would intervene with massive airpower, perhaps even tactical nuclear weapons, to save France from a defeat that President Dwight D. Eisenhower well knew was likely to bring down the government in Paris and lead France to jettison its colonial empire in Indochina all of a piece. The United States, which had bankrolled France's war against communism in Indochina to the tune of $2.5 billion between 1950 and 1954, found itself on the horns of a dilemma. Eisenhower was deeply troubled by the Cold War ramifications of a French exit from Southeast Asia and a communist government in Vietnam, but he was also dead set against unilateral American intervention on the grounds that it would taint the United States with the stigma of French colonialism, thus damaging American prestige not only in Indochina, but throughout the developing world.

Britain, America's staunchest ally, was adamant in its refusal to participate in a multilateral relief force. The Korean War had ended less than a year earlier. Britain lacked the resources or the political inclination to involve itself in another land war in Asia. Besides, the British failed to see why the Americans felt it so important to prevent Vietnam from falling to the communists. It seemed a sideshow in the Cold War best left alone by outsiders. In the end, President Eisenhower declined to intervene.

For all intents and purposes, the fall of Dien Bien Phu brought the French Indochina War to an end. A new socialist government assumed power in France with the unambiguous intention of securing peace at the Geneva Conference, already underway as the guns fell silent at Dien Bien Phu. Flush from its spectacular victory in northwest Vietnam, the Vietminh delegation at Geneva had high hopes for a favorable negotiated settlement. However, because both the Soviet Union and the People's Republic of China were anxious to court better relations with France and the United States for complicated geopolitical reasons of their own, the Vietnamese communists were pressured by their allies into agreeing to terms far less generous than they had hoped for, given the strength of their position on the battlefield.

Vietnam was temporarily partitioned into two states. The Democratic

Republic of Vietnam (the DRV, or North Vietnam), north of the 17th parallel, with its capital in Hanoi, was governed by Ho Chi Minh's Communist Party of Vietnam. A pro-Western state, soon to be known as the Republic of Vietnam (the GVN, or South Vietnam), with its capital in Saigon, was established under Emperor Bao Dai in the south. A vaguely worded Geneva declaration, left unsigned by Bao Dai or the United States, called for free elections to unite the country within two years under one government.

The Geneva Accords didn't so much establish a lasting peace in Vietnam as set the stage for renewed warfare. Just a few months after the diplomats had departed from Geneva, Hanoi sent orders to ten thousand clandestine Vietminh operatives who remained in South Vietnam (in violation of the Geneva Accords) to begin a political agitation and subversion campaign against the South Vietnamese government. Meanwhile, the National Security Council in Washington called for the use of "all available means" to undermine the communist regime in Hanoi, and "to make every possible effort . . . to maintain a friendly noncommunist government in South Vietnam and to prevent a Communist victory through all-Vietnam elections."[16] As 1954 drew to a close, a CIA team under counterinsurgency guru Colonel Edward Lansdale implemented a decidedly ineffective clandestine subversion program against Ho Chi Minh's government in North Vietnam. The Americans had taken up the reins of the anti-communist crusade from the French in Indochina.

CHAPTER 2
THE ORIGINS OF AMERICA'S WAR

America's war in Vietnam had an unusually complicated and protracted gestation period. The origins of the conflict lie in the unyielding commitment of both Hanoi and Washington to establish a society in their own image in South Vietnam. Hanoi viewed the reunification of Vietnam under its authority as a sacred mission, the fulfillment of the Vietnamese people's destiny, and it pursued that mission with an uncommon admixture of ruthlessness and religious intensity. To that end, North Vietnam provided material and moral support, as well as overarching strategic direction, to the successor insurgency movement to the Vietminh in the South. The Americans and their Vietnamese allies called members of this insurgency movement the Vietcong—a derisive term in Vietnamese for "Vietnamese communist." Members of this insurgency organized themselves into the National Liberation Front in 1960 under Hanoi's orders, and referred to themselves typically as revolutionaries, or soldiers of the resistance.

The NLF was an umbrella political front movement, a coalition of independent political parties and interests with a large and growing base among the (generally apolitical) peasantry. But the Front, like the Vietminh, was tightly controlled by the Communist Party. It had a military arm, the People's Liberation Armed Forces, which consisted of local and regional guerrilla bands at first, and later, by 1963, full-time "main force" conventional light infantry battalions.

Throughout the war, the communists claimed the NLF and its forces functioned independently as the only legitimate voice of the people of South Vietnam. In fact, neither the Republic of Vietnam nor the NLF was a truly independent entity. South Vietnam was utterly dependent on American aid and support from its inception until its collapse in 1975. The NLF was certainly a more self-sustaining organization than the government in Saigon, but it was nonetheless under the control of the North Vietnamese politburo. Historian William Duiker says it best: "The insurgency was a genuine revolt based in the South, but it was organized and directed from the North."[1]

Between 1954 and 1964, the United States and North Vietnam went to extraordinary lengths to achieve their objectives in the South *without* deploying combat units from their own conventional armies. By the end of 1961, Washington had poured more than $1 billion in military and economic aid into South Vietnam. By that time the struggle in Vietnam had taken on the vestments of a full-fledged American crusade. It was referred to by various policy makers and journalists as both a "test case" of America's commitment to defending free nations against communist aggression, and an example of the kind of nation building that would strengthen the international world order against the evils of communist subversion.

The Eisenhower administration threw its support behind a mysteriously aloof Vietnamese ascetic, a former civil servant in Emperor Bao Dai's government in the 1930s named Ngo Dinh Diem. Unfortunately, the most talented and democratically oriented nationalists in Vietnam had either been killed in a vicious 1946 purge of rivals orchestrated by General Giap, or they were too tainted by their association with the former French administration to be seen as legitimate in the eyes of the people. At the time of Diem's rise to power, there seemed no truly promising pro-democratic leader in Washington's eyes. Diem was a devout Catholic. He had a number of influential American friends, including Senator John F. Kennedy from Massachusetts, and the highly visible cardinal, Francis Spellman. Diem spoke English well. Most important, he hated communists with a passion.

Not long after being appointed prime minister of South Vietnam by Emperor Bao Dai in South Vietnam's first government in 1954, Diem rigged a popular referendum, "won" more than 98 percent of the popular vote, and declared himself president of the Republic of Vietnam. He aggressively pursued rival factions, defeating a powerful crime syndicate, the Binh Xuyen, in a major battle in the streets of Saigon in 1955, and subduing the private armies of two long-prominent religious sects, the Hoa Hao and Cao Dai. The Eisenhower administration had been initially skeptical of Diem's abilities, but Ike and his advisers were deeply impressed by Diem's seeming resolve and determination in consolidating power.

As the leader of a fledgling republic, Diem, a celibate Vietnamese mandarin who distrusted other politicians reflexively, was well out of his depth. An ardent patriot, he was nonetheless hostile to democratic values and institutions, and out of touch with the powerful social and political forces sweeping over his own country. What's more, he was strangely indifferent to the suffering of the long-exploited peasantry the communists were courting so assiduously. In fact, Diem had a strong authoritarian streak. "Compromise had no place" in his political universe, writes Bernard Fall, "and opposition of any kind must of necessity be subversive and must be repressed with all the vigor the system is capable of."[2]

Diem launched a "Denounce the Communists" campaign in 1956. Over the next two years, the government's secret police exterminated some twelve thousand suspects, and jailed about forty thousand more. As it turned out, a great many of these people were simply political opponents of the Diem regime with no affiliation with the Communist Party whatsoever. Nonetheless, the insurgency suffered grievously. Under great pressure from the southern revolutionaries, Hanoi at last called for the implementation of armed resistance in January 1959, as well as the continuation of the political subversion campaign against Diem.

Saigon's response to the sharp rise of violence was lethargic and inept. In part this was the fault of the American advisory effort to the Army of the Republic of Vietnam (ARVN), which focused not on counterinsurgency tactics, but on training in conventional operations to repel an invasion like the one the North Koreans sprung on their southern brethren in June 1950. But a much more important factor was the chronic political instability and intrigue that pervaded politics in Saigon. With few exceptions, the senior generals in the ARVN were demonstrably more interested in securing power and influence for themselves than in fighting the VC. Nor were they known to care very much about the welfare of the ordinary troops under their command—a fact not lost on the South Vietnamese enlisted men. Desertion rates in the ARVN were extraordinarily high in the early 1960s, and remained so throughout the Vietnam War. ARVN officers were promoted based on their loyalty to those above them, not on their performance in combat, and only a tiny percentage hailed from the peasantry.

John F. Kennedy and Vietnam

Two weeks before a handsome and charismatic senator from Massachusetts named John F. Kennedy became president of the United States, the gruff and voluble Soviet premier, Nikita Khrushchev, delivered a militantly anti-Western speech, promising Soviet aid for communist-led "wars of national liberation" in the developing world. Khrushchev's primary intended audience was the people of the developing world. He wanted to challenge Mao's claim that China was in the vanguard of support for revolution. Kennedy, though, took the speech as a direct challenge to the United States, and he responded with alacrity.

Jack Kennedy had long been interested in enhancing America's tools for dealing with communist insurgencies and other brushfire wars. In an oblique criticism of Eisenhower's military policies, Senator Kennedy stated in a 1959 speech that "in practice, our nuclear retaliatory power is not enough. It cannot deter communist aggression which is too limited to justify atomic war. It cannot protect uncommitted nations against a Communist takeover using local or guerrilla forces. It cannot be used in so-called 'brush-fire' wars. . . . In short, it cannot prevent the Communists from nibbling away at the fringe of the free world's territory or strength."[3]

John Kennedy and the "best and the brightest" foreign policy advisers he brought to Washington were a supremely confident bunch, infused with a toughness of spirit born of service as junior officers in World War II, and an abiding faith that a crucial American mission was not only to defend democracies, but to expand the boundaries of freedom in the world. As Kennedy famously said in his first inaugural address, "Let every nation know, whether it wishes us well or ill, that we shall pay any price, bear any burden, meet any hardship, support any friend, oppose any foe, in order to assure the survival and the success of liberty." The new crusade required an innovative defense doctrine focused on deterring Soviet- or Chinese-inspired aggression across the entire spectrum of conflict, especially in Third World brushfire conflicts. Kennedy's personal military adviser, an urbane and sophisticated retired army general named Maxwell Taylor, was the chief architect of "flexible response." It called for expanding conventional forces, which had languished under Eisenhower, as well as an intensive focus on meeting the communist challenge in the sphere of political and social development programs in the developing world. To support the expansion of democracy in the Third World, the Kennedy administration created several new government agencies, including the Peace Corps, the Agency for International Development, and the Alliance for Progress.

Kennedy, a former PT boat skipper who had been decorated for valor after a Japanese destroyer sunk his boat in the South Pacific, was an avid supporter of the Special Forces, which bore responsibility for training indigenous forces in guerrilla warfare, and for conducting a wide array of unconventional operations, including counterinsurgencies and psychological operations. The young American president even created a special counterinsurgency group within the National Security Council. Soon after assuming office, he ordered Secretary of Defense Robert McNamara to divert $100 million of his budget from other programs to expand Army Special Forces. It was John Kennedy who enthusiastically authorized their use of special headgear—the now instantly recognizable green beret. He did so, it should be noted, against the wishes of the army brass, which did not share his enthusiasm for such forces. Army general Earle "Bus" Wheeler, chairman of the Joint Chiefs of Staff, dismissed counterinsurgency forces as a "fashionable idea." Vietnam, he told the president, was simply too important for experimentation. Conventional troops possessed the capability to fight and win brushfire wars.[4] The army bureaucracy did what it could to slow down the service's turn toward "special operations" under both Kennedy and his successor, Lyndon Baines Johnson, despite the fact that the country found itself engaged in a hybrid war of both conventional and unconventional operations, in which political warfare—part of the Special Forces' bailiwick—was more important than military operations of any type.

The first months of the new presidency were marred by Cold War setbacks. Kennedy approved a disastrous CIA-led invasion of Castro's Cuba, and then Khrushchev moved to close off West Berlin from East Berlin by building a wall right down the middle of the city. These events (and several others) heightened JFK's determination to rise to the communist challenge in the Third World, and the most difficult challenge, without question, was Vietnam.

In May 1961, JFK signed National Security Action Memorandum (NSAM) 52, formally committing the United States "to prevent communist domination of South Vietnam; to create in that country a viable and increasingly democratic society; and to initiate on an accelerated basis" a series of "mutually supporting" military and political actions to achieve that objective.[5] This watershed document, though, left open the nature and scope of those actions, because doubts and disagreements remained within the upper reaches of the White House about the very nature of the war; about whether or not Diem's government in Saigon was a viable partner in the effort to save the country from communist domination, and even whether South Vietnam was of sufficient strategic significance to justify deepening American support.

Kennedy's advisers had varied opinions on these questions. Broadly speaking, the advice broke down along two lines. Deputy National Security adviser Walt Rostow, whom Kennedy joked could write faster than Kennedy could think, was the leading hawk. He didn't see much percentage in exploring the subtleties of Vietnamese history and politics in order to formulate an American policy there—an attitude he shared with most of the leading members of the Vietnam team in the White House. Rather, he saw the war as a classic Moscow-directed effort to expand the boundaries of the communist world, requiring a vigorous and assertive response. Rostow also felt the insurgency in South Vietnam, per se, was not the heart of the problem. He simply refused to believe that ordinary people would gravitate toward a communist regime of their own accord. The nub of the problem, he believed, was North Vietnam's determination to conquer the South. Rostow pressed Kennedy to punish the North with a graduated campaign of air and naval attacks, and to make a public commitment to using US troops as a sign of American resolve.

The "doves," who were far less prominent in number and influence than the hawks, were leery of extending the American commitment to defend South Vietnam too far, on the grounds that the regime in Saigon was fatally corrupt and inept, and that perhaps Vietnam wasn't worth risking US prestige at all. Undersecretary of State George Ball was the leading spokesperson for this group, and also the most eloquent. Ball felt that Rostow and the hawks misunderstood the very nature of the conflict. Aggression from the North wasn't the central problem. South Vietnam was in the midst of a civil war. Diem's repression and lack of popularity were serious stumbling blocks to legitimacy. Ball worried that if the US began its own ground war there, it would soon fall into a quagmire. He told the president, presciently, "If we go down that road [i.e., commit American ground troops], we might have, within five years, 300,000 men in the rice paddies and jungles of Vietnam and never be able to find them."[6]

Yet JFK, for his part, was deeply committed to holding the line in Vietnam. He rejected pretty much out of hand those in the State Department who advocated finding a political solution to the struggle in Southeast Asia. He had agreed to do so in neighboring Laos soon after taking office. To do so in Vietnam as well would give the appearance of weakness. Besides, there was a powerful consensus among the chief Kennedy advisers that political negotiations, no matter how skillfully carried out, would result in the long run in a Vietnam ruled by communists from the Ca Mau Peninsula in the Mekong Delta all the way up to Cao Bang Province on the Chinese border, where Ho's independence movements had been born in 1941. There simply had to be a better way.

Kennedy was also deeply reluctant to commit to using American forces directly in the fighting, even in principle. It was Saigon's war, he opined. Not America's. The United States could only support the South Vietnamese effort. In mid-1961, he ordered a rapid and considerable beefing up of the American advice and support effort. Accordingly, the number of Americans in Vietnam rocketed upward from 3,200 in December 1961 to 9,000 a year later. Army Special Forces A-Teams of twelve soldiers each went into the Central Highlands to train Vietnam's ethnically distinct mountain tribesmen—known as Montagnards to both French and American soldiers—to defend their own communities, and lead them in combat in guerrilla-style raids on enemy forces there. Regular army and marine advisers joined ARVN units down to the battalion level, and American helicopter pilots began to ferry ARVN units in air assaults against enemy-controlled combat villages. Kennedy also approved a CIA plan to form guerrilla forces among the Hmong (also called Meo) people in Laos to challenge the growing presence of North Vietnamese troops in that country, and to try to choke off Vietnamese infiltration through Laos.

The young president was elated to see the normally unreceptive Diem embrace a US-conceived counterinsurgency plan called the Strategic Hamlet Program in early 1962, in which a large number of South Vietnam's seven thousand hamlets were selected for fortification against VC attacks with trenches, concertina wire, and fighting positions, to be manned by the local militia forces. The United States provided funds for economic and social development projects with a view to binding the peasants to the government. Diem built the new hamlets at an unusually energetic clip. About three thousand were constructed in 1962.

Saigon made grand claims about the government's progress in the countryside. Within a year or so, though, it became quite clear to the American mission in Saigon that the program was turning into a fiasco. The government had tried to do too much too fast, and most hamlets received very limited help in the way of development funds and basic health and social services. By late 1962, the VC were destroying dozens of these hamlets and their defenders each month with infantry assaults. Others they took by internal subversion, which the VC had turned into a kind of high art. As an American official at the time remarked, "You could have all this visible apparatus of control outside and at the same time be controlling nothing inside."[7]

Diem and the Slide Toward Chaos

Despite lavish American support during the Kennedy years, Diem steadfastly resisted pleas by US officials and important South Vietnamese political constituencies like the university students and the Buddhist monks to institute social and political reforms. He was all too well aware the United States needed him just as much as he needed them, so he was able to dig in his heels. One old State Department hand in Vietnam quipped cynically that Diem had become "a puppet who pulled his own strings—and ours as well."[8]

In the countryside, corruption and nepotism in the government administration was rampant. The communists matched the American escalation of the war under Kennedy with one of their own. PLAF battalions were regularly chewing up ARVN units in combat, even though the South Vietnamese units were kitted out with American heavy weapons, including helicopters, armored personnel carriers, and field artillery. In early January 1963, a reinforced regiment of three thousand ARVN troops sporting all those weapons was mauled by a mere three hundred or so Vietcong regulars in a village forty miles southwest of Saigon called Ap Bac. The ARVN commander inexplicably delayed the attack for a day, giving the enemy a chance to prepare excellent defensive positions. Once the battle commenced the next morning, the airborne assault crumbled under withering automatic-weapons fire. Five US helicopters were downed in the fight. A tough, hard-driving American adviser to ARVN forces at Ap Bac, Lieutenant Colonel John Paul Vann, implored the ARVN commander of an armored personnel carrier unit to attack, but he refused to do so, claiming he would lose too many men. Then, after killing more than sixty South Vietnamese soldiers and wounding about a hundred, the VC escaped because another ARVN commander refused to close off the VC's route of withdrawal. A bitter John Vann later described the battle as "a miserable fucking performance, just like it always is."[9]

The top American commander in Vietnam at the time, General Paul Harkins, described the debacle as a victory, because the Vietcong had withdrawn from the battlefield. Vann thought Harkins was living in a dreamworld, as indeed he was. An American reporter who covered the Battle of Ap Bac described Harkins as a "general with a swagger stick and cigarette holder . . . who would not deign to soil his suntans and street shoes in a rice paddy to find out what was going on."[10] Like so many other American senior officials in Saigon, Harkins had a strong inclination to dismiss bad news out of hand, knowing it was not appreciated by the men in charge in the Pentagon and the White House. Indeed, Harkins was an early example of a classic American type that appeared with depressing regularity during the war—men who were arrogant, complacent, and lacking in curiosity about the people they were supposedly trying to save from communist slavery. They suffered from a form of victory disease that developed in the wake of America's enormous military and economic success during and after World War II. The disease was in no sense restricted to the upper reaches of the military in Vietnam. It affected the civilian leadership in government as well. "American society had become a victim of its own achievement," wrote Neil Sheehan, a veteran war correspondent who knew Harkins and his type well. "The elite of America had become stupefied by too much money, too many material resources, too much power, and too much success."[11]

John Vann soon resigned from the army for personal reasons, but his views about the weaknesses of the ARVN, and the American command's tendency to whitewash its performance, made a big impression on Sheehan and a number of other young reporters. Increasingly, their writing expressed skepticism about the official narrative of events in Vietnam.

Political instability continued to plague Saigon. In early 1963, Buddhists and university students rose up in protest over increasingly repressive measures instituted by the imperious Diem. Increasingly isolated from South Vietnam's political class, Diem came to rely almost exclusively on his family for political and military advice. His closest adviser was his brother Nhu, who was in charge of the government's secret police. Unfortunately, Nhu was an opium-smoking megalomaniac. In May 1963, Nhu's security forces shot and killed eight students for displaying outlawed Buddhist flags in a demonstration against government repression. On June 11, a Buddhist monk named Thich Quang Duc immolated himself on a busy street corner in Saigon. The gruesome image of his burning corpse sent shock waves through the world, further undermining Diem's legitimacy in the eyes of his own people, as well as his patrons in the White House. After Diem failed repeatedly to make conciliatory gestures toward the Buddhists and rival political parties, President Kennedy gave his tacit consent to a clique of ARVN generals to mount a coup against him. Rather than arresting the South Vietnamese president and expelling him from the country, as the White House had been led to expect would happen, the generals killed him, along with his brother Nhu, on November 2, 1963.

A military junta under the phlegmatic and taciturn General Duong Van Minh took up the reins of power, but not for long. Several governments would follow in quick succession in the coming months. The country's leadership, if indeed it could be called leadership, was in profound disarray.

Lyndon Johnson Assumes the Presidency

Three weeks after Diem's death, JFK was assassinated in Dallas. His successor, Lyndon Baines Johnson, promised to stay the course Kennedy had set in Vietnam. He sought by all means to keep American combat forces out of the fighting, and increased substantially economic aid and military assistance to Saigon. A master politician of towering ambition, Johnson had an almost morbid fear that he would be forced into deploying American troops to Vietnam, and that a nascent American war there would lead to the collapse of his ambitious domestic reform legislation, which aimed to provide education to the disadvantaged, health care to the poor and elderly, and eliminate poverty.

Insecure and inexperienced in the arena of foreign policy and diplomacy, Johnson decided to focus public attention on his ambitious domestic agenda during his first year in office. He wanted to put off major decisions on Vietnam until after he had defeated the Republican hawk Barry Goldwater in the November 1964 election and gained a strong popular mandate. In the meantime, Johnson appointed William C. Westmoreland, a handsome, self-assured West Pointer with a fine leadership record in World War II and Korea, to replace the ineffectual and perpetually optimistic Paul Harkins as head of MACV. The number of advisers in Vietnam increased from 16,300 at the end of 1963 to 23,300 by December 1964, and another $50 million was earmarked for economic assistance to Saigon. Like Kennedy, Johnson warmly embraced a variant of the domino theory, positing that the fall of South Vietnam would lead to the fall of other Asian countries and have a devastating effect on American credibility in the world, causing allies and potential partners to lose faith in Washington's leadership.

Meanwhile, the insurgency continued to gain in strength, thanks largely to diligent work by NLF recruiters, a stunning series of victories in battalion-size battles against the ARVN, and to perpetual political turmoil in Saigon. The Johnson administration from its first days was well aware that a crisis was coming to a head in Southeast Asia, but it downplayed the seriousness of the situation to Congress and the American people for its own political ends. LBJ presented himself as the peace candidate who, unlike the bellicose Goldwater, would keep American boys out of the jungles of Southeast Asia, and refrain from provoking World War III by going to war in Vietnam.

In part to counter Goldwater's charge that he was soft on challenging communist aggression, and in part to send a message to Hanoi, the Johnson administration provoked a North Vietnamese navy attack on American destroyers in the Gulf of Tonkin in early August, and launched dramatic retaliatory air strikes against military targets in North Vietnam. On August 7, after presenting the Tonkin Gulf incident as an *unprovoked* act of aggression by North Vietnam, Johnson obtained from Congress a resolution granting him wide authority "to take all necessary measures" to defend US forces in Southeast Asia. The Gulf of Tonkin Resolution served as the legal basis for the deployment of American forces in Vietnam for the rest of the war. Congress never formally declared war against North Vietnam. In effect, the resolution gave the president an open checkbook to escalate the war as he saw fit. "It's like my grandmother's nightshirt," quipped Johnson. "It covers everything."[12]

In Hanoi, Ho and his colleagues read the Gulf of Tonkin Resolution correctly as a signal of Johnson's intention to shift the conflict in Vietnam from a "special war" (in Hanoi's parlance), waged by the South Vietnamese with US support, to a "limited war" fought with American as well as South Vietnamese military forces. Hanoi began to prepare defenses against an American invasion in the North, as well as for the participation of its own army, the People's Army of Vietnam, in a major ground war in the South.

South Vietnam's political and military fortunes continued their downward spiral in late 1964. US Army and Marine advisers looked on in dismay as ARVN forces were outclassed time and time again in clashes with the more disciplined Vietcong. ARVN casualties jumped from one thousand a month in January 1964 to three thousand a month by year's end. Something had to give, and soon.

Vietnam in American Foreign Policy, 1945–1964

In the minds of virtually all the key players in the formation of American foreign policy from the Truman through the Johnson administrations, Vietnam's importance lay in the simple fact that it was a theater of Cold War competition, not because the country, in and of itself, had any strategic significance. To put it another way: Vietnam needed defending because the communist giants, the Chinese and the Soviets, were giving Ho both material and moral support with a view to expanding the "communist bloc." The communists had already succeeded in biting off the northern half of the country in 1954; it was thus critical (the thinking went) for the United States to preserve South Vietnam as a pro-Western bastion in Southeast Asia. A victory for the communists in South Vietnam was sure to inspire other adventures, thereby changing the balance of forces in the global Cold War in favor of the "Reds," and doing grave damage to America's credibility at the same time. Communist "wars of national liberation" had to be stopped. The future of the entire Free World seemed to lie in the balance.

With few exceptions, American policy makers thought the French defeat in Indochina had very little to do with the wide popular appeal of Ho's movement or the soundness of its politico-military strategy, and a great deal to do with a lack of political will in Paris and French military lassitude in the field. Unlike France, the United States, they felt, had the political know-how and the military power to get the job done right. How could an army of rice farmers led by a cadre of communist fanatics frustrate the will of the greatest power on the face of the earth?

In retrospect, it is truly astonishing how little credit American decision makers gave to Ho Chi Minh's ability to harness Vietnamese nationalism to his own ends. Ho's movement had also displayed impressive strategic prowess, deftly integrating guerrilla warfare, conventional operations, and political work. The failure of American policy makers to recognize the deep and broad appeal of Ho's revolutionary movement to ordinary Vietnamese people longing for both unity and freedom from foreign domination would have immense repercussions in the years ahead.

CHAPTER 3

WASHINGTON: THE COMPLICATED POLITICS OF ESCALATION

On November 3, 1964, Lyndon Baines Johnson was reelected president of the United States in one of the greatest landslides in American electoral history, winning the highest percentage of the popular vote since the election of 1820. Democrats won overwhelming majorities in the House and the Senate as well. LBJ had his long-awaited mandate from the American people, gained in no small measure on his marginally qualified promise *not* to do what Republican rival Barry Goldwater advocated: send American troops into the jungles of Southeast Asia to kill communist guerrillas.

It was a promise LBJ would have dearly liked to keep, but by late summer of 1964, neither he, nor any of his senior advisers, expected he would be able to keep it for long. What neither the American people nor their representatives in Congress knew as they went to vote in early November was that their president had already reached several conclusions. The first was that South Vietnam was on the precipice of complete collapse. The second was that only a significant interjection of American military power could prevent its fall. The third was that the fall of South Vietnam would have catastrophic consequences for all the non-communist countries in Asia, for American prestige around the world, and, implicitly, for his own political and historical reputation.

Therefore, under no circumstances could he permit South Vietnam to be allowed to fall. Johnson and his advisers had also reached a provisional consensus on their options going forward. The United States should not pursue a negotiated settlement in Vietnam while South Vietnam was prostrate, for any settlement they could imagine negotiating was bound to lead first to a coalition government in Saigon, and then to communist domination.

When the administration officials told the press and Congress the president had no intention of deploying US combat forces in Vietnam, they were dissembling.

A great many people within and outside the government foreign policy bureaucracy had provided the advice and expertise, oral and written, on which these conclusions had been affirmed. But in making these determinations, President Johnson relied to an extraordinary degree on three men whom he had asked to stay on from the Kennedy administration: Secretary of State Dean Rusk; Secretary of Defense Robert McNamara, and the special assistant to the president for National Security Affairs, McGeorge Bundy. "It's not just that you're President Kennedy's friends," he'd pleaded with them in the grim days after JFK's assassination, "but you are the best anywhere and you must stay. I want you to stand with me."[1]

Lyndon Johnson was a very persuasive individual. All three men agreed to stay put. Without these advisers, Johnson told one of his biographers, "I would have lost my link to John Kennedy, and without that I would have had absolutely no chance of gaining the support of the media or the Easterners or the intellectuals. And without that support I would have had absolutely no chance of governing the country."[2]

The collective influence of these three individuals on the set of presidential decisions that committed the United States to a major war in Vietnam between the fall of 1964 and the summer of 1965 was so great that historians have long considered each of them architects of the conflict in their own right. Together with Johnson, one of the most dynamic and hard-driving politicians in American history, they constituted a kind of "war council" that tended to filter out, or marginalize, advice about Vietnam that did not jibe with their preconceptions.[3] So much so, in fact, that a kind of "group think" enveloped White House discussions over Vietnam in this crucial period of decision-making between November 1964 and June 1965, when the administration secretly approved General Westmoreland's plan for a major American ground campaign in South Vietnam.

Johnson constantly sought both consensus and reassurance from the war council advisers for his Vietnam decisions, and with striking consistency, he got both. Tom Wicker, the White House correspondent for the *New York Times* during this period, put it well. Johnson "would look around him and see in Bob McNamara that [his Vietnam policy] was technologically feasible, in McGeorge Bundy that it was intellectually respectable, in Dean Rusk that it was historically necessary."[4]

Who were these men?

Dean Rusk, the secretary of state, described himself as looking like the neighborhood bartender. He did. Growing up poor in rural Georgia, he was the son of a Calvinist preacher-farmer, from whom he learned the values of modesty, hard work, and service to a cause greater than oneself. "We were rather a quiet family about expressing our emotions under any circumstances," Rusk recalled. "Perhaps it comes from the tough battle with the soil in the family that has to wrest a living out of not too productive soil."[5] Rusk worked his way through Davidson College in North Carolina, and joined the ROTC program, in which he excelled. Both of Rusk's grandfathers had been Confederate officers, and Dean had a lifelong fascination with the military. A brilliant student, he won a coveted Rhodes Scholarship and went on to study international relations at Oxford.

During World War II, Rusk served with distinction in the China-Burma-India Theater as a staff officer. In one of the war's many ironies, it was Colonel Rusk who approved the OSS parachute drop into Ho Chi Minh's headquarters in May 1945. Rusk's superb staff work caught the eye of no less a figure than George Marshall, chief of staff of the Army, and the Americans' "organizer of victory" in World War II. When the great general became Harry Truman's secretary of state, he personally recruited Rusk to the department. At State, Rusk rose rapidly through the ranks, working on a variety of United Nations issues, including allied strategy during the Korean War, and developing a reputation as a highly effective diplomat. At State, and later as head of the Rockefeller Foundation, he earned the admiration and respect of many towering figures in the foreign policy establishment, including Dean Acheson and John Foster Dulles—two secretaries of state with very different views of the nature and purpose of American power.

It was widely said in the early 1960s that JFK wanted to be his own secretary of state and that he chose the self-effacing Rusk for the position because of his proven facility to implement rather than make policy. Dean Rusk was certainly a much more cautious and self-contained person than either Mac Bundy or Bob McNamara, both of whom had towering egos. He felt—very deeply—that the United States had a special role to play, a moral obligation in fact, in bringing democratic institutions and the rule of law to the developing world. The great lesson he took away from World War II and his extensive experience with Cold War crises was that if a course of aggression was allowed to gather momentum, it was sure to mushroom into major conflict. The "Munich analogy" was an unshakable article of faith with Rusk. So was his belief that any commitment the United States made to the defense of another nation must be honored, whatever the cost. Too much was at stake to violate that principle, as he made crystal clear in a July 1, 1965, memo to Johnson a few weeks before the president formally approved a massive troop deployment to Vietnam, along with General Westmoreland's master plan for victory: "The integrity of the U.S. commitment is the principal pillar of peace throughout the world. If that commitment becomes unreliable, the communist world would draw conclusions that would lead to our ruin and almost certainly to a catastrophic war. So long as the South Vietnamese are prepared to fight for themselves, we cannot abandon them without disaster to peace and to our interests throughout the world."[6]

America had overcome adversity and succeeded in World War II and in the Cold War through patience and persistence, and those traits, Rusk believed, were bound to pay off against Chinese expansionism in Asia. Early on in the Kennedy administration, Rusk had been ambivalent about the crusade in Vietnam, doubting whether that ancient Southeast Asian nation was strategically important enough to defend. But by the time Johnson assumed the presidency, the doubts had evaporated. Vietnam was not a civil war among Vietnamese in the secretary of state's estimation, but a conflict caused by North Vietnamese aggression against a pro-Western South Vietnam. By checking communist expansionism and holding the line in South Vietnam, Rusk believed the United States could avoid a much more destructive conflict against China down the road.

Dean Rusk believed in protocol, doing things by the book, and loyalty. Loyalty to the president one served, showing deference for his decisions, was a vital part of public service. So was a willingness to defend those decisions to the bitter end. Once LBJ committed America to war in Vietnam, for Rusk, there could be no going back.

LBJ and Rusk were both southerners who had grown up in humble circumstances. They had learned similar lessons from World War II and the early struggle against communism. Rusk, with his Buddha-like countenance and vast store of foreign policy experience, seemed to be a source of strength and reassurance for a president who was deeply ambivalent about Vietnam. "When you're going in with the Marines," said LBJ, Rusk is "the kind you want at your side. . . . And he's also the man you look to when you're all set on something to speak up calm and say, 'Now just a minute.' He's the just-a-minute man around here, not feisty like McNamara and Bundy."[7]

Many historians have criticized Rusk for downplaying the State Department's role in shaping policy in Vietnam. It is easy to see why. This courtly, self-effacing Georgian was strongly inclined to believe that until the communists in Hanoi were ready to come to the negotiating table from a position of military weakness, Vietnam was essentially a military problem. And so when the administration faced crucial policy decisions in late 1964 and early 1965, Rusk tended to defer to McNamara and Mac Bundy, reacting to their proposals rather than putting forward his own. Dean Rusk was a man of great integrity, but he was also intellectually rigid. As one of his early biographers astutely noted, he failed to grasp the extent to which "the 'aggression' of a national liberation movement [was] much more complicated morally and much harder to cope with politically and militarily than the aggression of a great power."[8]

Born in San Francisco in 1916, Robert Strange McNamara was educated at Stanford and the Harvard Business School. As a staff officer in the Army Air Corps in World War II, he developed innovative logistical systems for the bombing campaign in Europe. After the war, he returned to Harvard Business School, where he conducted groundbreaking research on statistical and systems analysis. Recruited by Ford Motor Company, he applied some of the new systems and techniques he had developed at Harvard, and was widely credited with revitalizing a struggling organization that was deep in the red. A few months after he became president of Ford—the first non–family member to reach that prestigious post—John Kennedy asked him to become secretary of defense in his new administration.

At the Pentagon, McNamara used state-of-the-art business management techniques to cut massive amounts of bloat and redundancy in weapons procurement and personnel programs. He also brought a team of young academic strategists to work in the department, the "whiz kids," who challenged the traditional military way of doing things, and earned the resentment of most of the senior officers in the services in the process. McNamara and the whiz kids held the naive belief that warfare could be managed and controlled, just like any other business. It only required the correct organizational techniques and the application of quantitative and statistical analysis once the "process" of war was broken down into its constituent parts. Vietnam, a strange, unconventional conflict that was at least as much a political as a military struggle, was no exception—at least as Bob McNamara saw it. And woe to the official, military or civilian, who challenged a McNamara argument in a public forum. "He was brilliant and forceful at obliterating others" in policy-making meetings, according to journalist David Halberstam. McNamara "was a ferocious infighter, statistics and force ratios came pouring out of him like a great untapped faucet. He had total control of his facts, and he was quick and nimble with them; there was never a man better with numbers."[9] Admiral U. S. Grant Sharp, the head of the military's Pacific Command from 1964 to 1968, once complained that every meeting he attended with McNamara ended up reaching the conclusions the secretary of defense wanted.

Along with General Maxwell Taylor, McNamara was a driving force behind Jack Kennedy's "flexible response" strategy, which called for reducing the nation's reliance on nuclear weapons in favor of employing a wide range of diplomatic, economic, and unconventional military assets to counter communist aggression. The new president held Bob McNamara in awe, referring to him as "the best Secretary of Defense in the history of this country." LBJ's friend and mentor, Senator Richard Russell, head of the Armed Services Committee, thought the secretary of defense exerted a hypnotic influence on the president.

More than any other senior adviser in 1964 and 1965, McNamara expressed confidence in the American military's capacity to compensate for the weaknesses of Saigon and to break the back of communist resistance through "gradually increasing military pressure." He exuded self-confidence, and was convinced that the United States could find a technological fix to whatever problems were at hand, Vietnam included. "He had the sincerity of an Old Testament prophet," recalled veteran journalist James Reston, "but something was missing; some element of personal doubt; some respect for human weakness; some knowledge of history."[10] Later, in 1966, McNamara would be the first of the key advisers to realize his confidence in America's crusade in Vietnam had been misplaced.

When David Halberstam in the early 1970s coined the term "the Best and the Brightest" to describe the men who led America into the Vietnam War, Mc-George Bundy was his archetype. The first person to obtain a perfect score on the entrance examinations to Yale, Bundy majored in math, graduated first in his class, and wrote a highly popular political column for the *Yale Daily News*.

Shortly after graduating from Yale, the Harvard Society of Fellows offered Mac a prestigious junior fellowship. These positions were normally awarded only to the nation's most brilliant, newly minted PhDs. At Harvard, Bundy began to publish influential essays on topics in American government and foreign policy in the leading journals of opinion like *Foreign Affairs* and the *New Republic*. By the time his graduate studies were interrupted by army service in World War II, he had become one of the nation's most articulate thinkers on foreign policy. Mac Bundy was particularly fascinated with the question of how the United States should employ its awesome power, especially its military power, to create order, stability, and progress in the international arena.

Bundy was the quintessential New England WASP, with a deep commitment to establishment institutions, democratic values, and public service. His father, a prominent Boston lawyer, had many influential friends in government and business. He was especially close to Henry Stimson, secretary of state under Hoover and secretary of war under FDR. Young Bundy formed a close relationship with Stimson. He coauthored the statesman's memoirs in the late 1940s. Like his mentor Stimson, Bundy believed it was the responsibility of the world's leading democracy to bring progress, prosperity, and Western institutions to the developing nations in Asia and Africa, and to resist the spread of communism with all the energy and resourcefulness it could muster. Like Stimson, Bundy was an ardent believer in American exceptionalism. As Mac once remarked to a colleague, "The United States was the locomotive at the head of mankind, and the rest of the world the caboose."[11]

After working briefly on the Marshall Plan, Mac was offered a professorship in the government department at Harvard; soon thereafter, at the ripe old age of thirty-four, he became dean of the faculty. An inspiring teacher and highly effective administrator, Bundy worked hard to make Harvard a merit-based university, as opposed to the bastion of WASP privilege it had been for three centuries.

John Kennedy, who had known the Bundy family while growing up in and around Boston, appointed Mac his assistant for National Security Affairs in early 1961. The Harvard dean, writes one scholar, "was intellectually and temperamentally the ideal Kennedy man—tough, pragmatic, but with liberal instincts, and highly intelligent."[12] With JFK's support, Bundy transformed the National Security Council into a lean, highly efficient "Little State Department" within the confines of the White House that could respond quickly to any crisis. As Kennedy once quipped, "Damn it, Bundy and I get more done in a day than [the State Department] does in six months."[13]

Bundy was the first national security adviser to act simultaneously as the president's gatekeeper on foreign policy, and as a leading adviser on the substance of policy. Next to Robert McNamara and the president himself, Mac Bundy probably had more influence on shaping the policy agenda and the key decisions that led the United States into Vietnam than any other human being. "To an uncommon degree," writes Halberstam, Bundy "possessed the capacity to sense what others wanted and what they were thinking, and it would serve him well."[14] He was well aware by early 1964, for instance, that Johnson had a morbid fear that withdrawing from Vietnam would lead to his own political downfall and thus sabotage his dreams of implementing the Great Society. And so Bundy deflected several very persuasive memoranda arguing for disengagement from the president's eyes. He passed others along with razor-sharp rebuttals he dashed off himself. Undersecretary of State George Ball penned a cogent and prescient memorandum in October 1964 arguing that continued support for a shaky, authoritarian regime in Saigon would lead to an American quagmire. Moreover, once US troops were deployed, events would take on their own momentum. As Ball memorably put it, "Once on the tiger's back we cannot be sure of picking the place to dismount."[15] Bundy made sure this memo didn't reach LBJ's desk until it was too late to matter much.

Like Rusk and McNamara, Bundy took the "lesson of Munich" as gospel.

Under no circumstances should aggression by one nation against another be met with acquiescence, or even compromise, for to do so would only encourage further aggression. He believed, for instance, that the use of force against Germany and Japan when they first began to violate international norms of behavior in the 1930s might well have prevented World War II.

Supremely self-confident, and sanguine about the efficacy of American power, many colleagues found Bundy cold and arrogant, yet he generally got along well with other senior people in the administration, including the generals. George Ball nearly always disagreed with him about Vietnam, but he was amazed by Mac's "extraordinary facility to grasp an idea, summarize or analyze it, and produce an orderly response as fast as a computer."[16] Yet for all his brains, Bundy comes across in the documentary record as pretty much oblivious to the social and political complexities of the revolution going on in Vietnam in the 1960s.

And then there was the president of the United States, Lyndon Baines Johnson of Texas. Russell Baker of the *New York Times*, who covered the Johnson White House and came to know the president very well, described him as "a human puzzle so complicated nobody could ever understand him."[17] It would be difficult to find a serious student of Johnson's presidency who would disagree. Johnson lived for politics. Little else held his attention. He was a consensus builder, horse trader, and master manipulator, and widely considered today to be the most effective majority leader the US Senate had ever seen.

To describe LBJ's personality as domineering somehow seems an understatement. Johnson bent strong men to his will with the sheer force of his personality, employing a high-test blend of flattery, intimidation, thinly veiled threats, and less-than-gentle persuasion. He had "a genius for reading a man instantly, for knowing how far he could go, how much he could push, what he could summon from the man, when to hold on and when to let go."[18] The White House staff even had a name for Johnson's manipulation technique. It was called "the Johnson treatment." Ben Bradlee, longtime editor of the *Washington Post*, recalled that Johnson "never just shook hands with you. One hand was shaking your hand, the other hand was always someplace else, exploring you, examining you."[19]

Raised in the hardscrabble hill country of central Texas, the thirty-sixth president was intensely ambitious from the time he was in his late teens. The young Johnson craved influence, respect, admiration, and perhaps most of all, power. Power to do great things for "his" people, whether that meant bringing electricity and paved roads to the poor folks in his Texas congressional district in the 1930s, or delivering health care to the elderly and education to the under-privileged in America's bustling cities as president. Like his hero, FDR, Johnson had supreme faith in the power of government to improve ordinary people's lives, and to solve the most intractable social and economic problems. Clark Clifford, his close friend, and McNamara's successor as secretary of defense, described LBJ with tongue in cheek as a "con man" who would use "the con approach in a good cause and bring people along."[20]

The bluster, the inclination to intimidate and even embarrass colleagues in one-on-one meetings—he often insisted that male visitors accompany him to the toilet when nature called so he could continue his discourse while relieving himself—belied deep insecurity about his worth and his abilities. He felt he had been inadequately educated, and that his achievements had been underappreciated in Washington. He was given to bouts of self-pity and rage. Mac Bundy recalled that he seemed to have an "I'll show them" attitude that sometimes distorted his judgment.[21]

This master of domestic politics felt acutely out of his depth in matters of foreign policy. He was the first to admit to close friends that he didn't really understand foreigners, didn't get what made them tick. The opaque and indirect language of diplomacy baffled and frustrated him. Because he felt ill at ease in dealing with international affairs, he didn't trust his own considerable political instincts, and tended to rely heavily on his senior advisers' opinions. Foreign policy, of course, had long been the province of the Eastern Establishment types, Ivy Leaguers like John Foster Dulles, Dean Acheson, George Kennan, and Mac Bundy. He felt these people, along with Jack Kennedy's crowd of stylish sophisticates and intellectuals, looked down on him for his crude language and earthy manner. In policy meetings on Vietnam, writes Halberstam, Johnson was

> prone to limit discussion, as if somehow the discussion might show up his weaknesses. . . . [D]ecisions were made at the very top, in part because of his almost neurotic desire for secrecy. The more men who participate, the more gossip there is going to

be, the more rumor that maybe Lyndon Johnson himself didn't make those decisions, that he needed people to make them for him, or worse, that there was disagreement at the top level of government. . . . So the way to control secrecy was to control the decision making, to keep it in as few hands as possible and make sure those hands were loyal, more committed to working with the President than to anything else.[22]

No one ever had to remind LBJ what happened to the Democrats in 1949. Truman had "lost" China to the communists, and ever since, his beloved Democratic Party had been tarred with the brush of being soft on communism. Two days after Kennedy was assassinated, Henry Cabot Lodge, the ambassador to South Vietnam, told the new president things weren't going at all well with the war. Johnson responded with a statement that would become his mantra for the next four years: "I am not going to lose Vietnam. I am not going to be the president who saw Southeast Asia go the way China went."[23]

The prospect of communist victory in Vietnam haunted the president from Texas deep, deep down in his bones. To be sure, though, it wasn't that he possessed any particular affection or loyalty to the Vietnamese people. He had visited Vietnam on orders from JFK back in 1961. On that trip he had described Ngo Dinh Diem as the "Churchill of Southeast Asia" to a group of reporters, but when asked off the record if he had really meant what he'd said by journalist Stanley Karnow, he replied, "Shit, man, he's the only boy we got out there."[24] In private, Johnson called Vietnam "that pissant little country," and castigated its senior generals and political officials for their incessant plotting and bickering, for their failure to pull together and work as a team. Like pretty much everybody else in the White House, LBJ worried far more about the effect of Vietnam on domestic and international politics than he did about the fate of the Vietnamese people, or the nature of America's communist adversaries.

LBJ saw Vietnam as a kind of experiment, in which Moscow, Beijing, and Hanoi were out to demonstrate the efficacy of communist "wars of national liberation," and the weakness of American resolve to meet the challenge. But in Johnson's mind, the communist challenge to America in Vietnam was also interpreted as a direct personal affront that called into question not only his personal resolve, but his manhood. The Chinese, he told aide Bill Moyers over a generous glass of scotch, "will think with Kennedy dead, we've lost heart. So they'll think we're yellow and don't mean what we say. . . . The fellas in the Kremlin will be wondering how far they can go."[25] On another occasion, the president famously remarked, "If you let a bully come in and chase you out of your front yard, tomorrow he'll be on your porch and the next day he'll rape your wife in your own bed."[26]

The record is clear. Lyndon Johnson did not want to take the United States to war in Vietnam. Deep down, he didn't think America belonged in the fight. One of the enduring mysteries of Johnson's thinking process is why his fears of the results of disengagement and withdrawal were so much greater, so much more pronounced, than his fear of initiating a major ground war in Asia that several senior military advisers told him would probably take half a million men five years to win—if it could be won at all. But there is simply no question this was the case. The enduring power of that fear—and the failure of LBJ's senior advisers or the president himself to focus on the likely long-term consequences of deploying US military power in Southeast Asia—must rank high on the list of factors that led to America's disastrous campaign in Vietnam.

The Vietnam Working Group
Lays Out the Options

Two days before the 1964 election, the president established an interagency working group of eight mid-level officials from State, Defense, and the CIA under Assistant Secretary of State for Far Eastern Affairs William P. Bundy— Mac's brother, another one of the "best and brightest"—to conduct a major reevaluation of American policy in Vietnam, and to recommend a number of options to a group of LBJ's senior advisers, the "principals" on the National Security Council. Those men—the war council advisers, along with General Earle Wheeler, chairman of the Joint Chiefs of Staff; CIA director John McCone; and several others—would recommend a specific course of action to the president.

Bill Bundy, like his brother, was also educated at Yale. He went from New Haven to Harvard Law School, and then to a stellar career as an intelligence analyst in the CIA, and to several prominent positions in the Pentagon. Before joining State in March 1964, he had managed the military assistance program to South Vietnam. Although Bill would claim that his Working Group was meant to undertake "the most comprehensive" review of the Vietnam problem since Kennedy had come into office, there was nothing comprehensive about it. LBJ's oft-repeated assertion that he would not be the first president to lose Vietnam, and his proclivity for marginalizing the opinions of anyone who preached the wisdom of a political solution in Vietnam, ensured that the Group would focus virtually all of its attention on military actions the United States could take to prevent the fall of South Vietnam. There would be remarkably little discussion of the political settlement option by the Working Group, because disengagement had already been defined by Johnson himself as national and personal humiliation. The president became visibly irritated and impatient when the topic was raised.

For three weeks, the Working Group pored over intelligence reports and a welter of briefing papers and other studies. On November 24, Thanksgiving Day, Bundy's group put forward three policy options for consideration to the principals:

A. Increase military assistance and advice, while undertaking limited strikes on the Ho Chi Minh Trail in Laos and stepping up ARVN covert action against North Vietnam. In essence, option A was to continue on the current path, only do a bit more of it.

B. The "full/fast squeeze" approach. Escalate military pressure against North Vietnam sharply until Hanoi agreed in principle to halt supporting the insurgency in the South. This was an option looked upon favorably by the Joint Chiefs, who felt that the enemy would only respond favorably to highly destructive levels of violence, and had been pressing Johnson hard to take the gloves off in dealing with Hanoi.

C. Graduated military pressure against North Vietnam in two phases. First, limited strikes against the Ho Chi Minh Trail in Laos, and reprisal strikes against North Vietnam for any attack on American installations. In the second phase, an open-ended campaign of progressively more intensive air strikes against military targets in North Vietnam, "with appropriate U.S. deployments to handle any contingency."[27]

These three options were exhaustively discussed in a series of meetings in the last week in November among the principals. A clear consensus developed quickly around the third option, which also happened to be the choice of the two most influential members of the Working Group, Bill Bundy and John McNaughton, a Harvard Law professor who was McNamara's right-hand man in the Pentagon. "The whole sequence of military actions" in option C, said the official National Security Council paper detailing the policy, "would be designed to give the impression of a steady, deliberate approach, and to give the United States the option at any time . . . to proceed or not, to escalate or not, and to quicken the pace or not."[28] Option C, then, can be read as a classic example of "flexible response" in action.

President Johnson approved this option in principle during an afternoon meeting on December 1, but it was clear he did so with hesitancy, and a certain sense of foreboding. Johnson complained vehemently about the political circus in Saigon. The generals had to pull together, he told Ambassador Maxwell Taylor in no uncertain terms. The gradually intensifying air campaign against the North, said the president, could not begin until the South Vietnamese put their house in order. Ambassador Taylor was instructed to dangle the prospect of bombing North Vietnam as a carrot to encourage the disparate Saigon factions to work as a team. And under no circumstances, said the president, should the substance of this new policy leak to Congress or the public, except at his explicit direction.

In the final written summary of the agreed plan a few days later, Bill Bundy deleted the reference to "appropriate US deployments to handle any contingency," an oblique reference to ground forces, probably because if that language had leaked to Congress it would have set off a firestorm of protest and demands for a debate.

But its deletion from the official summary in no sense meant LBJ had ruled out deploying ground troops. He and the other principals were plainly thinking that US ground forces would be needed, and soon, for a simple reason. The latest CIA reports predicted that an American bombing campaign against the North would almost certainly trigger a significant escalation of Vietcong combat activity, as well as the deployment of fully equipped North Vietnamese army infantry battalions and regiments to the South. The only viable response to the introduction of PAVN combat units, if South Vietnam was to remain a going concern, would be the introduction of American ground forces.

The Meaning of Johnson's December 1, 1964, Decision

"It would be hard to overestimate the importance of the presidential decision" of December 1, 1964, writes Fredrik Logevall, the most meticulous historian of the high-level decision-making in the early years of the American war. "Johnson opted to fundamentally alter the American involvement in Vietnam" from one of advice and support to active participation.[29] More than a week later, Johnson remained uncomfortable over his decision. He sought out the counsel of his old friend Mike Mansfield, the Senate majority leader, knowing that Mansfield would not reveal the substance of their discussion with anyone in the press or Congress. On December 9, Mansfield wrote Johnson a prescient letter, urging him to reverse course. Option C, he said, would take the United States "further and further out on a sagging limb. We are now in the process of putting together makeshift regimes in much the same way that the French were compelled to operate in 1952–54 . . . an extension of the war may well saddle us with enormous burdens and costs in Cambodia, Laos, and elsewhere in Asia, along with those in Vietnam."[30] Troubled by the force and persuasiveness of Mansfield's letter, the president instructed Mac Bundy to pen a rejoinder. Comforted by Mac's response, Johnson stuck to his guns.

On December 14, as US fighter-bombers struck the Ho Chi Minh Trail in Laos in the first day of phase one operations, Saigon was again buffeted by major political turbulence. General Nguyen Khanh, who had been the most powerful figure in intrigue-infested Saigon for the past year, disbanded the legislature and threw several rival generals in prison with the help of the "Young Turks," a group of officers led by ARVN general Nguyen Van Thieu and air force colonel Nguyen Cao Ky. Ambassador Taylor was furious, and threatened to withdraw American support if Khanh didn't back down and restore the legislature. He did so, reluctantly, but that didn't end the chaos. In Hue and Saigon, signs of restiveness among the Buddhists and politically active student population were everywhere.

And then, at the end of the year, came another staggering setback for the Americans and the South Vietnamese.

The Battle of Binh Gia

On December 28, PAVN general Nguyen Chi Thanh, commander of all Vietcong forces in the South, sent elements of the 9th PLAF Division, the first division-size communist unit in the South, to attack a large government-controlled village about forty miles southeast of Saigon, in picturesque Phuoc Tuy Province on the coast. The village was called Binh Gia.

Early that morning, a VC battalion rapidly overwhelmed several platoons of South Vietnamese militia and seized the village, home to about six thousand Vietnamese Catholics. Another VC battalion deployed along the main avenue of approach to Binh Gia and awaited the inevitable arrival of elite ARVN relief forces. They weren't disappointed. The ARVN 30th Ranger Battalion was airlifted into the area and ripped to shreds in a Vietcong ambush within minutes after disembarking from their landing zone. Next day, another Ranger battalion arrived, landing south of the village, and attempted to assault the communist defensive positions in the village proper. They took heavy casualties from recoilless rifles and heavy machine guns that the Vietcong had managed to smuggle into the village the previous night by boat.

On December 30, the 4th Battalion of the South Vietnamese marines arrived on the scene—they, too, were an elite, emergency response unit. The marines quickly entered the village, encountering no resistance, but early that evening they came under a furious, sustained attack and were almost overrun. The VC shot down a helicopter, killing all four Americans on board.

Early on the morning of December 31, a company of South Vietnamese marines lost twelve men in the process of recovering the Americans' bodies, and then the entire 4th Marine Battalion was attacked by elements of two VC regiments—some 1,500 men in all—and fought a desperate battle until nightfall, when the remnants of the marine battalion fought its way through the Vietcong cordon into the jungle. Of the twenty-six soldiers inside USMC adviser Philip Brady's perimeter that day, precisely eleven escaped death or capture. Brady was one of them. Phil Brady had arrived in Vietnam the previous month. He recalled many years later that General Westmoreland "told us we were at the five-yard line" when he first arrived in-country. "Then I went out, and I got on the ground, and I found out we were losing this war. . . . The Vietnamese officers I talked to in the [South Vietnamese] Marine Corps figured they had six months before the end."[31]

The Battle of Binh Gia, in which five Americans lost their lives, sent shock waves through Saigon and Washington. US intelligence was surprised to learn the PLAF was capable of fielding an entire main force division, let alone one capable of eviscerating some of the finest units in the ARVN. Another American adviser remarked that "the Vietcong fought magnificently, as well as any infantry anywhere. But the big question for me is how its troops, a thousand or more of them, could wander around the countryside so close to Saigon without being discovered. That tells something about this war. You can only beat the other guy if you isolate him from the population."[32] The battle had rather a different meaning for Nguyen Chi Thanh. It marked the beginning of a new phase in the war in the South, in which guerrilla operations were combined with conventional, regimental-size assaults.

The Year of the Hawk Begins

The first month of the New Year was marked by several events of special interest to the American people. On New Year's Day, the University of Michigan Wolverines defeated the Oregon State Beavers in the Rose Bowl, 34–7. A day later, the Reverend Martin Luther King Jr. initiated a drive to register Black voters in Selma, Alabama, where only 1 percent of the voters were Black in a town where Blacks constituted slightly more than half the population. President Johnson spoke eloquently of his dreams of a Great Society in his State of the Union Address on January 4. On January 9, the Beatles' album *Rubber Soul* hit number one on the bestseller list, and stayed there for nine weeks. On January 30, Winston Churchill was laid to rest after a profoundly moving funeral service in the parish burial ground of St. Martin's Church in Bladon, England. He was the last of the Second World War's "Big Three" to leave the world. It seemed to mark the passing of an era to all those who had endured the extreme trials of World War II.

For the Americans in Vietnam and for their president, January 1965 was shaping up into a full-bore crisis. On January 6, five days after the Battle of Binh Gia, Maxwell Taylor, former chairman of the Joint Chiefs of Staff, now ambassador to South Vietnam, sent a cable from the US embassy in Saigon to LBJ:

> *We are faced here with a seriously deteriorating situation char-*
> *acterized by continued political turmoil, irresponsibility and*
> *division within the armed forces, lethargy in the pacification*
> *[counterinsurgency and social and economic development] pro-*
> *gram, some anti-US feeling which could grow, signs of mounting*
> *tensions by VC directly at US personnel and deepening discour-*
> *agement and loss of morale throughout SVN. Unless these condi-*
> *tions are somehow changed and trends reversed, we are likely*
> *to face a number of unpleasant developments ranging from*
> *anti-American demonstrations, further civil disorders, and even*
> *political assassinations to the ultimate installation of a hostile*
> *government which will ask us to leave while it seeks accommoda-*
> *tion with the national liberation front and Hanoi.*[33]

Taylor, who'd seen heavy combat in World War II as the commander of the 101st Airborne Division at the Battle of Normandy, wasn't engaging in hyperbole. After ten years of steadily increasing US military and economic aid, America's "test case" for defeating communist wars of national liberation was on the verge of collapse. While the Vietcong continued to ratchet up pressure against South Vietnamese forces in the countryside, most of the ARVN's senior generals seemed more concerned with lining their pockets with graft than with fighting communists. Between the fall of Diem and the establishment of a reasonable degree of stability in Saigon under Nguyen Van Thieu and Nguyen Cao Ky in June of 1965, half a dozen governments would come and go in Saigon. Little wonder the Vietcong were gaining ground so impressively in the countryside. The war seemed a distinctly secondary priority to the men in charge of waging it in Saigon.

In late 1964 and early 1965, it is fair to say there was no *functional* government in Saigon, let alone much of a government presence in the country's forty-four provinces, at least ten of which were entirely under communist administration at this time. Bill Bundy, who had spent most of the last decade analyzing the conflict, located South Vietnam's political and military troubles squarely on the country's tumultuous history. It was a nation, he wrote, that had much to overcome, including a "bad colonial heritage of long standing, totally inadequate preparation for self-government by the colonial power, a colonialist war fought in half-baked fashion and lost, [and] a nationalist movement taken over by Communists ruling in the other half of an ethnically and historically united country, the Communist side inheriting much the better military force and far more than its share of the talent."[34] In Saigon, said Bundy, dissent didn't express itself through legitimate political processes, but in "conspiracies of small clandestine groups dissatisfied with one another and the government."[35]

On January 27, Nguyen Khanh ousted Prime Minister Tran Van Huong in a bloodless coup, replacing him with a pliable civilian figurehead, Nguyen Xuan Oanh. That same day, President Johnson met with his senior advisers to discuss a memo prepared by Mac Bundy that spoke for himself and Bob McNamara. There was a palpable sense of urgency in Bundy's presentation of the "fork in the road" memorandum. The South Vietnamese were showing no signs of pulling together, and the government and the people were losing hope. The United States now had to make a choice:

> *What we want to say to you is that both of us are now pretty well convinced that our current policy can lead only to disastrous defeat. What we are doing now, essentially, is to wait and hope for a stable government. Our December directives make it very plain that wider action against the Communists will not take place unless we can get such a government. In the last six weeks that effort has been unsuccessful, and Bob and I are persuaded that there is no real hope of success in this area unless and until our own policy and priorities change. The underlying difficulties in Saigon arise from the spreading conviction that the future*

is without hope for anti-Communist policy. Our best friends have been somewhat discouraged by our own inactivity in the face of major attacks on our own installations. The Vietnamese know just as well as we do that the Viet Cong are gaining in the countryside. Meanwhile, they see the enormous power of the United States withheld and they get little sense of firm and active U.S. policy. . . .

The uncertainty and lack of direction which pervade the Vietnamese authorities are also increasingly visible among our own people, even the most loyal and determined.[36]

According to the memo, the United States faced a hard choice: either it could use its military power to force a change in communist policy, or all resources should be deployed "along a track of negotiation, aimed at salvaging what little can be preserved with no major addition to our present military risks."[37] McNamara and Bundy favored the former. It was soon quite apparent that the president did as well. "Stable government or no stable government," said Johnson, "we'll do what we have to do. I'm prepared to do that. We will move strongly."[38] Dean Rusk, who entered the meeting in disagreement with the thrust of Bundy's memo, appeared to be swayed, too. He was ready to go to phase two of option C. Rusk signed off later that day on a cable from LBJ to Taylor in Saigon, in which Johnson vowed "to make it clear to all the world that the U.S. will spare no effort and no sacrifice in doing its part to turn back the Communists in Vietnam."[39]

There was more than a bit of hyperbole in this cable, for Johnson had been working tirelessly behind the scenes, using his considerable persuasive powers, and a bit of bullying, to keep Senators Russell and Mansfield, among others, from initiating public hearings in the Senate on Vietnam policy, on the grounds that such a debate would give comfort to the communists. His efforts were remarkably successful. The public would have to wait more than two months for the news of the change in policy. Needing some sort of pretext for military escalation, Johnson authorized the resumption of destroyer patrols in the South China Sea—the first since September 1964—with a view to provoking the North Vietnamese into launching another attack.

At once resolute and cautious, determined yet reluctant, the president clearly would have rather postponed escalation in Vietnam until more of his domestic legislative agenda had passed Congress. But the Bundy memo convinced him that he had run out of time in Southeast Asia. And so Johnson ordered Mac Bundy to fly to Vietnam to determine *exactly* what should be done with the help of Ambassador Taylor and the American mission in Saigon. Perhaps he sent Bundy to give himself a few more days to pull the trigger on phase two of the escalation plan. Perhaps he simply wanted Bundy to confirm that the United States had run out of wiggle room with his own eyes. Remarkably, Mac Bundy had never set foot in Vietnam before. We shall never know the president's exact motives for sending the erstwhile Harvard dean to Vietnam during the first week of February.

In Vietnam, Bundy was deeply troubled by what he saw and heard. The Buddhists were heavily engaged in anti-American protests; the US Information Agency Library in Saigon had been sacked; the intelligence services and the American press in Saigon confirmed what Bundy probably already suspected: support for greater American intervention among the South Vietnamese was very weak, weaker, in fact, than it had ever been before. On the other hand, the Vietcong's position in the South had never been stronger. Striking evidence of that strength came in the form of yet another attack on American forces in Vietnam.

Just before 0200 hours on February 7, three hundred men of the PLAF's 409th Battalion launched a spectacularly successful raid on an American helicopter base near Pleiku, on a barren Central Highlands plateau. Using mortars, AK-47s, and explosive charges, the VC damaged or destroyed twenty-five aircraft, killed nine Americans, and wounded a hundred more. In terms of casualties it was the most costly attack on American forces yet, and confirmed MACV's doubts about the ability of the ARVN to protect American bases. The AP bureau chief in Saigon, Malcolm Browne, flew into the base just hours after the VC had made their escape, and produced this account:

> *The air base was attacked by two groups [of Vietcong]. One had carried six American-made 81-millimeter mortars into a hamlet 1,000 yards outside the barbed wire ringing the post. The residents of the hamlet never gave the slightest hint to Saigon*

*or American forces about the Viet Cong mortars being moved
in. . . . The six mortars were set up inside the huts of the hamlet,
since the hamlet itself was in clear view of the air base. Imprints
of the base plates of these mortars were found in the mud floors of
the huts later. The Viet Cong had taken their time setting everything up carefully, and when the time came for the attack, they
merely lifted the thatched roofs from the huts and opened fire.*

*Afterwards, the entire Viet Cong group got away without
casualties and with its mortars.*

Browne recalled how the commandos that formed the second Viet Cong
group cut through barbed wire to enter the base, "carrying pole and satchel
charges made from bamboo sticks, and TNT." The commandoes fired their
weapons and "put their charges on one aircraft after another, blowing them
up in order." The mortar shells, not the charges, caused the majority of the
casualties. The AP correspondent considered that this costly attack at Pleiku
"resulted from the rock-bottom morale of the Vietnamese forces supposed to
be protecting the base, American laxity, the political skill of the Viet Cong in
getting the local population to help them, and the sheer guts of the guerrillas
themselves.[40]

Early the next morning, Mac Bundy flew to the scene of the raid and was
visibly shaken by the extent of the destruction. When he spotted a bit of brain
tissue on a cot inside one of the barracks, he quickly exited the building and
threw up. After consulting with Taylor, Westmoreland, and General Khanh,
Bundy called the White House and urged immediate retaliation. In a hastily assembled meeting of the National Security Council in Washington, only Senator
Mansfield objected to launching retaliatory raids against North Vietnam. He
was worried that retaliation might provoke the Chinese to intervene. Johnson
was having none of it. "We have kept our guns over the mantel and our shells in
the cupboard for a long time now," said the president. "I cannot ask our American soldiers out there to continue to fight with one hand behind their backs."[41]
Within twelve hours of the Pleiku raid, American fighter-bombers flying off the
decks of two aircraft carriers in the South China Sea attacked the PAVN barracks at Dong Hoi, just north of the DMZ, and several other military targets.

More raids followed the next day. The Pleiku attack was read in Washington as a signal from Hanoi to the United States to back off. Ironically, Hanoi hadn't known about the raid until after the fact. The NLF had planned and launched the raid on its own initiative.

Immediately after flying back to Washington from Saigon, Bundy delivered his report. Well aware that as Vietcong strength surged so would the inclinations of the Buddhists and other factions in Saigon to enter into negotiations with the communists, Bundy argued aggressively for moving immediately to phase two, the "sustained reprisal" bombing campaign against North Vietnam:

> *The stakes in Vietnam are extremely high. The American investment is very large, and American responsibility is a fact of life which is palpable in the atmosphere of Asia, and even elsewhere. The international prestige of the United States, and a substantial part of our influence, are directly at risk in Vietnam. There is no way of unloading the burden on the Vietnamese themselves, and there is no way of negotiating ourselves out of Vietnam which offers any serious promise at present. It is possible that at some future time a neutral non–Communist force may emerge, perhaps under Buddhist leadership, but no such force currently exists, and any negotiated U.S. withdrawal today would mean surrender on the installment plan.*
>
> *The policy of graduated and continuing reprisal . . . is the most promising course available, in my judgment. That judgment is shared by all who accompanied me from Washington, and I think by all members of the country team [Ambassador Taylor and his subordinates in Saigon].*[42]

Johnson, Rusk, and McNamara were impressed by the sense of urgency imbedded in Mac Bundy's report, and plainly leaning toward supporting the move to phase two operations, when the Vietcong weighed in with another "spectacular." On the night of February 10–11, a bomb went off inside the US barracks at Qui Nhon on the central coast, killing twenty-one American servicemen. Two days later LBJ cabled Ambassador Taylor, informing him he had approved Operation Rolling Thunder, "a program of measured and limited air action jointly with the GVN against selected military targets in the DRV south of the 19th parallel until further notice."[43] Among the senior advisers, only George Ball, the undersecretary of state, voiced strenuous objection. Years after the war was over, Ball penned this damning critique of the reasoning behind the decision to bomb North Vietnam:

> As though to demonstrate how harassed but ingenious men can turn logic upside down, my colleagues interpreted the crumbling of the South Vietnamese government, the increasing success of the Viet Cong, and a series of defeats of South Vietnamese units in the field not as one might expect—persuasive evidence that we should cut our losses and get out—but rather as proving we must promptly begin bombing to stiffen the resolve of the South Vietnamese government. It was classic bureaucratic casuistry. A faulty rationalization was improvised to obscure the painful reality that America could arrest the galloping deterioration of its position only by the surgery of extrication. Dropping bombs was a pain-killing exercise that saved my colleagues from having to face the hard decision to withdraw.[44]

The first Rolling Thunder mission was delayed by a variety of circumstances until March 2. The weather was uncooperative, and yet another game of musical chairs in the Saigon government made it impossible for Taylor to get South Vietnamese concurrence on the bombing program quickly, even though it was a fait accompli. The end result of this particular chapter of turmoil in Saigon: General Khanh was forced into exile in the United States by the Armed Forces Council, dominated by Nguyen Van Thieu and Nguyen Cao Ky. February 1965 turned out to be the bloodiest month yet in the ARVN war on the VC. South Vietnamese forces suffered 4,140 casualties, including 870 killed. But the long civil war in South Vietnam had reached an inflection point that would alter the destinies of the American and Vietnamese people forever.

CHAPTER 4
CREEPING TOWARD
MAJOR WAR

A few days before the first Rolling Thunder mission commenced—on February 26, in fact—Lyndon Johnson approved General Westmoreland's request for two battalions of US Marines to defend the sprawling air base at Danang, where many of the Rolling Thunder air strikes would originate. Elements of the 9th Marine Expeditionary Brigade arrived on the shores of Red Beach in Danang on the bright, clear-blue morning of March 8. Their mission, Westmoreland announced, was strictly defensive. It wouldn't be for very long.

A day after the marines landed at Danang, Westmoreland received authority from Washington to order US airstrikes in South Vietnam when and where he saw fit. Even as the administration made a series of public pronouncements in March indicating that it had not altered course in Vietnam, it committed American ground troops and airpower to the fighting in the South. It began an open-ended bombing campaign against North Vietnam, the intensity of which could be dialed up or down, depending on Hanoi's behavior. Marine and army planners, meanwhile, stepped up their contingency planning for a host of possible missions. More marines were cruising the waters of the South China Sea in their amphibious assault ships, ready to step into the breach within a matter of hours. The military, in short, was laying the foundation for engaging in a major ground war, but the White House refused to say such a war was in the offing.

At the tail end of March, Westmoreland sent his aide, General William DePuy, to Washington with an urgent request for the deployment of one South Korean and two US Army divisions to Vietnam. By this point, DePuy told the president and the senior advisers, Hanoi had already sent several fully equipped, specially trained regiments of PAVN troops into the Central Highlands. One of the allied divisions was needed as a reaction force to challenge an anticipated communist offensive around Saigon; the other two were required to check a possible PAVN thrust from the Central Highlands to the coast, which had the ominous potential to sever South Vietnam in half. Ambassador Taylor objected to this proposed rapid increase of forces on the grounds that the logistical base "in-country" was too anemic to support them.

On April 1, Johnson deferred MACV's three-division request, but approved the deployment of two more marine battalions and an additional eighteen thousand to twenty thousand support troops to begin work on infrastructure development. Most significantly, he approved a change of mission for the marines in Vietnam. The 9th Marine Expeditionary Brigade was authorized to conduct offensive operations within fifty miles of wherever they were based along the coast in the northernmost five provinces of South Vietnam, soon to be known to Americans as I Corps (pronounced "eye" corps). It was agreed that for the time being, the marines would employ a classic counterinsurgency technique called the oil slick (or oil spot) strategy. Originally articulated by French general Hubert Lyautey, who had served in Indochina at the end of the nineteenth century, the oil spot concept called for infantry troops to move out from a secure base area into hostile territory, gradually extending their control over more and more terrain, just as spilled oil extends out from a center point on the ground. The British had used the strategy with great success in their campaign against communist guerrillas in Malaya in the 1950s. The Marine Corps, which had conducted a great many extended counterinsurgency operations in Central America and the Caribbean during the first three decades of the twentieth century, believed this approach was sound for a war that was ultimately about control over the country's 2,600 rural villages.

Three days after Johnson issued these new directives, the CIA released a top secret intelligence report to the senior players. The Rolling Thunder strikes thus far had had no appreciable effect on North Vietnamese morale, and only marginal effects on Hanoi's war production capacity. Additional PAVN units were moving into I Corps to challenge the marines, and the 101st Regiment of the 325th PAVN Division had begun to move into the Central Highlands. Pressure was building daily for additional American ground forces.

In a major speech at Johns Hopkins University in Baltimore on April 7, LBJ placed the conflict in Vietnam in the menacing context of Chinese expansionism. "Over this war—and all Asia—is another reality: the deepening shadow of Communist China. The rulers in Hanoi are urged on by Peking. This is a regime which has destroyed freedom in Tibet, which has attacked India, and has been condemned by the United Nations for aggression in Korea. It is a nation which is helping the forces of violence in almost every continent. The contest in Vietnam is part of this wider pattern of aggression."[1]

Indeed, by spring of 1965, the entire war council took it as gospel that China had malevolent designs on Southeast Asia. Fears of Beijing were inevitably heightened in Washington after the Chinese exploded their first atomic weapon in October 1964. By early 1965, Beijing "had replaced Moscow in the minds of U.S. policymakers as the wellspring of communist subversion," writes historian Brian VanDeMark. "Mao had replaced Stalin as the fomenter of world revolution."[2] We now know, of course, that in 1965, China was on the verge of a convulsion known as the Cultural Revolution. Mao had no master plan to establish hegemony over other Asian nations. In fact, Beijing encouraged Hanoi to press forward with the revolution in the South, but to do so cautiously and methodically. Above all, Mao wanted to avoid a direct confrontation with the United States. He was willing to provide aid and military specialists to Hanoi, but not ground forces, unless, that is, the United States launched a ground attack on North Vietnam. In short, the dragon of Chinese expansionism was largely a figment of the administration's collective imagination.

The Hopkins speech also revealed how poorly Lyndon Johnson understood the mindset of North Vietnam's leaders, particularly their level of commitment to reuniting the country. Johnson tried to lure Hanoi into giving up its quest to unite the entire country under its own rule by dangling a billion-dollar development plan for the Mekong River under its nose—a Vietnamese New Deal that would bring industry, health care, and education to the impoverished people of North Vietnam. It was a classic nonstarter to the men in khaki shirts on the politburo. Hanoi wanted all of Vietnam under its domain, not American-sponsored economic development. It couldn't be bought off. Within twenty-four hours of the speech, North Vietnam's prime minister, Pham Van Dong, laid out the conditions for peace talks: a complete American withdrawal from South

Vietnam; cessation of Rolling Thunder; and reorganization of the government of South Vietnam "in accordance with the program" of the National Liberation Front. The Johnson administration understood those terms to amount to surrender, and never formally responded.

Johnson did, however, approve General Westmoreland's request to deploy the 173rd Airborne Brigade as soon as possible to Bien Hoa, just twenty miles northeast of Saigon, as a rapid reaction force. US Army combat forces were at last going to war.

Ambassador Taylor in Saigon objected to the deployment of the 173rd on the grounds that it was simply too much too fast. LBJ ordered McNamara, Taylor, William Bundy, and McNaughton to meet with General Wheeler, General Westmoreland, and Admiral Sharp in a major conference in the Pacific Command Headquarters at Pearl Harbor, Honolulu, on April 20. He wanted the group to sort out exactly where American forces were needed, and when. At the conference, the flag officers steamrollered over Ambassador Taylor's objections to the rapid pace of additional deployments. It was already quite clear that bombing alone was not going to accomplish much, said the generals. Only a major infusion of American ground combat power could reverse the downward trend. After a lengthy and at times heated discussion, it was agreed to increase the number of maneuver battalions to fifteen, and to increase total troop strength from sixty-five thousand (there, or en route) to eighty-two thousand by the end of June.

Upon his return to Washington, McNamara presented the case for escalation to the other NSC principals. The United States, he said, must seize the initiative from the communists. It would be unwise to attempt to fix any time limit to the war. Johnson remained deeply ambivalent, just as he had been about every incremental step toward major war, but he approved the deployments agreed upon in Honolulu in any case, and instructed the army to prepare for the deployment of three full combat divisions to Vietnam.

Westmoreland's Strategy of Attrition

General Westmoreland liked the way the Marine Corps had hit the ground running in I Corps. General Lew Walt, the Marines' top field commander in

Vietnam, had established a good working relationship with the South Vietnamese forces in the area. This was no easy trick, given the huge gap in cultures and background, and the awkward necessity of maintaining separate chains of command in order to avoid the appearance that Saigon's military forces were—in the parlance of the NLF propagandists—"imperialist puppets." MACV's commander was impressed with the marines' early counterinsurgency work around Danang. But Westmoreland was *not* happy with the marines' strong emphasis on pacification—the effort to improve the lot of the local population with various forms of government aid and services, and provide them with security against the predations of the local Vietcong. Westmoreland wasn't oblivious to the threat the marines saw as preeminent—the guerrillas and the political cadres in the villages. There was, said Westmoreland, "no doubt whatsoever that the insurgency must eventually be defeated among the people in the hamlets and the towns." First, though, he explained in a secret cable to Washington, "the hardcore DRV/VC forces had to be destroyed in reaction and search and destroy operations" by mobile American forces.[3] Counterinsurgency and other pacification-type operations were best left to the South Vietnamese forces, as they spoke the same language and came from the same place as the people in the villages.

Communist military initiatives in the late spring and summer of 1965 went some way toward confirming Westmoreland's conviction that engaging the enemy's main forces should be the main priority for Americans, as the number of those units in South Vietnam seemed to be growing at a menacing pace. Together with the guerrillas, these forces were engaged in a sustained offensive to crack the spine of the ARVN. In May, at Song Be in Phuoc Long Province and at the Battle of Ba Gia, just twenty miles south of Chu Lai, Vietcong units wiped out several ARVN battalions.

Just before midnight on June 9, the VC stormed a US Special Forces camp and adjoining GVN district headquarters at a critical road juncture in the town of Dong Xoai, fifty-five miles north of Saigon. After plastering both objectives with mortar and recoilless rifle fire, about two thousand VC troops launched a powerful ground assault against a force of two hundred ARVN and two companies of Montagnard Civilian Irregular Defense Group (CIDG) forces, led by a dozen US Army Special Forces troops. In the initial assault, part of the

Special Forces camp was overrun, and the dispensary and communications shack were obliterated by mortar fire.

The Special Forces soldiers, under the command of Lieutenant Charles Q. Williams, scrambled to organize the defense of their mountain tribesmen, beating off several more ground assaults, but the "Yards" took heavy casualties in the process. By 0130 on June 10, two hours after the battle was joined, Huey gunships were on station, pummeling the VC positions with machine-gun and rocket fire. Nonetheless, the enemy soon gained control over the entire camp, and Lieutenant Williams had to withdraw his beleaguered defenders into the district compound.

A furious melee ensued throughout the remainder of the night. In the morning one of the Huey pilots described the scene: "The town and the [SF] compound were in shambles. At least seven [VC] .50 caliber machine gun positions were located throughout the area. The VC even had flamethrowers . . . to attack the compound."[4] The 1st Battalion of the 7th ARVN Airborne Regiment was committed to reinforce the defenders on the morning of June 10. They were flown into two LZs about two miles from the big fight. Both columns were ambushed by elements of the 273rd VC Regiment, which had taken up positions along the primary avenues of approach to the town, and were badly shot up.

Late in the afternoon, two battalions of the 52nd ARVN Rangers landed in a soccer field, catching the VC unaware, and began to drive them away from their objective with the help of well-placed artillery and close air support. By the morning of June 11, the charred ruins of the camp and the district headquarters were back in friendly hands, but four hundred South Vietnamese and thirteen Americans had been killed, among them eight helicopter crewmen. The VC left 134 corpses on the battlefield, and probably lost more than two hundred killed over the course of the savage fighting.

General Westmoreland found this cluster of powerful, sustained attacks worrying, but he was even more concerned over developments in the Central Highlands. Increasingly numerous PAVN forces were gathering in the vicinity of Pleiku and Kontum. These units threatened to push eastward along Route 19 and link up with powerful PLAF main forces in Binh Dinh Province on the coast just south of I Corps, effectively cutting the country in half. Westmoreland strongly suspected that Hanoi was about to progress from stage two of the Mao-

Giap protracted war paradigm, widespread guerrilla operations, to stage three, conventional war, in the hopes of crushing the South Vietnamese regime before the Americans had sufficient combat power in-country to stop them.

By the third week in June, Westmoreland had put forward to the JCS and the president a detailed conception of his strategy to defeat the insurgency outright, and a three-phase plan to implement it. The oil slick concept that Washington had approved in April, and the marines up in I Corps were employing, had to be shelved. It represented, said the general, "an inglorious, static use of U.S. forces in an overpopulated area with little chance of direct or immediate impact on the outcome of events."[5] In its stead, he proposed to

> employ US forces, together with Vietnamese airborne and marine battalions of the general reserve, against hardcore North Vietnam/Viet Cong forces in reaction and search and destroy operations, and thus permit the concentration of [conventional] Vietnamese troops in the heavily populated areas. We will be conducting mobile warfare from fixed and defended bases. Some of these will be major logistics centers at ports and airfields such as Chu Lai and Cam Ranh. Others will be tactical bases such as An Khe or Pleiku. The tactical bases will move as necessary and that may be with some frequency as the battle develops.[6]

With a force of forty-four maneuver battalions and a total of 175,000 American troops, he would blunt the considerable momentum of the insurgency by the end of 1965 and stabilize the military balance in phase one of his campaign. In phase two, from January to June 1966, US forces would go on a sustained offensive, requiring the deployment of an additional twenty-four maneuver battalions and supporting forces for those units. The combat battalions would "find, fix, and destroy" enemy main force units in the mountainous hinterlands of southern I Corps, the Central Highlands, and in the major VC base camps near Saigon. American infantry would both locate and engage enemy main forces, fixing them in place. Most of the killing would be done through the immense firepower that supporting arms—artillery, aircraft, and naval gunfire—could bring to bear.

By the end of the 1966 offensive or soon thereafter, Westmoreland projected, the war would likely reach a crucial "crossover point," where the communists would be taking more casualties per month than they could replace on southern battlefields. Once Hanoi reached that grim plateau, Westmoreland reckoned, its will to continue taking punishment would weaken, and break. At that point, "mop-up" operations would begin, in which remaining enemy forces in the South, mostly local guerrillas and demoralized main force units, would be destroyed by American and South Vietnamese forces together. It's not entirely clear from the documents how long Westmoreland envisaged phase three would take to accomplish. At several junctures in the summer of 1965 he seemed to hint it might take as little as a year. In theory, at least, these "search and destroy" missions would minimize American casualties, thereby helping to sustain support for the war back home.

Since Westmoreland had only nine American and one Australian maneuver battalion in mid-June, he chose to check the enemy offensive largely with air strikes. Wherever communist main force units were located they came under sustained aerial attack, and not only by fighter-bombers. On June 18, B-52 strategic bombers dropped their payloads over War Zone D in the first "Arc Light" strikes of the war. For the first time in warfare, strategic bombers were used to support ground operations.

In a nationally televised news conference on July 28, three weeks after he had secretly given the green light to Westmoreland's strategy, President Johnson came about as close as he ever would to a public declaration of war against the communists in Vietnam. He announced to the American people, and to the world, he was sending an additional fifty thousand troops to Southeast Asia immediately, and that as more were needed, more would be sent. For political reasons, he did not mention that he had in fact already approved the deployment of a total of 175,000 Americans to Vietnam by year's end. Nor did he mention that an additional 100,000 had already been earmarked for deployment in 1966. Against the advice of his top advisers, the president refused to call up the reserves for fear of prompting a spirited national debate over the war. Indeed, the American president refused to say what was plainly true: the United States was no longer simply supporting the South Vietnamese in *their* war. He had committed the United States military to fight a major war against the communists in Vietnam.

The Critics

Outside the White House and the National Security Council, the winds had been blowing in a very different direction. Since mid-1964, a diverse chorus of voices—including America's leading European allies, the Canadian government, key Democratic leaders in the Congress and Senate, leading pundits like Walter Lippmann and Joseph Kraft, and national newspapers of record like the *New York Times* and the *Washington Post*—had been calling on the administration both publicly and privately to seek a political solution in Vietnam. In August 1964, retired brigadier general Robert Thompson, head of the British advisory mission in Vietnam and a longtime supporter of American efforts there, sat down at his desk and wrote his superiors in London: "I am now convinced that we are passing the point of no return. Defeat by the Viet Cong, through subversion and increased guerrilla activity, is inevitable."[7] The Americans, said Thompson, must seek negotiations or face the prospect of having to deploy combat troops merely to extricate themselves. Brigadier Thompson's opinion was important. He had run the counterinsurgency campaign against Chinese communists in Malaya in the 1950s, and emerged victorious. The Foreign Office in London concurred with Thompson. The Brits would never go public with their views and embarrass their most important ally, yet they refused to make even a token military commitment to South Vietnam's defense, despite enormous pressure from LBJ and the State Department to do so. The best the United Kingdom could do was offer decidedly tepid diplomatic support.

Charles de Gaulle of France had always viewed American prospects in South Vietnam as essentially hopeless. De Gaulle had called for the withdrawal of all foreign troops from South Vietnam in 1963, and had been an outspoken critic of the Johnson administration's policy since it had assumed office. In April 1965, after learning that LBJ had approved offensive operations for the US Marines in Vietnam, he told his cabinet officers that unless Washington halted military action immediately and pursued a political solution, the fighting would go on for ten years, and result in humiliation and disaster for the United States. It was one of the more prescient and haunting assessments put forward during these critical months.

In truth, the senior officials of Britain, France, Canada, and West Germany were all deeply puzzled by the hold Vietnam seemed to have over Johnson and his senior foreign policy team. They saw the struggle there much like the author of America's containment policy, George Kennan, did: it was at best peripheral to Western security concerns. Unfortunately, LBJ was deeply defensive about America's leading allies' opinions about American options in Vietnam. When British prime minister Harold Wilson learned to his very grave dismay that LBJ had decided to commence open-ended air operations against North Vietnam in February 1965, he practically begged Johnson during a phone call to hold off, and to meet with him face-to-face to discuss alternatives. Johnson told him in no uncertain terms not to come to Washington. There was nothing that he could do or say to change Johnson's mind. Meanwhile, Dean Rusk's State Department's "More Flags" campaign to enlist military support from America's leading allies got nowhere. Only Australia and South Korea were willing to provide more than a handful of combat troops.

Senate Majority Leader Mike Mansfield, former marine, former professor of Asian history, had been counseling withdrawal in private meetings with the president for months on the grounds that American forces could not win a civil war for a listless and ineffective Saigon government that showed little inclination to fight the insurgency aggressively itself. Senator Richard Russell of Georgia had gone so far as to suggest to his old protégé LBJ that the administration should unearth a high-ranking South Vietnamese general who could be convinced to demand an American withdrawal after a certain interval, thereby allowing the administration to "save face" as it exited Vietnam.

The *New York Times*, after years of supporting the American crusade in Southeast Asia, changed its tune in late 1964. So did scores of other newspaper editors across the country. According to an editorial in the *Washington Post* in late December, "it is becoming increasingly clear that, without an effective government, backed by a loyal military and some kind of national consensus in support of independence, we cannot do anything for South Vietnam. The economic and military power of the United States . . . must not be wasted in a futile attempt to save those who do not wish to be saved."[8]

Within the government bureaucracy, a cadre of mid-level officers who had worked intensively on Southeast Asia for years argued that no good would come of committing the United States to a ground war in Southeast Asia. In 1964 and early 1965, they felt increasingly isolated and frustrated by their inability to make an impact on the thinking of senior-level decision makers. A number of these old Asia hands, such as Paul Kattenburg and James C. Thomson Jr., were either nudged out of their jobs or left government service as it became clear that their opinions were being ignored or marginalized in the policy-making process.

Finally, another important constituency—this one a small group within the military with no direct access to decision makers—had serious reservations about Johnson's plan to expand the American mission so ambitiously. While at the Armed Forces Staff College in late 1964, just as the US Army was gearing up to deploy its own combat forces to Vietnam, Colonel Volney F. Warner attended a speech by the marine commandant, General Wallace Greene. Before he began his talk, General Greene asked his audience of a hundred majors and colonels a pointed question: "How many of you think that U.S. forces should be sent to fight in Vietnam and draw the line against communism there?" Virtually everyone in the audience raised their hands enthusiastically. Then Greene, a decidedly hawkish member of the Joint Chiefs of Staff, asked a second question: "How many of you do not think we should become involved [in combat] in Vietnam?"

Six officers raised their hands hesitantly. Warner was among them. "There are a few cowards in every bunch," quipped the commandant.[9] But those six officers were not cowards by any stretch. They were soldiers and marines who had recently returned stateside from tours of duty as advisers to ARVN units. They knew from firsthand experience what many in the senior leadership of the American armed forces did not: that the ARVN officer corps, like the government it served, was both corrupt and indifferent to the plight of the peasantry it was supposed to protect. Moreover, the ARVN was fighting a decidedly unconventional "people's war" against small units of guerrillas with tactics and doctrine developed by the US Army for conventional conflicts between regular armies. No wonder Saigon was losing.

CHAPTER 5

HANOI GOES FOR BROKE

In December 1963, just a few weeks after the coup against Ngo Dinh Diem, the Central Committee, the DRV's chief policy-making body, gathered in Hanoi amid an atmosphere of urgency and expectation. The question before the roughly fifty members of the committee: How should the revolution respond to Diem's recent demise? How could it best be exploited by the insurgents in the South? What could their brothers in the North do to aid in the struggle? We have no detailed record of the discussion, but we know it was both protracted and passionate, with committee members divided largely into two camps. We also have the text of the decision they rendered, Resolution 9.

Moderate party leaders, led by Ho Chi Minh and General Giap, thought the demise of the South Vietnamese president might well open the door to negotiations with the new military junta in Saigon, leading to the formation of a coalition government and the exit of the United States. They urged their colleagues on the committee to pursue such a course of action, at least long enough to determine whether a good outcome appeared feasible. Wouldn't it be better, they said, to take control of the South through gradual political struggle rather than brutal warfare against their own countrymen, and perhaps the Americans? The revolution had been going on for more than two decades already, and patience was among the most prized of Vietnamese virtues. A few more years, they argued, wouldn't matter much in the broad scheme of things.

In truth, Ho and the other moderates had consistently sought to limit the level of violent struggle in the South over the previous several years. They feared a major war in the South would retard the development of a successful socialist state in the North, a project that still had a long, long way to go, even ten years after the Geneva agreement. North Vietnam still had trouble feeding its entire population properly. Giap, for his part, was leery of committing the PAVN to a conflict that would involve the Americans before its divisions were fully modernized with new AK-47s, rocket forces, artillery, and motor transport from the Chinese. He also felt that the southerners had yet to develop a mature political understanding of the struggle that lay ahead, and were a bit too impulsive. Better to focus on political and organizational work than to get distracted by combat operations prematurely. Like other "North Firsters," Giap worried that an NLF conventional offensive in 1964 might well draw American forces directly into the fight, a prospect that Moscow had strongly urged Hanoi to avoid. It was not a good time to strain relations with the Russians.

The man with the most direct experience and knowledge of revolutionary activities in the South on the politburo in Hanoi was Le Duan, hands down. For several years now, he had been the driving force behind the militant "South First" faction, which had regularly lobbied the Central Committee to expand the North's support for NLF operations. By the time of Diem's assassination, Le Duan, who appeared to the outside world as a taciturn, unassuming bureaucrat, had become the most powerful North Vietnamese leader, eclipsing in influence even Ho Chi Minh and General Giap, the two great heroes of the French Indochina War.

The South First faction, which also included politburo members Le Duc Tho and General Nguyen Chi Thanh, believed the Saigon coup exposed the depth of Saigon's weakness and illegitimacy, as well as Washington's sinister domination over South Vietnamese politics. It seemed to them that the chances for direct American intervention with combat forces had never been greater. The instability and chaos that gripped Saigon in the wake of the coup, they said, provided the revolutionary forces with a golden opportunity to defeat the American-backed puppets. Time was of the essence. Revolutionary forces must strike, and strike hard. North Vietnam had to step up its military support as soon as possible, before the Americans arrived in strength. Le Duan and his supporters reckoned that the Americans were no fools. Once they saw South Vietnam's new regime crumbling under the weight of a powerful NLF offensive, they would come to realize that there was no military solution and seek a way out through negotiations. In response to Giap's concerns that the People's Army of Vietnam was not yet ready to go to war in the South, Le Duan said that if the "go for broke" strategy failed, the revolutionary forces could always regroup, rest, and resume guerrilla warfare while the PAVN expanded and modernized.

In Beijing, Mao weighed in behind the South First faction, and indicated a willingness to help Hanoi build up its forces for the fight. In part, Beijing did so because the Soviets were urging caution and supporting Ho Chi Minh's position. Mao wanted the peoples in the Third World to see China, not the Soviet Union, as the foremost advocate for wars of national liberation. The Sino-Soviet split of the early 1960s posed a number of problems for Le Duan and his colleagues that required delicate diplomatic work, but in the long run, the Vietnamese communists were able to play Moscow off against Beijing brilliantly in order to obtain more material aid than they might have done otherwise.

In the end, the South First faction's views carried the day at the crucial December gathering of the Central Committee. As historian Pierre Asselin has asserted, Resolution 9 was essentially a declaration of war against the government in Saigon and its American backers. It called on the North to fully support the war being waged against Saigon:

> *We are still weaker than the enemy militarily. Therefore the key point at the present time is to make outstanding effort to rapidly strengthen our military forces in order to create a basic change in the balance of forces between the enemy and us in South Vietnam. . . . If we do not defeat the enemy's military forces, we cannot overthrow his domination and bring the revolution to victory. To destroy the enemy's military forces we should use armed struggle. For this reason, armed struggle plays a direct and decisive role.*[1]

The military offensive, said the resolution, would be joined with an ambitious worldwide propaganda campaign to pressure the United States to withdraw its forces from the South.

This document also amounted to a shot across the bow at the North Firsters. It confirmed the necessity of stepped up violent action—immediately. Negotiating with lackeys, the document claimed, demonstrated weakness, and was tantamount to capitulation. Only war would enable Vietnam to achieve national liberation and unification. Hanoi hoped to break the back of the new military junta headed by General Duong Van Minh before the Americans could deploy sufficient numbers of their own forces to save Saigon from ruin. The flow of military supplies and PAVN specialists to expand the NLF's lethality had to be ramped up immediately, and so it was. (See the story of the Ho Chi Minh Trail in chapter 8.)

In the wake of Resolution 9, Le Duan and Le Duc Tho orchestrated a partial purge of mid-rank party officials who supported the North Firsters. Yet it should be noted that Giap, Ho, and several other "revisionists" retained substantial influence over communist strategy in 1964 and 1965. They continued to temper Le Duan's aggressive inclinations with pleas for caution and restraint. It seems clear from the limited sources we have, for instance, that Le Duan would have liked to begin sending PAVN units (as opposed to individual soldiers) to the South in early 1964, but Giap and Ho's reluctance to deploy the army was almost certainly responsible for delaying the arrival of the first North Vietnamese battalions and regiments in South Vietnam until the last few months of the year. But there is no question that the North First faction had considerably less influence in shaping war strategy than the South First group during 1965, and later.

Le Duan

Who exactly was Le Duan, this mysterious and reticent figure with "the perennially sad eyes and protruding ears"?[2] On the surface, he seemed a bland Party functionary who eschewed the public spotlight. In fact, he possessed a highly nuanced sense of revolutionary strategy and a decidedly Machiavellian approach to power politics. He was, indeed, a leather-tough revolutionary with an unyielding commitment to the liberation of the South. Among the hard men of his clique, "the Spartan ethic—a willingness to suffer in pursuit of a high purpose—reigned supreme."[3] According to Colonel Bui Tin, the PAVN officer who ultimately accepted the surrender of the South Vietnamese government in Saigon in 1975, he was also "very self-confident and thought a lot of himself."[4]

Born in humble circumstances in Quang Tri Province in 1907, Le Duan first became aware of the doleful effects of French rule on Vietnamese life when he traveled the length and breadth of the country as a railway clerk in the mid-1920s. Like Ho and Giap, Le Duan found his calling as a revolutionary early, joining several youth groups dedicated to the pursuit of independence in the late 1920s. He was a founding member of the Communist Party of Vietnam. Placed in charge of indoctrinating potential Party members in Tonkin—northern Vietnam—he was arrested by the French for subversion in Haiphong in 1931, and sentenced to twenty years in prison. His sentence was commuted by a new liberal government in Paris after he had served only six years. As he endured the vicissitudes of the French penal system, Le Duan developed an almost religious commitment to communism as a vehicle for national liberation. He took over the Party apparatus in Annam (central Vietnam), only to be arrested for subversion once again in 1940 and sent to the grimmest of Vietnam's prisons on Poulo Condor Island, where he languished through most of World War II.

During the long war against France, Le Duan was placed in charge of military and political operations in Cochinchina, where the French presence was strongest. He did so well at this truly mammoth task that he was appointed to the politburo in absentia in 1951, and remained in the South (with occasional trips to Hanoi to file reports and vote on key legislation) through the early 1960s. Widely recognized as the leading authority on the insurgency in the South to serve on the politburo, he was elected first secretary of the Party in 1960, thus outranking everyone except Ho himself. According to Colonel Tin, Le Duan had been chosen over Vo Nguyen Giap because of his deep knowledge of the South, and because he had "spent two long periods in prison. . . . This was a significant qualification for rising to the top of the Party, since it was considered that the more one had been put to the test, the more trustworthy one was. In fact, imprisonment was regarded as the university of politics."[5]

By late 1963, writes a leading historian of the Vietnamese side of the war, Le Duan's "revolutionary pedigree, commitment to Marxism-Leninism and self-abnegation were beyond reproach."[6] A vicious bureaucratic infighter, Le Duan expanded his power base through intimidation and fearmongering, with considerable help from "the Hammer," Le Duc Tho, his chief protégé on the politburo, and General Nguyen Chi Thanh, Giap's chief rival within the ranks of the PAVN. All three men considered the liberation of the South to be their sacred duty. All were loath to delay the full-throttle pursuit of that objective for the sake of building up the socialist experiment in the North. Le Duan in particular saw the liberation of the South as a seminal event in the worldwide "people's struggle" against imperialism and capitalism. It had significance well beyond Vietnam.

The Evolution of Hanoi's War Strategy

During the Vietnam War and for several decades afterward, American policy makers and historians of the war had only a hazy understanding of communist decision-making on war strategy. The conventional wisdom depicted the senior leadership in Hanoi as a dozen like-minded fanatical communists grimly determined to impose their political system and way of life on the South at virtually any cost. This demeaning perception neglected to account for the natural variance of opinion among a group of highly experienced, intelligent, and, above all else, deeply committed leaders. Though politburo archives still remain closed to Western researchers, by the 2010s, Hanoi had released a sufficient number of Party and military documents to give Western scholars of the war a much more richly textured picture of the decision-making than was available during the war years.

We know now that Hanoi pursued a policy of peaceful unification through the vehicle of a general election for more than two years after the Geneva Conference in 1954. The North Vietnamese were too preoccupied with domestic problems to engage in a shooting war in the South. After it became clear that no such election would be held, the senior leadership struggled continuously to balance competing but complementary objectives of building a viable communist society in the North, and providing political and military support to the revolutionary forces in the South.

Hanoi's road to war, like America's, was a halting and tortuous one. Le Duan was the only politburo member to remain in the South more or less continually from 1945 through the early 1960s. He witnessed firsthand the devastating effects of Diem's sweeping July 1955 "Denounce the Communists" campaign, which resulted in the killing of at least two thousand well-trained political cadres and the imprisonment or death of many thousands of the revolution's sympathizers. Morale among the faithful in the South plummeted, and many people deserted the movement. At Le Duan's urging, the politburo in early 1957 approved the use of violence against Saigon for the first time, but placed tight constraints on its implementation. Armed cadres were permitted to conduct selective assassinations and acts of terror against symbolic targets of government authority. Such acts, though, were not to be advertised as being carried out at the direction of the Party. Rather, they were to be presented as spontaneous reactions by "the people" to Saigon's repression.

Diem responded to VC terror and assassination tactics with a renewed anti-communist campaign that was so successful that communist historians refer to the period between 1957 and 1959 as the darkest time in the history of the movement in the South. Le Duan was hardly the only important Party figure in the South who genuinely feared that the insurgency might collapse under Saigon's pressure. In January 1959, the Central Committee began to debate Resolution 15, calling for the rapid buildup of military forces in the South, and selective attacks on ARVN units in the field by guerrilla companies. It implied that the southern revolutionaries should begin to form their first full-time, regular infantry units. And it called for the formation of a united front, a new iteration of the Vietminh, that would pull together all of the opponents of the Diem regime. The National Liberation Front was formed officially in December 1960.

The moderates on the politburo, though, weren't ready to launch a real war against Diem—not yet. Ho revised Resolution 15 by his own hand, deleting all references to "infantry attacks" and calling instead for the formation of a large number of Armed Propaganda Units (APUs) in the South. These were armed teams of between three and a dozen men whose primary duty was to expand and protect the nascent political infrastructure in the countryside, through a heady mix of persuasion, inspiration, and coercion. The APUs were not designed for offensive action. They did not go looking for fights, but they could defend themselves in the event of a government attack, and some of the units had cells that specialized in conducting assassinations of government officials and other troublemakers. Attacks against Saigon's local militia, or civil guards, were deemed permissible, but not attacks on the regular armed forces.

Having been given the green light to engage in "revolutionary violence," the southern communists initiated an assassination campaign aimed not only at GVN officials, but at health workers and teachers who served the people in the countryside. In 1959, there were 1,200 such assassinations. During 1961, the number mushroomed to about 4,000. Meanwhile, the PLAF steadily built up its strength in remote bases deep in War Zone C, west of Saigon near the Cambodian border; War Zone D, northwest of the capital city; and in the Ca Mau Peninsula in the Mekong Delta.

In early 1963, the moderates on the politburo were again successful in limiting the North's support for armed struggle. They importuned their southern brothers to concentrate on guerrilla warfare and political subversion. But Le Duan, ever impatient, maneuvered ruthlessly to secure control over the Party's internal security forces and solidify his power base with the help of Le Duc Tho and General Thanh. Unlike Giap, Thanh was more than ready to commit the North's regular army to the fight in the South.

The National Liberation Front's Leading Military Commander

Born very near Le Duan's home village in Quang Tri, Nguyen Chi Thanh also spent considerable time in French prisons during World War II. After his release, he commanded Vietminh forces in central Vietnam, and went on to write some influential pieces on strategy and motivation for the Party newspaper, *Nhan Dan*. Emboldened by the stunning success against the ARVN at the Battle of Ap Bac at the beginning of the year, and by Beijing's increasing willingness to support Vietnam's war of national liberation, the militant's views began to gain traction. Convinced that the Americans could not escalate the war fast enough to deprive the revolutionary forces of a major victory over the ARVN, Le Duan pressed his case for "going for broke" with a major offensive. In April 1964, PAVN units began to train for the arduous trip to the South. General Thanh was sent south during the summer to take command of the Central Office for South Vietnam (COSVN), the NLF command center near the Cambodian border in Tay Ninh Province. Accompanying Thanh on his journey was a retinue of high-level cadre with experience in building up main force units and leading big-unit combat operations.

The Tonkin Gulf incident, and the Gulf of Tonkin Resolution that followed on its heels on August 7, 1964, granted President Johnson a free hand to escalate the war as he saw fit. It also catalyzed the politburo to intensify its efforts to bolster revolutionary forces in the South. Within a few short weeks, the People's Army of Vietnam sent its first complete infantry regiment south along the Ho Chi Minh Trail. Another regiment left for the south in early October.

From his headquarters deep in the jungle, Thanh planned major combat operations in three areas: north of Saigon in War Zones C and D; on the coast in Binh Dinh Province, long a stronghold of revolutionary forces; and in the remote Central Highlands, in the vicinity of Pleiku and Kontum. The PAVN's most offensive-minded general also developed and implemented a political indoctrination campaign to stamp out a mushrooming "inferiority complex" among the troops as they anticipated meeting the Americans in battle.

Thanh, the PAVN general who would command COSVN until his death in the summer of 1967, not only pressed for a tight focus on main force operations against the ARVN; he also advocated main force operations in the (increasingly likely) event the Americans deployed ground forces, which was blasphemy among protracted war theory advocates. "To attack unremittingly is the most active and effective method to maintain and extend our control of the battlefield," wrote Thanh.[7] The superior fighting spirit of the revolutionary armed forces, maintained by constant indoctrination, would compensate for the revolutionary army's material deficiencies against the mighty Americans, or so General Thanh believed.

The objectives of Thanh's first offensive, which began at the tail end of 1964 with the dramatic Battle of Binh Gia (see chapter 3 for an account), were to break the back of the ARVN before the Americans arrived in strength; to destroy the strategic hamlets, and expand the liberated zone in the southwest of the country near the Cambodian border. PLAF units went on a kind of rampage, decimating a shocking number of ARVN battalions, and temporarily seized several provincial and district capitals. Thanh's offensive combined a relentless series of attacks on ARVN convoys and outposts, designed to draw Saigon's elite ranger and marine strategic reserve units into prepared killing zones. In Binh Dinh Province, several main force VC battalions captured a fortified district headquarters at An Lao in early December, and then fought off several counterattacks by elite ARVN units ferried to the fight in American helicopters. The ARVN took the headquarters back after three days of fighting, but they suffered some three hundred casualties in the process.

Several other major attacks were planned in the coming months as part of Thanh's offensive. VC sapper attacks against Pleiku (February 7) and Qui Nhon (February 10) resulted in heavy casualties for the Americans, shocked the Johnson administration, and triggered the initiation of Operation Rolling Thunder. After a lull in the fighting in March and April throughout the country, elements of the 9th VC Division pulverized an ARVN regiment in Quang Ngai Province in the Battle of Ba Gia in late May.

The tempo of VC operations, and the skill and bravado of the communist forces, worried General Westmoreland. In March 1965, he filed a very sobering report to Washington. If present trends continue, said the head of MACV, the Vietcong might well take over the country before the end of the year. Three months later, Westmoreland reported to his superiors at Pacific headquarters that Thanh's offensive was "destroying [ARVN] battalions faster than they can be reconstituted." South Vietnamese commanders "do not believe they can survive without the active commitment of U.S. ground forces."[8]

Strategies, Forces, and Key Warfighting Concepts

The sustained friction in the early and mid-1960s between the moderate and the militant factions within the politburo should not obscure the fact that the senior leaders in Hanoi possessed a common strategic mindset in confronting the daunting prospect of fighting the greatest military power in the world. They understood themselves to be fighting a revolutionary war, the central purpose of which was to break down the authority and the legitimacy of the "puppet" Saigon regime, and replace it with an administration that was responsive to the aspirations of ordinary Vietnamese peasants for independence from foreign domination. Despite the blizzard of heated rhetoric to the contrary in their propaganda literature, Hanoi's strategists never imagined they could force an end to American involvement in Vietnam by defeating the American army on the battlefield. They knew they could not match the American military's mobility and awesome firepower, even with substantial military assistance from the Chinese and the Soviets. But they were confident of their ability to best the Americans in the realms of overall strategy, political warfare, and organizational skill. Hanoi dismissed "the assumption that the principal and primary means test [of success in the war] must be military combat," observes Douglas Pike, a long-serving US foreign service officer in Vietnam during the war. "They realized . . . that it might be possible to achieve a change of venue and determine the war's outcome away from the battlefield."[9]

The communists' most important assets in the war against the United States were, first, a distinctly Vietnamese conception of Mao's protracted war strategy. It was called *dau tranh*, loosely translated into English as "struggle movement," and it involved the mobilization of vast numbers of people, especially peasants, against the GVN and the Americans along two broad tracks: political struggle and military struggle. Another crucial asset was the revolutionary movement's politically indoctrinated, three-tier army. A third key asset was the organizational vehicle for the execution of *dau tranh*: the National Liberation Front, that remarkably dynamic and cohesive "organization of organizations." As the Americans arrived in strength in spring and summer of 1965, the Front enjoyed wide and deep support in the countryside, where about 90 percent of the country's 16 million people lived, and was seen as the legitimate expression of the people's desire for national unity and freedom by much of the world, including a considerable number of American citizens, despite its communist leadership.

And finally a fourth crucial asset, in historian Jeffrey Record's phrase, was Hanoi's "superior strategic grasp of the political and social dimensions of the struggle."[10] As Vo Nguyen Giap often remarked, American military forces were far superior to his own by virtually every measure, but the Americans' strategic assessments of the nature of the war, of their own strengths and weaknesses and those of their adversaries, were markedly inferior to those of Hanoi and the NLF. Through the NLF, Hanoi effectively integrated a cluster of political and military initiatives to build up the strength of its shadow political infrastructure in the villages, while simultaneously frustrating the efforts of Saigon to do the same. The essence of *dau tranh*, writes Pike, was "people as an instrument of war. The mystique surrounding it involved organization, mobilization and motivation of people. . . . Violence is necessary to it but not its essence. The goal is to seize power by disabling the society, using special means, i.e., assassination, propaganda, guerrilla warfare mixed with conventional military operations, chiefly organizational means. In fact, organization is the great god of *dau tranh* strategy and counts for more than ideology or military tactics."[11]

Dau tranh can be conceived of as a kind of bear trap. The two "jaws" of political struggle and military struggle close in on the enemy, constricting his room for maneuver and response, inflicting psychological and physical punishment on him, and gradually sapping his morale as well as his material resources. The role of the Party leadership is to adjust continually the ratio of resources devoted to each type of struggle over time and space, as circumstances develop. *Everything hinges on the caliber of the strategic assessments behind the adjustments.* Neither form of struggle can be effective in isolation. It is only when the two are properly combined—what Pike calls "the marriage of violence to politics"—that success can be achieved.[12]

"Military struggle" for the Vietnamese communists meant a great deal more than conventional military operations. It included terrorism, sabotage, assassination, guerrilla warfare, even the avoidance of combat with a view to frustrating the enemy's desire to close in and attack his adversary. The major functions of the communists' military forces in the war against the Americans were to defend and expand the political infrastructure, and to protract the conflict by avoiding decisive, big-unit battles. They sought to inflict sufficient casualties to create a sense of doubt in the minds of the American troops, policy makers, and the American public that progress was being made. Over time, said the Vietnamese strategists, doubt would erode confidence, morale would begin to crumble and, eventually, America's will to continue would evaporate.

To carry out these missions, Hanoi had at its disposal a uniquely resilient fighting organization with three types of forces. Light infantry, main force units of both the PLAF and PAVN were typically deployed in operations in 1965 in battalion and regimental strength. They were full-time, well-trained troops. There were three infantry battalions of 450 to 600 men in a regiment, plus supporting units. Battalions were composed of three infantry companies, a combat support company that handled heavy weapons such as mortars and recoilless rifles, and separate platoons for signals (communications), reconnaissance, and sappers, or combat engineers who were responsible for clearing obstacles and leading attacks on fortified positions.

Unlike Western armies, the revolutionary forces in Vietnam were heavily politicized. All main force units of company size or greater were co-commanded by a military officer and a political officer, or commissar. The political officer, invariably a member of the Party, bore responsibility for maintaining good morale and "correct revolutionary thinking" in the ranks. They served as counselors and confessors to the troops, and conducted self-criticism sessions after operations, and indoctrination-education classes when their units were not actively deployed. At these sessions, recalled Colonel Bui Tin, "our thoughts, our awareness, our actions, all were called into question. So too were our relationships with our superiors and subordinates, with our peers, friends, family, and other soldiers. Our good points and shortcomings were all noted down in a record to promote self-improvement. The aim was to give prominence to the spirit and meaning of the Revolution."[13]

Xuan Vu, a gifted writer of fiction and nonfiction who served as a propaganda officer in the PAVN, recalled the crucial importance of self-criticism sessions as a way of ensuring the "correct thinking" communist strategists understood to be essential for military success:

> If you were educated in a French school you had to describe how your thoughts had been formed by the colonialists. If your parents were business people or owned land you had to tell about how they had acted against the interests of the people—and how you yourself had profited from it. If you had made any mistakes of your own, you had to include those in your confession. . . . Maybe you had fought alongside the French for a while, or maybe you had chosen to continue your studies rather than join the Vietminh. . . . Even if you couldn't really think of anything, you had to exaggerate some inconsequential incident or make something up. What they wanted was for you to deny yourself and to accept the consciousness of the Party. You had to root out everything that was part of you that didn't conform to the correct way of thinking.[14]

Below the main force units were the VC regional guerrilla forces. These, too, were full-time soldiers, usually deployed in company strength (100 to 120 men), and typically controlled by the provincial military committee of the NLF. Most of the men in these units had been recruited locally, and they seldom fought outside their own province. They conducted limited independent raids and ambushes, and were quite often attached to main force units in larger, sustained operations, where they provided crucial intelligence on the enemy dispositions and knowledge of the local terrain. Proven regional guerrillas were often recruited into main force PLAF units.

The third type of force was the local guerrillas, sometimes called the militia. These were the part-time fighters, "farmers by day, soldiers at night," whose primary responsibility was to provide a continuous armed presence in the villages, to collect intelligence there, and to build village fortifications. Most of these people were either too young or too old to fight in regional or main force units. The three-tiered structure of the armed forces was devised to permit Hanoi to conduct flexible and varied types of operations at varying degrees of intensity in different regions, while simultaneously defending the Vietcong infrastructure. Broadly speaking, in 1965, guerrilla operations dominated in the lowlands near the coast, and main force operations were carried out in the Central Highlands and northwest of Saigon, near the large communist base areas.

Outside of the northernmost fourteen provinces of South Vietnam, which remained under the direct operational control of the Central Military Party Committee in Hanoi, military operations in South Vietnam were commanded by PAVN general Nguyen Chi Thanh's Central Office for South Vietnam, but Thanh took broad directions from the CMPC. The guerrilla forces, both local and regional, played an indispensable role in protecting and growing the political infrastructure, the intricate network of village, district, and provincial committees and subcommittees that organized and directed the activities of the people who lived under its sway. The guerrillas and the local population, supported often by a combat engineer or two from North Vietnam, had by 1965 constructed hundreds of "combat villages" in the South, replete with tunnels, trenches, myriad fighting positions, and sometimes even underground hospitals. In these villages, recalled AP chief correspondent Malcolm Browne, one could find "cleverly concealed fortifications. . . . Innocent seeming paddy dykes studded with gun ports; apparently accidental holes in the corner of fields [for] machine gun positions; tall trees contain sniper's nests, and even graveyards became enormous bunker systems."[15] Since the end of the war, official Vietnamese historians tend to gloss over the differences between the PAVN and PLAF forces, seeing them as two parts of the same revolutionary army. During the war, it was a different story, as Hanoi went to great pains to contradict Washington's assertion that Hanoi controlled the insurgency. Hanoi presented the PLAF as an independent army controlled by the NLF that enjoyed moral and material support from North Vietnam. During 1965, the burden of combat in South Vietnam was carried out by PLAF main forces and guerrillas, but the majority of these units were reinforced with individual PAVN officers and noncommissioned officers.

Yet the rapid escalation of PLAF military operations in 1964 and 1965, however, was due largely to ramped-up recruiting *within* South Vietnam, not to PAVN infiltration, as the Johnson administration wanted the public to believe—and perhaps convinced itself it believed. NLF political cadre Trinh Duc had fought with the Vietminh against the French, and had stayed behind in the South to help run the clandestine revolutionary apparatus there. As the first American ground forces arrived in the spring of 1965, he was a recruiting officer. "There were a great number of volunteers [in the South]. The Americans had finally brought their own forces into Vietnam, and one of the results was a huge outpouring of young people who wanted to fight against them. During one period I was able to bring five hundred recruits out just from [the city of] Cholon. . . . They came because they were willing to sacrifice themselves to save the country."[16]

After three months of training in the vicinity of COSVN in Tay Ninh Province, those recruits were put into the field. Trinh Duc recalled that a great many had been killed by year's end. "Rather than being intimidated by American escalation," observes historian Brian VanDeMark, the NLF and the North Vietnamese "pushed back, demonstrating determination rather than intimidation, and moving nimbly as mice in response to the lumbering American elephants."[17]

The passionate desire of so many members of the insurgency to fight against the Americans in the South, it must be said, was rooted primarily in the Vietnamese peoples' age-old resentment at foreign intrusion. They did not, in any meaningful sense, adopt communism as an ideology, nor did the Vietnamese Communist Party attempt to teach conventional Marxist-Leninist communist doctrine to its followers. In late 1964, the RAND Corporation began a field study of Vietcong defectors and prisoners, attempting to understand, in the words of the army liaison officer for the study, why they forsook Saigon and the material benefits of working with the Americans in order "to go and breathe under the reeds" and "live in the tunnels at Cu Chi."[18] The study, issued in early 1965, asserted that the VC were generally "selfless, cohesive, dedicated soldiers who saw themselves as patriots, particularly within the context of a corrupt South Vietnam and a disintegrating army."[19]

Perhaps the most effective tactic employed by communist forces in the war against the Americans concerned their effort to control the tempo of fighting in general, and to choose the time and place of individual engagements. According to one US military study, 88 percent of engagements during the entire war against the Americans were initiated by the communists.[20] Naturally, Vietcong and PAVN units alike struck when and where their commanders thought the circumstances were favorable. Often, that meant a sharp, fierce hit-and-run firefight, followed by a well-planned withdrawal along several routes to a prearranged reassembly point.

The PLAF guerrillas were taught the "one slow, four fast" method of combat: slow preparation; fast attack; fast exploitation and pursuit; fast clearing of the battlefield; fast withdrawal to an agreed-upon site. When main force units did stand and fight for protracted periods of time—a rare event in Vietnam in 1965—they invariably tried to fight their adversaries at close range, in order to limit the Americans' use of air and artillery support fire. Colonel Huong Van Ba, a PAVN artillery officer, remarked after the war that

> *in order to fight the Americans, you had to get close to them. You couldn't fight them from a distance. The best way to attack them was while they were on the move, or at night when they were all stationed together. So our tactics were different from theirs. Their idea was to surround us with ground forces, then destroy us with artillery and rockets, rather than attacking us directly with infantry.*[21]

To avoid detection, the VC and the PAVN moved often and with stealth, seldom remaining in one camp for more than three or four days. Main force and guerrillas alike displayed a truly extraordinary ability to traverse long distances undetected by breaking down into small groups and arriving at a common assembly point at an agreed time. They were masters of camouflage and silent marching. Troops relied for sustenance on NLF-controlled villages, many of which had hidden caches of food and ammunition buried in tunnel complexes, and remote base camps in western Vietnam, Laos, and Cambodia, some of which were never discovered by the Americans or the South Vietnamese.

Revolutionary forces did not have the traditional logistical "tail" of Western armies. Supply and engineering units prepared the battlefield in advance of major operations clandestinely, building fortifications, tunnels, communication trenches, and supply dumps. The Vietnamese had fought off other foreign invaders in this manner for more than a thousand years. Broadly speaking, communist regular forces were superb at building and defending positions with well-prepared escape routes. As one American officer commented, "I have talked to small-unit commanders all over Vietnam ... who have slugged it out with a fanatical enemy in these positions. From these detailed after-combat interviews, I have concluded that it is impossible to penetrate, flank, or envelop these fortifications without taking extremely heavy casualties. To fight the enemy in these positions is analogous to cornering a tiger in his lair and then trying to stalk him with only a Bowie knife."[22]

Main force communist troops received superior training to American forces in camouflage and concealment techniques, as well as night combat operations. Many American infantrymen who saw extensive combat against the VC and PAVN have expressed grudging admiration for their tenacity and resourcefulness. Charlie Beckwith, an Army Special Forces officer of some renown who saw extensive combat in Vietnam, described the Vietcong main force troops "as the best infantry I've ever seen."[23] One of the most highly decorated marine officers during the war, company commander (and many years later, US senator from Virginia) Jim Webb, commented that the North Vietnamese

> had great fire discipline and good marksmanship skills. They built excellent fortifications, incredibly impressive trenches and emplacements. They used a "grab and hold" tactic: their ideal scenario was to wait until we were so close to them that we couldn't use supporting fires for fear of hitting our own men. That required tremendous fire discipline on their part—to hold off until

we were so close. They were able to spring very effective and sizeable daytime ambushes in the trenches and tree lines adjacent to wide rice paddies. . . . When the NVA controlled the terrain or when we stayed too long in one spot, they were deadly; when we could use maneuver and fire support, we did a number on them.[24]

Political Warfare

Political struggle, says Douglas Pike, was conceived of by revolutionary strategists as three discrete but interrelated "action programs":

1. *Dich van*—action among the people controlled by the enemy, and in the world at large, especially people controlled by the South Vietnamese government and the people in the United States. *Dich van* involved the production and distribution of propaganda tracts, leaflets, cartoons, radio broadcasts, newspaper stories, and the like, conveying key revolutionary themes, and disputing the American government's main narrative about the war, in order to shape perceptions of the conflict as a "David vs. Goliath" struggle, in which the revolutionary forces were seen as virtuous liberators of the people. The *dich van* program was meant to instill confusion and doubt within the population controlled by Saigon and among the American public. Organizing political demonstrations and exploiting local grievances in face-to-face meetings with villagers was a crucial part of the program. Meeting with American antiwar activists, which began late in 1965 and continued for years, was a key element in the *dich van* campaign.

This account by a government village chief in Long An Province, southwest of Saigon, conveys a sense of the perseverance and sophistication of the *dich van* program:

> *The Vietcong were very smart. If they knew that Binh's family had been ill-treated by the government, they would work on that weak point. Perhaps Binh had had money extorted by an official—in his heart he had to feel resentment. So they would come by from time to time and say, "You see how bad the government is, it calls itself*

nationalist, but in the end it steals your money. . . . Are you just going to do nothing?" So, like fanning a flame, Binh's resentment would grow to anger, and his anger to hatred, and his hatred to revolt. Or maybe Xoai would be building a house. The Vietcong would come by and help him put it up, meanwhile talking about their life—no pay, living in the swamps, being shot at all the time. Naturally, Xoai would take pity on them, so the next time they came by and asked for a meal, he would invite them in. But when they took a meal it was not like our soldiers' way: burst in, demand food, sit around while it was being fixed, eat, and finally grab a couple of chickens and run off. Instead, the VC would go into the kitchen, clean the rice, and while they were waiting for it to cook, they would sweep the house . . . and set the table. When the meal was over, they would clean up, and then thank everyone politely. . . . Naturally, he let the Vietcong eat at his house all the time. That is how the Vietcong gained the people's support. They simply built on the opportunity we gave them.[25]

2. *Binh van*—action among the ARVN and the Saigon government administration. Since most of the enlisted ranks of the ARVN were peasants, the political cadres of the NLF focused a great deal of attention on bringing them into the revolutionary fold, or at the very least convincing them to desert the army. Again, the chief method was to inundate prospects with social pressure and propaganda. Leaflets were distributed and radio broadcasts highlighting corruption and incompetence in the ARVN were a staple feature of the *binh van* efforts. One-on-one meetings with troops when they were on leave was perhaps the most effective method of conversion to the cause. VC cadres also put pressure on the families of ARVN troops to cease fighting for the government. Here is the text of a classic *binh van* leaflet:

Dear Friends in the Civil Guard and Regular Army,

The powerful forces of the Liberation Army have appeared in order to fight for the ideals of independence, democracy, reunification, and peace. The glorious and lofty mission of the Liberation Army is to exterminate the vicious traitor, Ngo Dinh Diem, and a small number of his stubborn lackeys, who have brought you here to fight against the Liberation Army, because of the forced draft, because you have had no choice but to enter the army in order to survive from day to day, or perhaps because you have been fooled by their . . . fake "nationalist republic." Clearly understanding your situation, and with a deep feeling for our nation and our race, we have no desire to fight with you, because that would just spill Vietnamese blood, while Diem and the foreigners sit by and harvest their profits. Thus we urge you to join with us in fighting against the common enemy of our people, the traitor Ngo Dinh Diem.[26]

The Front also had hundreds of clandestine agents serving in the ARVN and in the Saigon government who worked to sew dissention in the ranks and report on government initiatives with a view to sabotaging their execution.

3. *Dan van*—action among the people within the liberated zones. This was the vast, multidimensional effort to mobilize, motivate, and direct the energies of the people already under the sway of the NLF. Political cadres enlisted the people in "mass associations" of farmers, women, laborers, and students and engaged them in rigorous indoctrination classes and one-on-one meetings, where they stressed simple, clear themes. The Farmers' Liberation Association was by far the largest of these with 1.8 million members by early 1965. Cadres in their lectures to the local meetings of these groups held that the Americans were colonialists just like the French, but with more money and better weapons; they were there to rob the Vietnamese of their freedom. The South Vietnamese government was controlled by the Americans. Only the revolutionary forces had the dedication, patience, and wherewithal to free the country from its shackles, and to give the peasants the land they needed to feed their families, and to prosper. Thus, the NLF offered ordinary Vietnamese a way to find meaning and purpose in their lives as participants in a vast and important social movement. As one die-hard member of the NLF told an American researcher:

The Liberation had the answers for the most important problems that we all knew. They had an answer about land reform, which was that they would give land to the poor people. They had an answer about high taxes. They said the Liberation would spend the taxes only on the people, and would collect them without corruption. They said they would help the poor, and this was something else that made them very popular, because many people in the village were very poor.[27]

All the leading communist strategists—Le Duan, Ho, and Giap, among others—were convinced that they could mobilize and sustain the power of the masses through political and military struggle long enough, and with sufficient force, to demoralize the Americans and their Vietnamese allies, and frustrate their efforts to win the allegiance of the people.

Now, of course, all countries, including the United States, engage to some degree in "political struggle." The US mounted a massive propaganda campaign to shape perceptions about the war at home and abroad, but it was poorly executed and largely unconvincing, even to people who lived in Western democracies such as the United States. What seems different about the communists' political warfare campaign in retrospect is that Hanoi understood this work to be in many ways more important than military operations, and it was carried out, as Douglas Pike reports, on a staggering scale as a kind of "high art."

Although General Giap's role in the shaping of war strategy was far more circumscribed than Washington and MACV thought at the time, his writings remain a crucial source of insight into *dau tranh* protracted war strategy. "The Political and Military Line of Our Party" was published in December 1964, just a few months before the first marines landed at Danang. It offers a clear window into the strategic thinking of Hanoi at that crucial time:

Our people in the South enjoy a clear political superiority over the enemy; they also have traditions and experience in political struggle and armed struggle and are animated with ardent patriotism and high revolutionary spirit; the enemy are strong materially and technically, but the social basis of the reactionary forces in the service of the United States imperialists being extremely weak, they are in a state of complete political isolation, and their political weakness is irremediable. . . .

The war of liberation now being waged by our countrymen in the South is a revolutionary war . . . using simultaneously the two forms of struggle, regarding both as fundamental and decisive. . . . Armed struggle which becomes more and more vigorous does not make political struggle decrease in intensity but, on the contrary, gives it a stronger impulse; together they pursue the aim of annihilating and dislocating enemy armed forces, striking vigorously where the enemy is basically weak, on the political ground.[28]

The path ahead in the looming American war was sure to be long and arduous. Here one can see the relevance of Mao's protracted war strategy in Giap's thinking:

Our military art had determined the following strategic orientation: to promote a war by the entire people, a total and protracted war. We have to wage a long war in which our political superiority will prevail, and we can gradually increase our strength, pass from a position of weakness to a position of strength, change the balance of forces between us and the enemy and ensure victory. . . .

It is necessary to promote an extensive guerrilla war that will gradually develop into a regular war combined with a guerrilla war. Regular war and guerrilla war are closely combined, stimulate each other, deplete and annihilate enemy forces and bring total victory.[29]

Just as the war was about to escalate, Giap and the rest of the politburo were sanguine about the revolution's prospects, in large measure because they didn't believe American military power would prove effective in a protracted war context: "The organization as well as the composition and training of the American army, generally speaking, is more or less unfit to deal efficiently with our entire people's revolutionary war, not to mention great difficulties due to unaccustomed terrain and climate."[30]

Perhaps the greatest advantage the communists possessed in the looming fight with the Americans was their superior understanding of the kind of war in which they were engaged. While General Westmoreland saw the primary object of the war to be the destruction of the enemy's armed forces, and Washington clung to the politically convenient notion that it was primarily a war of aggression by North Vietnam against South Vietnam, Hanoi understood itself to be engaged in a revolutionary war of considerable complexity. "Such a conflict," wisely observes military analyst (and former US Marine) Samuel Griffith,

> is never confined within the bounds of military action. Because its purpose is to destroy an existing society and its institutions and to replace them with a completely new state structure, any revolutionary war is a unity of which the constituent parts, in varying importance, are military, political, economic, social, and psychological. For this reason, it is endowed with a dynamic quality and a dimension in depth that orthodox wars, whatever their scale, lack. . . . In the United States, we go to considerable trouble to keep soldiers out of politics, and even more to keep politics out of soldiers. Guerrillas do exactly the opposite. They go to great lengths to make sure that their men are politically educated and thoroughly aware of the issues at stake. . . . The end product is an intensely loyal and politically alert fighting man.[31]

The American soldier would find his adversary in South Vietnam to be a very tough and committed customer, about that there is no doubt at all.

PART II

THE FIGHTING ON DIFFERENT FRONTS

CHAPTER 6
MARINES AT WAR

Fire discipline had never been the strong suit of the Army of the Republic of Vietnam. The first rounds fired in the direction of the US Marine positions in the sparsely populated hills just to the west of the sprawling Danang Air Base were strays from a nearby ARVN base camp. The only hints of the enemy's presence in the area were the distant reverberations of artillery fire in support of combat missions for South Vietnamese army units, and the menacing whine of the odd sniper round near the air base perimeter. The only US Marines to glimpse the elusive Vietcong in the flesh during the first several weeks of deployment were the helicopter crews ferrying South Vietnamese infantrymen into and out of battle.

While General Karch and the 9th MEB staff busied themselves establishing protocols for coordinating operations with General Thi and sorting out a host of logistical problems with MACV and the navy, marine infantrymen struggled to acclimatize themselves to the torrid heat and humidity of the Vietnamese spring. The drudgery of building defensive positions had to be restricted to early morning and late afternoon to limit the number of heat prostration cases. In defensive warfare, there are invariably two major foes: the enemy, and boredom. The first days in-country, remembered First Lieutenant Phil Caputo, were all alike.

> *The sun rose about six, changing color as it climbed, from red to gold to white. The mists on the rice fields evaporated and the dawn breeze died away. By noon, nothing moved beneath the bright sky. Peasants left their fields for the shade of their villages . . . the trees stood as still as plants in a greenhouse. A wind fanned out*

of the mountains in the midafternoon, a hot wind that lifted the dust from the roads and the parched paddy fields lying cracked in the sun, where the rice had been harvested. . . . In the late afternoon, the mountains brought a premature twilight to the coastal plain, but this early dusk was the worst time. The wind dropped and the air was made stifling as the earth released the heat it had absorbed all day. We drank from our canteens until our bellies bulged, and tried to move as little as possible. Sweat ran down our sides and faces. The dust clinging to our skin thickened into a gummy film.[1]

Among the reinforcements approved by Washington in the early spring were sufficient marine ground and air forces to establish two more coastal enclaves in I Corps, both smaller than the Danang enclave, but substantial nonetheless. The first was at Phu Bai, about fifty miles north of Danang in Thua Thien Province. The other was at Chu Lai, in Quang Tin Province, which bordered Quang Nam to the south. The 2nd Battalion of the 3rd Marines deployed to Phu Bai, located about eight miles south of the beautiful old imperial capital of Hue, on April 10. Its initial mission: to defend a small airstrip and an army communications facility there.

During the first two weeks of May, three infantry battalions of the 3rd Marine Expeditionary Brigade crossed the sandy beaches near Chu Lai and began to establish a third enclave in I Corps. At Chu Lai, engineers and Seabees struggled in intense heat to assemble a piece of equipment unique to the Marine Corps: a short airfield for tactical support (SATS). Meant to relieve the extreme overcrowding at the Danang Air Base, SATS had a four-thousand-foot runway with an aluminum surface of interlocking, lightweight metal alloy planking, a catapult, and carrier deck–type arresting gear. A difficult job for the Seabees was made even harder by Chu Lai's fine-grained, sandy soil, which had the texture of refined sugar, and was inherently unstable. Nonetheless, two squadrons of Marine A-4 Skyhawk fighter-bombers arrived from the Philippines at the beginning of June and began to fly support missions for ARVN combat units from this temporary airstrip. In the months to follow, construction crews built a ten-thousand-foot concrete runway nearby to replace the SATS.

In early April, General Karch received a new "concept of operations" document from Westmoreland. Defense of the enclaves remained the top priority for the time being, but the marines should also begin to conduct deep reconnaissance patrols of the VC's avenues of approach to the marine bases. The marines should prepare to undertake, in coordination with General Thi's forces, "an intensifying program of offensive operations to fix and destroy the VC in the general Da Nang area."[2] The ban on offensive operations had been lifted, much to the relief of Karch and the entire brigade.

On April 20, the infantry companies finally began long-range patrolling at Danang, moving as far as six miles outside their tactical areas of responsibility (TAORs), accompanied by ARVN civil affairs officers to ensure a smooth introduction of the Americans to the local populace. Two days later, the marines made first contact with the enemy. An eighty-man patrol from D Company, 3rd Reconnaissance Battalion, clashed with a VC main force company near Binh Thai, nine miles southwest of Danang, and quickly found itself pinned down. Several ARVN scouts with the recon marines panicked and fled the scene. A company from 3/3 came to the rescue by helicopter, but upon their arrival, the Vietcong broke off their attack and withdrew. One marine was wounded in the fight, and one enemy soldier killed.

Two days later, a VC company attacked a fortified hilltop a mile and a quarter from the new base at Phu Bai. Two marines were killed before the enemy broke off the fight and vanished. Marine intelligence suspected the VC had mistakenly thought they were attacking an ARVN position, for it was quite clear at this early stage of things that the Vietcong were operating under orders to avoid clashes with the newly arrived Americans when they were in fortified positions.

In late April, in a desolate area a few miles southwest of Danang, dominated by a terrain feature called Charlie Ridge, C Company, 3rd Marines experienced its baptism of fire. The company conducted a classic frontal assault on a squad of VC, driving them off the ridge and into a swamp. After a sustained artillery barrage by 105 mm howitzers on the suspected enemy location, Lieutenant Caputo's platoon was ordered to clear the swamp of any remaining enemy troops. After an hour and a half of hard toil and confusion in and around the swamp, the marines uncovered a small base camp, a bundle of documents, and four enemy corpses.

Over the next several weeks, there would be other confused, inconclusive clashes for C/3, usually resulting in light casualties all around. Caputo remembered years later that:

> *There was no pattern to these patrols and operations. Without a front, flanks, or rear, we fought a formless war against a formless enemy who evaporated like the morning jungle mists, only to materialize in some unexpected place. It was a haphazard, episodic sort of combat . . . we did not see heavy combat . . . [b]ut we saw enough to learn those lessons that could not be taught in the training camps: what fear feels like and what death looks like, and the smell of death, the experience of killing, of enduring pain and inflicting it, the loss of friends and the sight of wounds. We learned what war was all about, and a callus began to grow around our hearts, a kind of emotional flak jacket that blunted the blows and the stings of pity.*[3]

In early May, Washington approved yet another expansion of the American presence in Vietnam at the request of MACV: the establishment of a new corps-level—that is, multi-division—command in Danang to oversee large-scale combat operations throughout all of I Corps' five provinces. With 2.6 million of South Vietnam's 16.5 million people in 1965, I Corps was the least populated of the country's four military zones. Running 225 miles from north to south and between thirty and seventy miles wide, it comprised about ten thousand square miles of territory, making it the smallest of the four politico-military regions of the country. Yet the strategic importance of I Corps far outweighed its size and population. First, I Corps lay just south of the demilitarized zone between North and South Vietnam. The terrain there heavily favored the enemy. It shared a border with Laos in the west—the rugged Annamite Mountains, which range in height from about five thousand to eight thousand feet. These mountains contained many communist base areas as well as multiple paths and roads of the Ho Chi Minh Trail. East of the mountains was a narrow, rolling piedmont region of hills and river valleys, which gave way to flat coastal lowlands. In these lowlands, and in the piedmont's river valleys, most of the people dwelled.

Within I Corps lay two of Vietnam's most important cities: Hue, the old cultural capital and home of the emperors, and of course, Danang, a major port and South Vietnam's second most populous city. By war's end, more American troops had been killed in I Corps than any of the other three military regions in South Vietnam.

The III Marine Amphibious Force was formally established on May 5, under the command of Major General William Collins, but Collins's thirteen-month tour in Asia was due to conclude in early June. He was relieved as commander of III MAF by a newly minted major general named Lewis William Walt. Unlike the US Army, the Marine Corps has a tradition of filling their most important flag officer billets from the small cadre of men with truly extraordinary records of performance in combat. "Uncle Lew" certainly fit the bill. A former halfback at Colorado State, Walt had served with distinction at Guadalcanal as a Raider under Merritt "Red Mike" Edson, earning a Silver Star. At Cape Gloucester in December 1943, he commanded the 3rd Battalion of the 5th Marines in the ferocious assault on Aogiri Ridge, where he earned his first Navy Cross, the second highest medal awarded for valor by the naval services. A second Navy Cross followed soon thereafter as a result of Walt's actions during the Battle of Peleliu. Walt and another marine made a daring night infiltration behind enemy lines to locate several missing companies and reposition them effectively to participate in a major assault the next morning.

Gruff, outspoken, and highly intelligent, Walt was widely admired throughout the upper reaches of the military establishment, and by the press as well. Every marine in Vietnam knew Lew Walt cared deeply about their welfare, and he conveyed an air of confidence and determination that was infectious. Al Gray, who served four tours in Vietnam as a marine officer and later went on to become the commandant of the Marine Corps, recalled Walt fondly in an interview with the author:

> As operations officer for the 12th Marine Regiment, I had frequent direct contact with General Walt. He was indeed a big, tough warrior, who'd been highly decorated in both World War II and Korea. He had a very hot temper, for sure, but he was pretty much always able to regain his composure quickly and deal

*with whatever matters needed attention effectively. What is less
well known about Walt, though, was that he was an extremely
compassionate guy. He used to visit wounded Marines every day
in the hospital in Danang. He loved his Marines, and, as I think
comes through in his book,* Strange War, Strange Strategy, *he cared very deeply about the ordinary Vietnamese peasant as
well.*[4]

Although Walt didn't consider himself an expert on counterinsurgency warfare when he assumed command, he soon would be. His chief mentors when he was a junior officer, Lieutenant General Chesty Puller and Colonel "Red Mike" Edson, had both served in counterinsurgency operations in the 1920s and '30s in the Caribbean and Central America, and shared their insights into unconventional warfare with their protégé on numerous occasions. Walt had read Giap's *People's War, People's Army*, the primer on Vietnamese revolutionary warfare, and talked at length with a great many marine advisers who'd served in Vietnam, as well as the Marine Corps' in-house expert on counterinsurgency, Lieutenant General Victor "Brute" Krulak.

The Marines' Initial Strategy

With minimal initial guidance from MACV early in its tenure in Vietnam, the Marine Corps relied on its own doctrine as expounded in *Fleet Marine Force Manual 21: Operations Against Guerrilla Forces*, its extensive experience in counterinsurgency operations in Latin America, and its reading of the dynamics of the war on the ground to determine its strategy and tactics. The main architects of the marines' war, at least in its first two years, were Generals Walt and Krulak.

Krulak, commander of Fleet Marine Force, Pacific, in early 1965, was one of the most dynamic and accomplished American military officers of the twentieth century. He had played a crucial role in the development of the landing craft that carried the marines and the army across the Pacific during World War II. After the war, he cemented a reputation for overcoming bureaucratic obstacles and supporting key innovations such as the "vertical envelopment" doctrine—the use of helicopters to move combat forces well behind the enemy and then maneuver them rapidly about the battlefield.

Krulak had also served as JFK's special assistant for counterinsurgency, and had immersed himself in the history and the literature on the subject, including the marines' own classic *Small Wars Manual*, the work of Sir Robert Thompson on the successful British counterinsurgency operations in Malaya in the 1950s, and the French soldier-scholar David Galula's *Counterinsurgency Warfare: Theory and Practice*. Moreover, he was thoroughly conversant with the extensive writings of Mao and Giap on "people's war."

Brute Krulak visited Vietnam eight times between 1962 and 1964. He believed that the primary target in Vietnam was not the Vietcong and the North Vietnamese soldiers, but the ordinary people of Vietnam. Krulak was convinced "that the central issue of the struggle was the reinstitution of [GVN] control over the rural areas," and that "lasting control would result only from indigenous political effort."[5] As a captain, Al Gray commanded Marine Advisory Team One in the remote northwestern frontier of I Corps from March to August 1964, where he monitored enemy communications transmission and provided reconnaissance on enemy infiltration routes into South Vietnam. Gray frequently briefed General Krulak on the situation on the ground in I Corps around that time, and a bit later on in the war, when Gray was serving as a regimental operations officer. According to Gray, Krulak had been instrumental in establishing counterinsurgency training camps for use by units of both the 1st and 3rd Marine Divisions at Camp Pendleton and on Okinawa. The primary lessons about counterinsurgency operations drilled home in these camps, recalled Gray, were: (1) take care of the civilian population as best you can, and (2) don't make more enemies than you already have.

In Gray's estimation, the marines were very well prepared to fight the sort of war they encountered upon arrival. A great many junior officers who served in I Corps in the early years of the war had been sent to the army's Special Warfare School at Fort Benning to absorb the latest counterinsurgency thinking and tactics. The marine command was under no illusion that success in I Corps would come fast or easily, even if the government in Saigon managed to stabilize itself and become more responsive to the needs of the populace. And there was very little the marines could do about that. But the senior leadership of the Corps was convinced there were a number of things the marines could do to improve the situation in the countryside.

First, the guerrillas' hold over the villages had to be broken. That meant aggressive sweep-and-clear operations, followed by rigorous small-unit patrolling, both through and around the hamlets. The purpose of intensive patrolling, Walt told his battalion and company leaders, was not only to keep the VC at bay, but to build trust and understanding between the local people and the marines. In time, that trust would pay tangible dividends in the form of local intelligence networks that would provide timely and accurate information on VC plans and locations.

Because the rural areas just beyond the towns and cities on the coast of I Corps were infested with VC guerrillas and political cadres, neither the American nor South Vietnamese agencies responsible for reconstruction and development projects had been able to make much headway by spring of 1965. It was simply too dangerous for civilians to venture out into the villages with security so tenuous. In truth, the extensive civic action programs developed by a host of American civilian agencies as well as the South Vietnamese government had yet to be implemented. For all intents and purposes, they remained on the drawing board.

The marines were well equipped to address the security problem, and thereby facilitate reconstruction and development within the villages. But Walt felt passionately that the marine role shouldn't be *restricted* to security, to clearing the guerrillas out of the village and keeping them out. He pushed hard to get III MAF into the civic action business, working closely with the South Vietnamese agencies as well as the USAID, the Catholic Relief Services, CARE, and the political advisory staff at the embassy to build small schools, medical dispensaries, improve agriculture, and provide basic goods in short supply, especially clothing, food, and soap.

The marines' approach to their new war, Krulak would later explain, "was to treat the whole patient," in other words, to go well beyond combat operations to eliminate guerrillas and main force conventional communist units, and to assist the South Vietnamese in "pacification"—the complex process of establishing security and responsive local government in the countryside, with a view to improving the economic and social welfare of the people.[6]

Walt and Krulak had seen enough of the ARVN to know that by training and inclination it was unsuited to counterinsurgency operations. The South Vietnamese army had been trained by the US Army to fight against a conventional invasion from North Vietnam. It knew little to nothing about counterinsurgency and would take time to learn. Thus, there seemed no point in trying to pressure General Thi into deploying his regular forces for pacification work. But it was a different story with the Regional (i.e., provincial) and Popular (village-level) Forces. These poorly trained, underdeveloped GVN organizations had a real stake in breaking the stranglehold of the communists in their own backyards. For better or worse, these militia forces were the government counterparts to the Vietcong's regional and local guerrillas, though in 1965, they clearly lacked their adversaries' zeal, tightly knit organizational structure, or military skill set.

So far as Walt and Krulak could see, the path to stability in rural South Vietnam rested on a foundation of viable local defense forces to keep the VC away from the hamlets and villages once the marines had cleared them out. The success of the marines' campaigns in Haiti (1915–1934), the Dominican Republic (1916–1934), and in Nicaragua (1926–1933) had hinged on developing savvy indigenous police and militia to maintain order and stability. Training of indigenous forces became an early and abiding preoccupation of the marine units in South Vietnam.

To deal with the war in the villages, the marines strongly favored the "oil spot," or "enclave" strategy, described in chapter 4. It had received provisional approval by the JCS and the president in April, but the staff at MACV in Saigon, it will be recalled, was busily engaged in a strategy of an entirely different color. Walt, Krulak, and Greene envisioned counterinsurgency operations against the guerrillas and civic action programs to improve the lives of ordinary villagers as the top priorities in a "balanced strategy" that also included conventional big-unit (battalion-size or larger) action against main force communist units. But unlike General Westmoreland and his MACV staff, the marines didn't see the main force units as the critical threat. The larger main force units needed to be challenged and destroyed, but only when they posed an imminent threat to the populated areas. By focusing on breaking the stranglehold of the guerrillas and the VC political infrastructure on the villages rather than the main force units, the marines reckoned they would eventually deprive the communist regulars of the taxes and foodstuffs they needed to operate effectively. Over time, they would wither on the vine.

The Marines Continue to Press for Counterinsurgency Operations

Walt, Krulak, and Greene were convinced by the Corps' experience in the first couple of months of the war that Westmoreland's determination to use American maneuver battalions to go after the main force communist units was wrongheaded in principle. Nor did marine intelligence analysts concur with MACV's strong suspicion that Hanoi was moving toward stage three of the protracted war paradigm. Walt hoped he could come to some sort of compromise with Westmoreland over the allocation of marine combat resources so that III MAF could continue to pursue its balanced strategy.

Just two days after Westmoreland's three-phase strategic plan had been formally approved by Washington, on July 30, Westmoreland arrived at III MAF headquarters in Danang with important news. As commanding general of III MAF, Walt would henceforth exercise operational control over all US forces in I Corps, and serve as senior adviser to the crucially important I Corps Advisory Group. As such, Walt took on the responsibility for managing all American military advice, assistance, and support to GVN forces in the five northernmost provinces. This crucial slot had previously been filled by an army general. Westmoreland made it clear that he expected Walt to increase the number of big-unit search-and-destroy operations against communist regulars deep in the hinterlands as soon as possible.

While the senior marine leadership and MACV worked on big-picture issues of strategy, logistics, and interpretation of reams of intelligence, marines in the maneuver units confronted an elusive and resourceful enemy in day-to-day operations. On occasion during these early days of the war, seemingly small clashes and other incidents made national headlines. Such was the case with the well-choreographed raid on the Danang Air Base by a thirteen-man PAVN sapper team early on the morning of July 1. After tunneling under the outer defensive wire at the south end of the base, the raiders, supported by about seventy VC troops with mortars, made their way to the tarmac and destroyed two C-130 transports and an F-102 fighter-bomber, in addition to damaging a number of other aircraft with satchel charges. With the exception of a single wounded PAVN officer, all the raiders made good their escape.

What explained the embarrassing lapse in security? The short answer: base defense the night of the attack had been perilously thin. Two of the four marine companies responsible for perimeter defense had been redeployed to conduct offensive sweeps. The raid confirmed what General Walt had suspected for a number of weeks: there were not enough marines in I Corps to meet the growing demand for offensive operations without making unacceptable compromises on security within the three enclaves. But a more serious problem, at least as Walt saw it, was that security for the areas immediately south and east of the base remained in the hands of the ARVN, whose protocols for static defense were notoriously lax. Many ARVN units had been infiltrated by VC sympathizers, to boot. A few days after the raid, Krulak and Walt finally succeeded in convincing General Thi to relinquish responsibility for the defense of the terrain just outside the base perimeter entirely to the US Marines.

Immediately after the raid, the marines began to conduct aggressive patrols by the hundreds in the countryside around the base. Contact with enemy guerrillas increased significantly. On August 3, D Company of the 9th Marines cautiously made its way toward the village of Cam Ne, about five miles southwest of the air base. Cam Ne was VC country, and long had been. In July, three marines had been killed and about a dozen wounded while patrolling in and around this cluster of hamlets, most of which were well fortified with spider holes, bunkers, trenches, and an eclectic assortment of booby traps. As the marines approached the village, they came under sporadic small-arms fire from several directions and were repeatedly pinned down. Once they'd managed to press their way into the village confines, they were bedeviled by sniper fire. The marines were itching for a firefight, but the VC disengaged, either fleeing into hidden bunkers and tunnels, or hiding their weapons and fading into the civilian population. Several marines were wounded, and the company commander ordered the troops to burn down any dwellings from which they had received fire. It was a nasty business. CBS News correspondent Morley Safer and his crew happened to be attached to the patrol that day. The camera was rolling as a number of dwellings burned. At one point, an old woman pleaded with a marine rifleman not to burn down her home. Indifferent to her entreaties, the leatherneck proceeded to set her hooch alight with his Zippo lighter.

When Safer's report aired on the *CBS Evening News*, it set off a wave of protest and debate, for it exposed the nation in dramatic fashion to the cruel ambiguities of the village war. Collateral damage was inescapable in a war where the enemy and the civilian population were for all intents and purposes indistinguishable. Safer's report emphasized the seemingly wanton destruction inflicted by the marines on the villagers' property, but made no mention of the earlier American casualties or that the patrol that day had taken fire from within the village.

The marine senior command complained bitterly to CBS executives that the story lacked balance and context. Many more such protests to the press from the services, and from the White House, would follow in the months and years to come. The Cam Ne story made it all too clear to the Johnson administration and to MACV that unrestricted media coverage of combat, particularly the raw immediacy of television coverage, was going to have a strategic impact on the war in Vietnam.

A week after Cam Ne came another ugly incident. Lance Corporal Marion McGhee, a fire team leader in the 3rd Battalion of the 3rd Marine Regiment, walked out of his unit's perimeter to a nearby village and attempted to rape a fourteen-year-old girl. When the girl's father tried to intervene, McGhee killed him. Marion McGhee was the first American serviceman in Vietnam to be convicted of unpremeditated manslaughter. He served six years in a military prison.

In mid-August, III MAF launched Operation Starlite. Thus far in the war, the communist forces had studiously avoided sustained engagements with American forces of battalion size or larger. That changed abruptly on the steamy, sun-drenched morning of August 18, the day of the first regimental-size battle between American and communist regular forces in the Vietnam War. On that day, the VC decided for the first time in the new American war to defend vigorously a cluster of heavily fortified combat villages against a powerful assault from air, land, and sea. It turned into a chaotic slugfest that cost both sides dearly in blood. Both adversaries would claim victory, and as was so often the case in a war cluttered with irony, paradox, and contradiction, both sides could make a good argument that they were right.

A number of independent sources, including an NSC signals intelligence officer in Saigon and a VC defector, identified the location of the 1st VC Regiment on the triangular-shaped Van Tuong Peninsula, twelve miles south of Chu Lai. No one knew what the unit's intentions were, but it was entirely conceivable that it was preparing to launch a powerful strike against the marine airfield at Chu Lai. The 1st PLAF Regiment had already earned the respect of the allies, having destroyed a number of ARVN battalions in previous engagements. The unit contained some of the most experienced combat troops in the PLAF. The 1st was led by Colonel Le Huu Tru, who had commanded a battalion of Vietminh at the Battle of Dien Bien Phu. As it happened, the colonel was away from his regiment at the time of Starlite, so chief political officer Nguyen Tinh Tuong orchestrated the defense of the Van Tuong combat villages.

According to a *New York Times* correspondent who arrived at Van Tuong during the operation's second day, "the Vietcong were protected by well-fortified bunkers, tunnels and foxholes. . . . Some of the bunkers were reinforced by concrete. . . . The countryside [consisted of] rugged terrain of plowed rice paddies crisscrossed by dense rows of trees, and rolling hills covered by rock outcroppings and patches of scrub brush that afforded the Communists good concealment."[7] The rice paddies were surrounded by dikes and hedgerows, severely constricting the avenues of approach to the key villages for American tanks, amphibious tractors, and Ontos—tracked vehicles sporting six 106 mm recoilless rifles—a superb weapon for bunker busting.

Starlite was planned at a frenetic clip by the 7th Marine Regiment staff, under the command of Colonel Oscar Peatross, a former member of Carlson's Raiders who'd earned a Navy Cross fighting an outsize Japanese force on Makin Island during World War II. Peatross went on to fight with the famed 28th Marines on Iwo Jima—the unit that had secured Mount Suribachi and raised the American flag atop that mountain. As with most ground operations in Vietnam, the 7th Regiment had under its operational control units that belonged to other marine regiments—in this case, the 3rd Battalion of the 3rd Marines, and the 2nd Battalion of the 4th Marines. The 3rd Battalion of the 7th Marines was in reserve on ships off the coast. As luck would have it, Colonel Peatross knew the battalion commanders from the 3rd and 4th Marines who would be fighting with him—Lieutenant Colonels Joe Muir and Bull Fisher, respectively— better than he knew his own battalion commanders, which boded well for the operation. Like Peatross, they were experienced combat veterans.

For the first time in military history, an amphibious assault would be combined with a vertical envelopment of the enemy by helicopter. The scheme of maneuver called for one battalion, 3/3 under Joe Muir, to make an amphibious landing southeast of the peninsula and attack west and north toward the sea. Meanwhile, 2/4 under Bull Fisher would be helicoptered to three landing zones southwest of the enemy's cluster of combat villages and punch to the northeast into the enemy defenses, and on to the coastline. The plan called for the sea and heliborne marine infantrymen to converge by early afternoon on the enemy, clearing the hamlets and driving the enemy toward the sea. The infantry could expect a plethora of fire support from three flamethrower tanks, seven standard M-48 battle tanks, and more than two dozen armored amphibious tractors, as well as the Ontos and helicopter gunships.

The night before the assault, M Company of the 3rd Marines came down from Chu Lai by road and set up blocking positions to prevent the enemy from escaping to the north (see map).

At dawn on August 18, about thirty amphibious tractors crossed the line of departure about two thousand yards out to sea and motored slowly toward the shoreline. Just as they crossed the beach, the VC set off a massive command-detonated mine, but it went off a few seconds too early, sending debris and smoke everywhere, but failing to impede the amphibious attack. The first objective, an ancient fishing village called An Cuong 1 by marine planners, was secured very quickly by 3/3's infantrymen. A VC hospital was uncovered. There were lots of bloody bandages, but no patients.

Marines struggling through the soft sands toward Van Tuong village, a mile and a half northeast of An Cuong 1, began to take heavy fire from a delaying force of enemy troops—the VC were in the process of moving their command post from Van Tuong to a more defendable locale. They had been anticipating an attack, but it had come earlier than expected. At 0645, fifteen minutes after the amphibious assault commenced, CH-34 choppers began to swoop into the three landing zones. All went well at the northernmost two LZs. The arrival of the

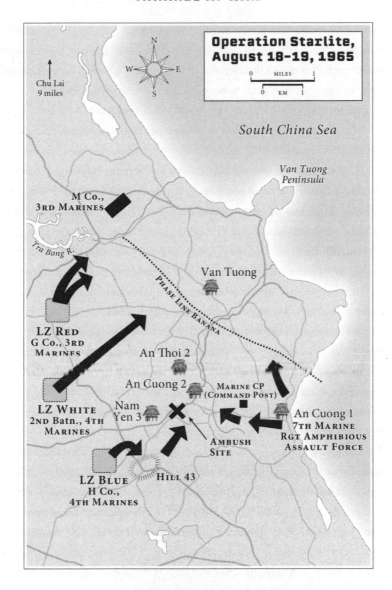

Americans was greeted by desultory fire, but it did not prevent the marines from forming up and pushing forward into the maw.

At LZ Blue, it was a different story. Hotel Company, 4th Marines landed within the defensive perimeter of the 60th VC Battalion. The enemy opened up with blistering rifle, automatic weapons, and mortar fire. Several marines were killed within seconds, and many more were wounded. Heavy fire poured down on the marines from Hill 43, just a few hundred yards to the east. Fierce fighting would continue all day and through the early evening all over the peninsula, but the most vicious, grinding combat occurred in the southern sector of the battle-field, in and around Hill 43, Nam Yen 3, and An Cuong 2.

As helicopters swooped down onto the peninsula with the last elements of Lieutenant Homer "Mike" Jenkins's H Company, a crew chief in one of the CH-34s, Coy Overstreet, spotted two enemy soldiers racing directly toward his aircraft. As he swung his M60 machine gun their way, he was astonished to see about twenty small bushes jump up and join the attacking soldiers in their run. The "bushes" were well-camouflaged PLAF infantrymen. Overstreet let go with a long burst, killing several of the VC in the lead wave and scattering the rest. Then a shell of some sort hit the chopper, and Overstreet took to the controls and struggled to clear the LZ and head back toward Chu Lai. He made it.

Mike Jenkins quickly regrouped his forces and attacked the Hill. The assault was stopped cold near the base of the hill by sustained enemy fire. Then Lance Corporal Ernie Wallace spotted a large number of enemy soldiers moving down a trench line toward the marines' rear. He rushed at them, firing his M60 from the hip, killing at least a dozen, perhaps more. The tempo of fire from both sides steadily ascended. About an hour later, and after several very accurate air strikes, Jenkins's three platoons took the Hill.

At 1100, Lieutenant Jenkins's Hotel Company, now augmented by five tanks and three Ontos, pushed forward to the east of another fortified hamlet, Nam Yen 3, thinking it had already been cleared by a marine company attacking from the beach. It had not. Enemy fire, small arms, and mortars swept through his ranks. Jenkins ordered the armored vehicles to form a circle for protection, and then set up an assault. One platoon laid down a base of fire as the other attacked toward the village. As they got within fifty yards or so of the hamlet perimeter, "fire poured into Jenkins's men. Without warning plants came to life," writes the battle's leading American historian. "Every place the Marines looked there were dozens of bushes moving in all directions. The situation became very, very intense. The VC shot at the Marines from spider holes, hooches, and bunkers. The Marines countered with gunfire and grenades."[8]

Many of the houses in the hamlet, in fact, were disguised bunkers. The sides of these dwellings suddenly dropped down to reveal VC machine guns and recoilless rifle positions. Two young marines, Corporal Dick Tonucci and Private First Class Ronny Centers, managed to take out three bunkers in rapid succession, killing a dozen or so enemy troops. But it was not enough to break the resolve of the defenders. Jenkins was forced to withdraw his men from the village. He called in an air strike. Two more assaults would follow, leading to heavy casualties on both sides, but the enemy still held the village when a battered H/4 was withdrawn around 1400 and returned to LZ Blue, on orders from battalion commander Bull Fisher.

As Jenkins tried in vain to take Nam Yen in late morning and early afternoon, Captain Bruce Webb's India Company/3rd Marines, which had come in across the beach, approached the hamlet of An Cuong 2. According to First Sergeant Art Petty of India,

> *Captain Webb moved the 1st Platoon out and across the semidry river bed in and over a Viet Cong trench and into an area occupied by the Viet Cong. He was determined to not let the Viet Cong escape with their wounded and weapons. The many times in the past they had fired on us and escaped. . . . There was a lot of action—exploding grenades, the tanks firing, machine guns, mortar rounds were landing, and a lot of small arms rifle fire.*[9]

The hamlet contained twenty-five to thirty huts, many spider holes, and camouflaged trench lines connected by interlocking tunnels. Not long after the marines penetrated the hamlet proper, Webb was killed by a grenade thrown by a wounded VC soldier playing dead. Seconds later a 60 mm mortar round landed among a squad of Americans, wounding three. The fighting was close and intense in An Cuong 2 for several hours before I/3 fully eliminated resistance there. About fifty enemy soldiers were killed in the fight for this one hamlet alone. Another sixty VC were killed that morning when they were spotted running in the open, and then shredded by naval gunfire and air strikes.

In the thick of the fighting in and around An Cuong 2, an India Company squad leader, Corporal Robert E. O'Malley, exhibited extraordinary initiative under heavy fire, as his Medal of Honor citation attests:

Corporal O'Malley raced across an open rice paddy to a trench line where the enemy forces were located. Jumping into the trench, he attacked the Viet Cong with his rifle and grenades, and singly killed eight of the enemy. He then led his squad to the assistance of an adjacent Marine unit which was suffering heavy casualties. Continuing to press forward, he reloaded his weapon and fired with telling effect into the enemy emplacement. He personally assisted in the evacuation of several wounded Marines, and again regrouping the remnants of his squad, he returned to the point of the heaviest fighting. Ordered to an evacuation point by an officer, Corporal O'Malley gathered his besieged and badly wounded squad and boldly led them under fire to a helicopter for withdrawal. Although three times wounded in this encounter, and facing imminent death . . . he steadfastly refused evacuation and continued to cover his squad's boarding of the helicopters while, from an exposed position, he delivered fire against the enemy until his wounded men were evacuated.[10]

Shortly after noon, a resupply column consisting of five amphibious tractors ("amtracs" for short) and three flame tanks lost its bearings as it pushed westward from the beach, only to be ambushed by a reinforced company of Vietcong, supported by recoilless rifle fire, and stopped dead in its tracks. The lead tank was knocked out, along with several amphibious tractors. There it remained until the following morning. Its crew and a handful of other marines desperately fought off a series of VC attacks.

At 1305, a rescue force spearheaded by an M-48 tank made its way from the landing beach (Green Beach) in the direction of the ambushed supply column. It, too, came under a powerful and well-organized enemy attack. Unbeknownst to the marines, the VC had employed a number of high school and college students who spoke English to monitor American communications. The enemy knew the relief force was en route. The column stalled, and the volume of enemy fire rapidly ascended. Within a few minutes, five marines were killed and seventeen wounded. Major Andrew Comer led the armored rescue force from the Green

Beach area. He recalled later how the battle was shaping up in the afternoon. "It was obvious that the VC were deeply dug in, and emerged above ground when we presented them with an opportunity and withdrew whenever we retaliated or threatened them."[11] Comer called in artillery and air support, causing a sharp diminution in enemy fire. Elements of another company joined his relief force and they pressed forward in search of the ambushed supply column. As night fell, the whereabouts of that column remained in doubt.

By midafternoon, the VC had taken a real beating, with perhaps three hundred men killed, but they had also inflicted heavy casualties on the marines—very heavy by Vietnam War standards at that time. Perhaps thirty-five Americans had been killed and more than 150 wounded. More important, the enemy, with sound knowledge of the terrain and real-time access to American communications, had short-circuited Colonel Peatross's effort to coordinate the movement of his battalions. The fighting, in essence, had broken down into a series of individual company and platoon firefights, punctuated by air strikes. The marines were having a very tough time reducing enemy resistance in most of them, despite their highly destructive supporting arms and aggressive assault tactics.

Around 1500, Colonel Peatross committed his reserve battalion, 3/7, to the fight. One company came ashore that afternoon. The other two landed late that night.

Spooky illumination flares lit the darkness dimly all night. The ambushed marines in and around the supply column felt sure they were going to be completely overrun, but they hung on grimly, successfully fending off a series of probes. Just after sunrise, American aircraft at last located the site of the ambush. Peatross immediately sent elements of the 3rd Battalion, 7th Marines to the rescue. The rescue force encountered only light small-arms fire en route. More than sixty enemy corpses were scattered all around the ambush site. One tank and an amtrac were too badly damaged to repair, and they were left on the battlefield. The rusting hulks of these vehicles remain where they were hit to this day as part of a Vietnamese memorial to the battle.

Meanwhile, the companies of 2/4 and 3/3 pressed forward to the east, toward the coast, eliminating an enemy delaying force. Lima Company of 3/7 joined in the drive. As it pressed on toward the hamlet of Van Tuong, its commander called in an air strike. Twenty to thirty enemy infantrymen dispersed under the air attack, and marine troops cut most of them down with rifle and machine-gun fire.

Mopping up operations on the peninsula continued for several days. During the operation, the marines claimed to have killed 614 enemy troops and taken 9 prisoners. But it had been a costly victory: 45 marines died in Operation Starlite, and 203 had been wounded. In conventional Western terms, Starlite was a tactical victory for the marines. They had forced the enemy to withdraw from the battlefield, and shown great resolve and bravery in attacking such well-defended defensive positions. Yet the marines' performance had been far from perfect. The 1st PLAF Regiment had been chewed up, but it had not been destroyed. Several hundred of its 1,500 soldiers had escaped to fight another day.

A marine artillery officer who participated in the operation told the author that marines in Lieutenant Colonel Fisher's battalion believed the colonel had failed to coordinate his companies' assaults against the enemy's fortified positions, causing them to suffer unnecessarily heavy casualties. In addition, this officer—who chooses to remain anonymous—believes the scheme of maneuver for the entire operation had been unnecessarily complicated, involving too many different ground units. All of the accounts I have read of the battle leave one with the distinct impression that this officer's assessment is on target. After the war, Major Andrew Comer was haunted by what he had seen during the battle. He watched in disbelief as a marine tank commander let go with a burst of machine-gun fire directed at a ten-year-old boy. Luckily Comer was able to rescue the boy before he was hurt. He could do nothing for the five wounded marines killed by a panicked amtrac driver who ran them over several times with his tracks. Insecure communications on the radios had given the enemy the luxury of knowing where and when the American maneuver units were going.

The marines' impressive kill ratio also had the effect of buttressing General Westmoreland's conviction that his attrition strategy was working, and would continue to do so. After the battle, he pressed General Walt to put more emphasis on such operations, at the expense of pacification. Walt cooperated, but only up to a point.

The enemy had performed with extraordinary tenacity and skill, making masterful use of the terrain and camouflage. Back at the Central Office for South Vietnam, the NLF's field headquarters deep in the jungle of western Tay Ninh Province, and in Hanoi, senior military officers were very pleased with the performance of the 1st Regiment in the battle, and they had good reason to be. The Vietcong regulars, clearly, could stand and fight when ordered to do so. Much remained to be learned among the Americans about fighting a seasoned, well-entrenched enemy force on his own turf.

Pacification and Fall/Winter Big-Unit Operations

Although MACV pressured III MAF to focus more resources on major search-and-destroy operations, a byzantine US command system prevailed in Vietnam, and that "system" limited Westmoreland's influence on the marines. III MAF was under the operational control of MACV, but it was under the administrative and logistical control of the Fleet Marine Force, Pacific, commanded by General Krulak. Brute Krulak was not shy about giving General Walt strategic advice at odds with Westmoreland's directives. Moreover, Krulak had the sympathetic ear of Westmoreland's immediate superior, Admiral U. S. Grant Sharp, commander in chief of all American forces in the Pacific. Given this situation, and Westmoreland's generally congenial personal relationship with Walt, the commander of III MAF retained a considerable degree of latitude in shaping his operational agenda—especially during the first fifteen months or so of the war.

During the late summer and fall of 1965, the marines did mount several major search-and-destroy operations against VC regular units, but for the most part the enemy refused to engage in sustained combat. Walt's focus, for the remainder of the year at any rate, remained firmly fixed on consolidating the management of the pacification effort in I Corps. He established a Joint Coordinating Council (JCC) with US and GVN agencies responsible for executing the rural development program throughout I Corps, including USAID, the State Department political adviser to I Corps, and the ARVN, among others. The JCC met weekly, and subcommittees were established to coordinate specific aspects of the pacification program, such as public health, food distribution, infrastructure development, and psychological operations. In 1966, the JCC would assume responsibility for coordinating combat operations with the pacification program.

So committed was Walt to the pacification program that he ordered the Plans and Programs section of his III MAF headquarters staff to devote its attention exclusively to civic action initiatives, in other words, using marine resources and organizational expertise to improve the lives of the people in the villages. Before long, the division, regimental, and battalion staffs in III MAF followed suit.

In early May, a month or so before Walt had taken command, the marines had embarked on an important pacification experiment. The village of Le My was located on the banks of the Cu De River, eight miles northwest of the Danang Air Base, and had been under the thumb of the Vietcong for years. The commander of the 2nd Battalion, 3rd Marines, Lieutenant Colonel David Clement, wanted to extend his defenses to cover the village in order to better protect the air base from attack. On May 11, 2/3 cleared two platoons of VC guerrillas out of Le My after an extended firefight, and sent fifty suspected Vietcong sympathizers back to III MAF for questioning.

Over the next several weeks, the battalion set up defensive positions in and around the village, and began to train a Popular Force platoon composed of Le My villagers to prepare defensive positions and execute small-unit patrols. Civil affairs officers and engineers began work on a small medical dispensary and a schoolhouse, and Clements's marines ran regular patrols in and around Le My. The goal, according to Clements's civil affairs officer, was "to create an administration, supported by the people, and capable of leading . . . feeding, and protecting themselves by the time the battalion was moved to another area of operations."[12]

A VC company attacked Le My on the night of May 20. After a sustained firefight, the marines and the Popular Force platoon repulsed the attack, killing four enemy soldiers in the process. Throughout the summer, a steady stream of senior officials from the Department of Defense and other Washington agencies toured the village to learn what they could about the marines' nascent pacification techniques.

The most celebrated and promising of the Marine Corps' innovations in the pacification war was concerned at once with improving village security, implementing civic action programs, and fostering close cooperation between marine infantry and the Popular Forces militia. The "combined action platoon" idea had its origins in the Corps' experience in Haiti in the early 1930s, when marine officers trained and led patrols of the local gendarme in counterinsurgency operations. Lieutenant Paul Eck, a Vietnamese speaker and avid student of Vietnamese culture, was tasked with integrating four PF platoons in and around Phu Bai with four squads of handpicked marines into combined action platoons (CAPs). Eck provided the marine volunteers with a crash course in basic Vietnamese language and customs. Then, in early August, the first few CAPs were formed.

Each marine squad took up full-time residence within a particular hamlet, and began cross-training with a Popular Forces platoon. The Americans taught the Vietnamese basic small-unit tactics, military discipline, and population control techniques, while the Vietnamese militia taught the Americans about local customs, terrain peculiarities, and communist tactics and techniques. The CAPs worked with the Vietnamese National Police as well as the local populace to root out communist cadres; they protected the villages through constant patrolling, and worked on small civic action projects. The local people provided invaluable information on enemy activity to the Americans. Bit by bit, the villagers came to know and trust the marines through simple, day-to-day interactions. "By the end of 1965," writes General Walt, CAPs "were saturating wide areas of the densely populated lowlands with thousands of patrols and ambushes, day and night watches—and the Viet Cong were being hit where it hurt most."[13] Over the coming months, the effectiveness of the program was widely heralded by counterinsurgency experts, and, with the consent of General Thi, CAPs were soon established in the other two marine enclaves.

Two other types of pacification operations made their first appearance in the fall of 1965 in I Corps. One of them came at the request of the chief of the village of Hoa Hai, Huynh Ba Trinh, in a rice-rich region just south of Danang. After the 1st Battalion, 9th Marines under Lieutenant Colonel Verle E. Ludwig had soundly defeated a VC company in a firefight near his village, Trinh asked Ludwig if the marines could offer protection against teams of Vietcong rice collectors. Every harvesting season, the VC came into the local villages in the area and took a not inconsiderable percentage of the farmers' rice crops for their own use. Colonel Ludwig gathered together the chiefs from four villages within his battalion's tactical area, and it was agreed that 1/9 would protect the farmers against the predations of the VC through active patrolling, ambushes, and sweep operations as they gathered the rice harvest. After the rice was successfully harvested, the marines helped bring it to market via truck and helicopter.

And so "Golden Fleece" operations were born. Battalions from both the 9th and 3rd Marines, which operated northwest of Danang, were steadily engaged in Golden Fleece operations throughout September and October. Other III MAF units conducted similar operations outside of Chu Lai, and General Walt ordered his staff to implement a repeat performance during the spring 1966 harvest season.

Another pacification innovation in the fall of 1965 coordinated the efforts of marines with local village chiefs and GVN civic action personnel supplied by the provincial chief and the national police. Marine companies would cordon off a hamlet suspected of harboring VC at night. Vietnamese officials would call on the entire village population via loudspeaker early the following morning to gather at a central assembly area, where they would be given food and medical care by marine civic action personnel. The villagers' identity papers would be checked by the GVN officials, with a view to identifying suspected enemy agents and guerrillas. Then marines and Popular Force troops would search the village for guerrillas and arms caches. These "County Fair" operations became a regular feature of the marines' pacification effort over the next several years.

Operation Harvest Moon

From December 8 through December 20, the marines conducted their first major search-and-destroy operation in cooperation with the ARVN. It marked the marines' first foray into the Que Son Valley about forty miles southwest of Danang, a locale that would see very heavy fighting between the marines and the PAVN at various junctures over the next couple of years. The Que Son Valley stretches westward from the lowlands on the coast to the foothills of the Annamite Mountains. About eighty thousand peasants, mostly rice farmers, dwelled in clusters of hamlets along the valley floor. A marine veteran of the fighting there described the landscape evocatively as

a sea of paddies, green, golden, fallow, wet or dry, divided by
dikes according to centuries-old pedigrees of ownership. Route
534 lies the length of the valley floor, bisecting it like vertebrae.
Here and there are huge, black rocks, scattered around . . . with
the randomness of watermelon seeds. Villages rise from the sea
of paddies like atolls in a confusion of hooches, coconut trees, and
family vegetable plots patrolled by chickens, with small, scabrous,
yellow dogs and squadrons of ducks. . . . Bamboo, sixty feet high
or more with many stalks four inches think, girds the little com-
munities and barricades them against sudden entry, channeling
foot traffic into narrow passages. There are ancient trails where
countless feet have pounded their surfaces a foot or more below the
surrounding terrain. [14]

The town of Hiep Duc serves as the western gateway to the valley. On November 16, 1965, the ARVN garrison there was completely overrun by the 1st Vietcong Regiment. Intelligence reports in early December indicated the enemy was planning on marching northeast, with a view to sweeping away the small ARVN outposts in the towns of Que Son and Viet An. Generals Walt and Thi agreed it was time to wrest the valley from enemy control in Operation Harvest Moon.

The operation got off to an extremely rocky start when not one but two separate ARVN Ranger battalions were ambushed as they pressed their way into the valley. "They attacked in a mass and hit us from all sides. . . . People were dropping around us right and left," recalled a US Army adviser attached to one of the Ranger battalions.[15] In fifteen minutes on the afternoon of December 8, that battalion lost a third of their strength and were effectively finished as a fighting unit. The next day, the other Ranger battalion met with similar bad luck.

The original scheme of maneuver called for the marines to conduct a series of heliborne assaults and to converge on the enemy forces once they had been located and engaged by the South Vietnamese. Now the marines' mission morphed from trapping and destroying the enemy to rescuing their South Vietnamese comrades. On the afternoon of the ninth, the 3rd Battalion, 3rd Marine Regiment air-assaulted to several LZs within quick striking distance of the ARVN Ranger units, only to run into at least two well-armed companies of VC. For more than four hours a wild firefight raged. At last light, the VC broke off the fight. About seventy-five enemy troops lost their lives in this engagement. Eleven marines were killed and seventeen had been wounded.

Early on December 10, Brigadier General Melvin Henderson's effort to trap the enemy in a vice faltered when two other marine companies were pinned down by heavy mortar and machine-gun fire. By the time the fighting was over that day, the marines had lost a total of twenty men killed and eighty wounded. The enemy had shown uncanny ability to anticipate where the marine helicopters would land the assault units and to maneuver in strength pretty much undetected by aerial surveillance.

The VC had seized the momentum. Henderson was relieved of command. Brigadier General Jonas Platt took charge of the fight. Platt flew over the valley the morning of December 11. Much to his surprise, his helicopter drew no enemy fire. Suspecting that the enemy had withdrawn to the Phouc Ha Valley about four miles to the southeast, Platt received clearance from MACV to call in B-52 strikes on the valley floor before sending in two marine battalions to clear it of enemy forces. For a week after the Arc Light B-52 strikes, the two marine battalions combed the area, drenched by monsoon rains day and night. They searched in vain for the enemy, but several dozen marines had to be evacuated after developing sores and blisters on their feet as a result of constant patrolling in mud.

Harvest Moon had been an operation of nasty surprises, drenching monsoon rains, and a couple of days of very hard, inconclusive fighting. Casualty figures were reported as 407 enemy killed and 33 captured. The marines had lost 90 killed, 218 wounded, while the South Vietnamese lost 91 men killed and 141 wounded. In reviewing the operation, the marine command identified a number of problems. Hasty planning, lousy weather, and the rapid pace of ground operations had hampered ground-air coordination. Casualties could have been reduced with better reconnaissance on the ground. Plainly, the marines were up against a tenacious enemy who knew how to use the terrain and the weather to compensate for his lack of heavy weapons and air support.

As the year came to a close, General Krulak prepared yet another cogently argued "strategic reappraisal" of the war in which he again respectfully challenged the underlying assumptions of Westmoreland's "big unit" attrition strategy. The marine general was particularly skeptical of the "crossover point" concept at the heart of Westmoreland's strategic concept. No one really knew how many men the North Vietnamese were willing to throw into the fight to compensate for PLAF losses in the South. How could MACV possibly gauge when the crossover point might be approaching?

Krulak went on to propose an alternative approach to reducing enemy combat power than the current attrition strategy: vigorously step up attacks on North Vietnamese ports, war production facilities, and the Ho Chi Minh Trail. US airpower had to stanch the flow of men and matériel to the battlefield. Simultaneously, the United States should "shift the thrust of our effort to the task of delivering the people from guerrilla oppression, and to protecting them thereafter...."[16]

Brute Krulak's report received a generally tepid reception from Secretary McNamara, and from most of the president's inner circle of foreign policy advisers. The major criticism was that the oil spot strategy the Marine Corps favored would take too many Americans too long to implement. The focus of American efforts would remain just where it was: on defeating the enemy's regular forces in the hinterlands.

Lew Walt was well aware the marines would be pressured into increasing the number of multi-battalion search-and-destroy operations in 1966. Yet Walt remained committed in principle to the Corps' balanced strategy in I Corps. His objective as the new year approached was "to link up the expanding areas of control for Hue, Danang, and Chu Lai, putting the bulk of the population and agriculture and all of the key roads and railroads in our area within a protective envelope, in which freedom of choice was up to the individual Vietnamese— without a gun at his temple."[17]

It was an admirable goal, but it would prove an unobtainable one.

CHAPTER 7

THE BIG BUILDUP AND THE "OTHER WAR"

Pressure to expand American ground forces outside of the marines' area of operation, I Corps, built slowly and steadily throughout the spring of 1965 in both Saigon and Washington. In April an advance party of the 173rd Airborne established a base camp in the high ground at Bien Hoa, twenty miles northeast of Saigon, facing the thickly forested Vietcong stronghold known as War Zone D. By early May the entire unit was in Vietnam.

The 173rd was the army's fire brigade in Asia and the Pacific, and thus better prepared for combat in Vietnam than most army organizations, having conducted extensive jungle-fighting training in Asia. Westmoreland wanted other units in place and ready to fight in the communists' key war zones surrounding Saigon, and in the Central Highlands, where North Vietnamese regulars had begun to assemble in considerable strength.

In early June, the 1st Battalion, Royal Australian Regiment arrived in the 173rd's area of operations (AO). The Australian army was widely recognized as one of the premier jungle fighting organizations in the world. Together, Australia and New Zealand ultimately contributed a brigade-size force. America's European allies, as we have seen, found Johnson's arguments for fighting in Vietnam to be less than compelling. They all refused to send combat forces to Southeast Asia, despite sustained pressure to do so from Washington's "More Flags" campaign. South Korea made the largest military contribution among US allies, sending an army division of some twenty thousand men to fight in Vietnam in 1965, and later, another ground division. The Koreans quickly established a reputation as tough soldiers who gave no quarter, and they were deeply feared by the enemy. So were the Aussies, but for different reasons. The "diggers" were widely considered more stealthy than the Americans, better marksmen, and more rigorously trained in small-unit patrolling.

In July, the 2nd Brigade of the 1st Infantry Division, the Big Red One, also deployed in the vicinity of Bien Hoa. The rest of the division was dispersed in five camps, guarding the approaches to Saigon. Soon thereafter, the 1st Brigade of the 101st Airborne Division deployed into the vital Central Highlands near An Khe. Their mission was to clear the area of enemy forces so the army's cutting-edge fighting force, the 1st Cavalry Airmobile Division, could build a gigantic base in the area to house its fifteen thousand men and four hundred helicopters. The Cav began to arrive in Vietnam in September. Westmoreland wanted the airmobile division to take on the North Vietnamese forces gathering in strength in the Central Highlands, and he looked forward to seeing that unit put its innovative airmobile doctrine and tactics to the test for the first time in combat.

Transforming the Landscape

Already under profound stress from twenty years of nearly continual warfare and political strife, Vietnamese society in 1965 was rapidly overwhelmed by the influx of tens of thousands of American troops, their war machines, and a vast supporting apparatus. The South Vietnamese found the material abundance of the Americans at once reassuring and disconcerting. Private construction companies, Navy Seabees, and army engineers transformed the landscape of the country, building mammoth base camps, each one the equivalent of a small city. Hospitals, fuel depots, office buildings, scores of tactical airfields, army camps, and helicopter pads soon dotted the landscape from the DMZ down to the Mekong Delta. In 1965, Vietnam was many things, including one gigantic construction project.

At Cam Ranh Bay, 190 miles north of Saigon, 2,500 army engineers arrived on June 9 and began a massive expansion of the port and airfield, with vast storage facilities for jet fuel, and a new ten-thousand-foot runway that could handle every aircraft in the American inventory. Seabees and civilian construction companies started work on five other deep-water harbors to handle the rapid influx of gargantuan cargo ships and naval vessels. A sprawling communications and transport network crisscrossed the country by year's end, and the building would continue for several more years. Bui Diem, Saigon's ambassador to the United States from 1965 to 1967, was among the most reflective and wise anti-communist Vietnamese politicians. He recalled the hectic days in Saigon at this time in his memoir, *In the Jaws of History*:

> *The war was now indisputably an American enterprise. . . . The Americans came in like bulldozers . . . and the South Vietnamese followed their lead without a word of dissent. After July 1965 the American buildup was so massive, so irreversible, and so fast that it simply left no room for doubt or second thoughts of any kind. . . . The marshaling of forces by the world's greatest power was an awesome sight. . . . U.S. Army tent camps—small towns, actually—sprang up everywhere. Around them swarmed Vietnamese businessmen and small-time entrepreneurs vying to provide necessary services and take advantage of the thousands of new opportunities the situation offered. Construction boomed. It seemed the Americans wanted to build everything at once. . . . U.S. contractors who arrived in the army's wake recruited thousands of workers overnight, sucking the labor pool dry. Traffic jammed the streets; prostitutes were all over the place. Transport planes and jet fighters roared in and out of the airports with a constant maddening din.*[1]

The new American arrivals, for the most part, were bursting with self-confidence, a "can do" spirit, and more than a little disdain for the South Vietnamese people they were there to help. Many of the Americans who arrived in 1965 seemed wedded to the idea that if the South Vietnamese couldn't rally to their own defense and transform their country into a democracy, the United States would do it for them. Along with jets, troops, and tanks came cadres of American political scientists and economists, as well as agricultural development experts and city planners to help South Vietnam transform itself into a modern society. Vietnam would be remade in the American image. That, in effect, was the plan.

Early US Army Operations

For the most part, VC regular forces avoided contact with US Army units in the spring and summer of 1965, much to the frustration of the officers and men of an American army anxious to get on with the war. David Ross, a medic with the 1st Division, remembers the typical frustrations Americans encountered out in the field:

> *The farmer you waved to from your jeep in the day who would be the guy with the gun out looking for you at night. They would come together and man a small offensive or probe attack, drop a few mortar rounds and go home and call it a night. We took more casualties from booby traps than we did from actual combat. The big problem was you couldn't find the enemy. It was very frustrating because how do you fight back against a booby trap? You're walking along and all of a sudden your buddy doesn't have a leg. Or you don't have a leg.* [2]

During the last week in May, the 173rd conducted its first battalion-size search-and-destroy mission about twelve miles northwest of the coastal town of Vung Tau in Phuoc Tuy Province. The brigade's artillery softened up the landing zones with fifteen minutes of prep fire; then came twenty minutes of air strikes. Three companies of American infantrymen debouched from their choppers unopposed. They spent the next two weeks hunting for enemy contact in the bush. For all their efforts hacking through the jungle under a scalding sun, and tracing narrow, dirt trails between villages, they were rewarded with a mere handful of fleeting contacts with the enemy. Eleven US Army sky troopers were wounded, most by booby traps. Seven guerrillas were reported killed over fourteen days of patrolling. More formidable than the enemy was the broken, thickly jungled terrain, and the enervating humidity.

In the second week in June, elements of the 173rd air-assaulted into an area near the town of Dong Xoai, fifty miles north of Saigon. A VC regiment near there had overrun a Special Forces camp garrisoned by a Special Forces A-Team and several hundred Montagnard troops, and then mauled the ARVN relief force. By the time the Americans arrived, it was too late to do anything. The enemy had vanished into the jungle. In late June and July, the 173rd made a number of deep penetrations into the enemy stronghold of War Zone D, twenty miles northeast of Bien Hoa. The only enemy contact consisted of a few snipers and the occasional incoming mortar round at night. The sky troopers did uncover large caches of rice, tobacco, and tea, signaling the enemy's presence. But in a pattern that would hold until the end of the war, the enemy kept his distance, and bided his time.

Between October and December, the 173rd conducted fourteen air assault operations of company size (about 150 to 200 infantrymen) or greater. Only one of these missions turned into a sustained combat engagement—the US Army's first battalion-size battle of the Vietnam War. The Battle of Hill 65—a daylong, bloody brawl, also known as the Battle of the Hump—occurred in War Zone D, north of the Dong Hai River. The fighting unfolded in menacing, thickly jungled terrain, laced with tunnel complexes, combat villages, and an imaginative array of VC fortifications, some of which had been originally constructed during the French Indochina War.

On November 5, US intelligence located a full VC regiment operating near the confluence of the Song Be and Dong Nai Rivers. The brigade commander, Brigadier General Ellis Williamson, sent Lieutenant Colonel John Tyler's 1st Battalion, 503rd Infantry and an Australian battalion attached to the brigade after them. Inserted into the area by chopper, the joint force struggled through triple-canopy jungles and broken ground, finding little over the course of three days' patrolling but a few deserted camps and fortifications, some of which were obviously new. Both the Aussies and the Americans encountered innumerable "wait-a-minute" vines as they hunted for the enemy. Lieutenant Al Conetto, a platoon leader in the 173rd, described the process of moving in the jungle through this terrain:

> These vines grow vertically as well as horizontally and invari-
> ably caught on pieces of equipment as we bent to go underneath
> them. They hooked onto almost anything; and as you moved for-
> ward, they restrained you then jerked you back. In other words,
> two steps forward, one step back. The point man in each unit used

a machete to cut a path through the jungle, but he could not get
all the vines. . . . Men cursed as the vines dragged them back, and
it echoed up and down the column. Progress was very slow. . . .
The jungle has never been a pleasant place for American soldiers
with 50 to 70 pounds of equipment on their backs and steel pots
[helmets] on their heads. And it never will be.[3]

Late on the seventh, Tyler's unit received confirmation from intelligence that the VC were deployed in strength less than a mile to the west of a prominent hill—Hill 65 on their maps. The battalion set up defensive positions a thousand yards east of the hill. The night was uneventful. Little did Tyler know that the commander of the 3rd Battalion, 271st Regiment, 9th PLAF Division knew where the Americans were and had received orders to attack them as they broke camp in the morning.

The VC infantrymen spent the night quietly preparing assault positions on and around the hill, undetected by Tyler's men. Soon after dawn, Tyler sent Bravo and Charlie Companies toward the hill in two columns. He wanted to gain the high ground so he could try and locate the enemy, close in on them, and attack. Tyler kept A Company in reserve. Around 0800 hours, not long after Charlie Company came upon a recently occupied hamlet, two of its three platoons stumbled into a well-executed VC ambush. It was the usual drill: heavy, concentrated automatic-weapons fire, machine guns, and captured American Claymore mines ripped into the flesh of the US soldiers. "The whole earth seemed to erupt furiously," remembered First Lieutenant Ben Waller of C Company, commanding the second platoon. "Claymore mines exploded all around the platoon, and interlocking machine gun fire rained down with deadly accuracy. Young men, who only seconds before had been strong and daring, now lay lifeless, their bodies torn apart, forever lost to this world."[4] Rifleman Niles Harris recalled in an interview that he was badly wounded in the opening seconds of the fight. "I can't remember if I was second, third, or fourth man in line. . . . Everybody [in my squad] was killed or wounded."[5]

The sky troopers tried desperately to get their bearings, hugging the ground and returning fire. Sergeants shouted directions and encouragement. Soon, it was clear the two platoons might well be cut off and annihilated. By 0930, B Com-

pany had maneuvered its way into a position where it could support Charlie
Company on the right flank with fire, preventing it from being overrun.

Over the next several hours, the enemy made several attempts to encircle
both Bravo and Charlie Companies. "Throughout the morning during the lulls
in the fighting we could hear the screaming pleas of the wounded to the left
and front of us," Chaplain James Hutchens remembered.[6] First Sergeant Edgar
Board pushed forward up the hill to assess the situation. He returned a few
minutes later. He'd found seven dead troopers and one wounded man with two
broken legs. Four men, including Chaplain Hutchens and Sergeant Board, tried
to rescue the wounded man and carry him back on a hammock, but one American
was killed and the other three, including Board and Hutchens, were wounded.
Later that day a squad succeeded in rescuing the wounded soldier.

Shortly after the Vietcong's second attempt to encircle Bravo and Charlie
Companies, Lieutenant Colonel Tyler, sensing disaster, committed A Company
to the escalating battle. Lieutenant Al Conetto recalled what happened just as
Alpha Company entered the fray: "The Viet Cong attacked the lead elements
of Bravo and Charlie in an ambitious maneuver designed to encircle both
companies. It was like a banzai charge. But the attackers were unaware of Alpha's
presence and assaulted with their backs toward us. While enemy bugles blared in
the jungle, our small arms fire mowed down the attackers by the dozens."[7]

Throughout the afternoon, the fighting ebbed and flowed in intensity as
small groups of combatants attempted to flank each other's positions. Much of
the combat was hand to hand. Tyler called in artillery fire on suspected enemy
assembly points around the hill to prevent the VC commander from reinforcing
the battlefield, as well as against enemy positions on the hill itself. No one knows
how many communist infantrymen were killed or wounded by this intense fire,
but scores were hit. So were a few Americans, for the adversaries were locked in
combat at very close range.

By dusk, the firing at last died down to sporadic bursts of machine-gun
and rifle fire. As darkness descended, the enemy withdrew from the hill, having
suffered well over four hundred casualties. Fifty Americans died in the fighting
that day. The toll would have been higher had it not been for some sustained
heroics by a medic, Specialist Lawrence Joel, attached to Charlie Company. Shot
in the thigh early in the fighting himself, Joel self-administered morphine and

then crawled from one wounded man to another to provide solace and medical help. For much of the time, he operated under direct enemy fire. Joel, from Winston-Salem, North Carolina, was the first medic in Vietnam to be awarded the Medal of Honor, and the first living Black man to receive that honor since the Spanish-American War.

Today, only the 173rd Brigade survivors, the relatives of the dead, and a small cadre of Vietnam War history buffs remember the hard struggle for Hill 65. The first sustained, multi-battalion engagement between the US Army and the People's Army of Vietnam, the Battle of Ia Drang Valley occurred a week after Operation Hump, consigning the 173rd's battle to an obscurity it does not deserve.

Battle of Bau Bang

The Vietcong had chosen to attack Lieutenant Colonel Tyler's troops. Four days later, Senior Colonel Hoang Cam sent a reinforced regiment from the 9th PLAF Division to attack a 1st Infantry Division battalion that was supported by a squadron of armored personnel carriers (APCs) along Highway 13, a few miles north of the enemy-infested Iron Triangle, another VC stronghold dating back to the 1940s. Lieutenant Colonel George Shuffer's 2nd Battalion, 2nd Infantry had bivouacked just south of the village of Bau Bang on the night of November 11 after providing security along Highway 13 for an ARVN unit's passage. A VC battalion managed to surround the American perimeter that night, undetected. Between 0605 and 0650, Colonel Cam launched three multi-company assaults on Shuffer's unit. The first two attacks thrust toward the Americans from the south; the last one from the east. Shuffer's APCs rushed out to meet the first assault. The shock of the counterattack, especially the carriers' highly destructive .50 caliber machine guns, stopped the VC assault cold. Riflemen and machine gunners along the perimeter's defensive line stopped the next two, but the defenders took heavy casualties in the process.

At 0700, Colonel Cam launched the most ferocious assault of the morning, determined to crack the perimeter. This time the attack came directly out of Bau Bang village. Up until this attack, Shuffer had been careful not to call in fire on the village proper, to prevent the shelling of civilians. But after he was sure mortar fire was coming directly from the village, he plastered it with artillery fire, and then came the coup de grâce: fighter-bombers dropped iron bombs, cluster bombs, and napalm across the entire village and then some, breaking the momentum of the attack. Nonetheless, NLF suicide squads were able to break through Shuffer defenses, where they killed two howitzer crewmen and wounded four others, but the breakthrough was quickly contained.

A final assault commenced at 0900, also from the north, but this quickly withered under intense air and artillery fire. The Vietcong left behind 146 bodies, according to the official American count. If history is any guide, the sad truth is that a fair number of those "enemy" bodies probably belonged to civilians living in Bau Bang. By the battle's end, the entire village was a fiery shambles, and gray-black smoke blotted out the sky. Ironically, American civil affairs teams had distributed rice, beans, and used clothing to the villagers just a few days before the battle. The butcher's bill for the 2nd Battalion, 2nd Infantry was 20 killed and 103 wounded.

Pacification and Its Problems

"We seem to have got past the big monsoon dangers," opined Mac Bundy in a summary of a September 11 meeting of the war council, "and we need to be sure we have an agreed program for the continuing contest of pacification. . . . All of us feel that this is the most important area of effort for the coming weeks and months."[8] At numerous junctures during the summer, the war council, midlevel advisers in both the State and Defense Departments, and a cadre of counterinsurgency gurus expressed understandable concern that Westmoreland's ground war strategy was not addressing adequately the politico-military struggle for control of villages. This contest was called different things by different people at different times. "Rural reconstruction," "revolutionary development," "the village war," and "the other war" were all synonyms one encountered in 1965 for what the French had called *pacification*, and what Americans today tend to call counterinsurgency. Bernard Fall provided a short but excellent definition of the concept: counterinsurgency = political reform + economic development + counterguerrilla operations.

When the Americans began arriving in strength to fight in Vietnam in 1965, Saigon's pacification efforts were in disarray. The political instability between the fall of Diem in November 1963 and the ascent of Thieu and Ky in spring 1965 had only exacerbated deep-seated problems with pacification that went back to the very beginnings of South Vietnam's short history: corruption, nepotism, and indifference in Saigon to the struggle every Vietnamese peasant endured just to get from one year to the next without being killed or starved. Every one of the short-lived administrations in Saigon had its own pacification priorities and key personnel. Plans adopted one month were suddenly off the table the next. "The war against the Viet Cong was all but forgotten in the uproar," observed AP Saigon bureau chief Malcolm Browne. "Political storms continued to drain the war effort."[9]

In their typical determined and resourceful way, the Vietcong took maximum advantage of the turbulence, seizing control of large swaths of the countryside, capturing thousands of American-made weapons in raids and attacks on Popular and Regional militia forces and, increasingly, in attacks on the ARVN. Once the VC political cadres had recruited and organized a government-controlled village, they put the entire population to work building fortifications, tunnels, and setting booby traps. Nguyen Huu Tho, a leading VC political cadre, estimated in December 1964 that three-quarters of South Vietnam's land and one-half of its population had been "liberated" by revolutionary forces. Browne, who by that time had spent several years covering the war for the Associated Press from the Ca Mau Peninsula all the way up to the DMZ, believed Tho's assessment was spot-on.

The "other war" had two broad, mutually reinforcing aims: to break the NLF's hold over the rural population and to generate popular support for the GVN through economic and social improvement programs. Village security was the province of the police, the Regional and Popular forces—the militia—and to a lesser extent, the ARVN. Nation-building projects were officially carried out by the GVN's Ministries of the Interior and Rural Development. That, in any case, was the theory, but as usual in Vietnam, theory and practice were at odds. By the time the American army arrived in force, pacification consisted of a bewildering array of poorly administered GVN programs sponsored by various American agencies and organizations. The most important of these were USAID, the CIA, and MACV. Some programs were designed to improve agricultural production. Others provided basic education and health care services, built schools, infirmaries, and village markets. Still others sought to improve the responsiveness of local government to the peasants' problems and concerns, and provide basic goods like food, clothing, and soap. One interesting initiative sought to train young Vietnamese to serve in development teams akin to those of the communists' political cadres when they went into a village and began to organize it for Hanoi's purposes.

Throughout the war, Saigon was officially in charge of implementing pacification programs of all stripes, but the Americans provided most of the funding, expertise, and logistical support, as well as some of the manpower. In fact, the Americans were the driving force behind the entire pacification program, because one of the few constants in Saigon's political culture throughout the war was studied indifference to the peasantry.

Not until 1967 were all civilian and military pacification programs placed under a single authority—Robert "Blowtorch Bob" Komer's Civil Operations and Revolutionary Development Support, or CORDS. CORDS's Phoenix Program, which focused on destruction of the VCI infrastructure using VC techniques such as terror and assassination, made a great deal of progress after the Tet Offensive of 1968, when programs were finally integrated, but it proved too little, too late.

From 1965 on, competing with the Vietcong in the countryside was a task of Herculean difficulty. Drawing on the Vietminh's trusty playbook, the Vietcong had developed an extraordinarily effective, systematic method for penetrating the villages, eliminating or marginalizing GVN officials within them, and enmeshing the people in the revolutionary enterprise in various political and military capacities. The process was spearheaded by highly dedicated Armed Propaganda Teams (APTs) of between three and twelve members, who served as propagandists, instructors, and role models for the peasants. The APTs were well supported by both part-time and full-time guerrilla units, manned almost entirely by local peasants. The Armed Propaganda Teams were in many ways more important in the "People's War" than the units that engaged the enemy in combat. Despite limited communications technology, the APTs were able to drench the rural population in pro-NLF messages and ideas. They staged pro-revolutionary skits and lectures, produced vast quantities of mimeographed literature and, most important, engaged in hour after hour of one-on-one conversations to convert the people into believers. The APTs would often set up a roadblock, stop a bus, and force the passengers to attend a few lectures on the evils of the "US-Saigon clique" and the virtues of the revolution that was using the power of the people to defeat the Americans and their "lackeys." The APTs were organizers and motivators of a revolution that prized organization and motivation more than military technology or power.

Here is an excerpt from the field manual of a highly successful APT leader who was killed in 1965 by GVN forces:

PROPAGANDA MISSION

Question: What is the importance of a propaganda mission? What should you do in carrying out this mission with the people?

Answer: A propaganda mission is designed to attract people's interest and stimulate their thoughts, and also to expand our party's policy and ideology.

Question: What are the four ways by which this is carried out?

Answer: 1. Increase feelings of discontent on the part of the people before trying to mobilize their patriotic sentiments. 2. Explain to the people the efforts being made by the enemy to divide us from the population. 3. Educate the people about our struggle in South Viet Nam; and 4. Stress the importance of our Front for the Liberation of South Viet Nam. . . . Also, educate the people about our party's basic policies, about North Viet Nam, about socialism, and other world news.

Question: What are the consequences of widespread application of propaganda at meetings and so forth, which, however, lacks work in depth?

Answer: No valuable result can be obtained if a propaganda mission is carried out in width only, that is, superficially, but not in depth. The public can never understand the subject well, because at most meetings you cannot explain everything in detail. Only by carrying out your propaganda mission secretly and at the grassroots level can you succeed. . . .

Question: What is the proper behavior of the propagandist?

Answer: A propagandist should be modest, he should learn from the people, and he should teach what he has experienced to the people. This helps to consolidate his position. He should be patient and his behavior should be exemplary.[10]

The GVN's rural administration in 1965 was a study in contrast to that of the NLF's shadow government. Government propaganda teams lacked depth, commitment, and training. A typical GVN cadre would show up at a village out of the blue and give a short talk about the evils of communism, the virtues of democracy, and then give away a few handouts on those two themes. Very little one-on-one persuasion went on at the hamlet level. "Under the best of circumstances, the GVN administration was characterized by a kind of paternalism in the French colonial manner that lacked the 'get up and go' that the Americans wanted," observes historian Eric Bergerud.[11] The culture of the GVN administration proved stubbornly resistant to efforts to reduce corruption and inefficiency. To survive within the dysfunctional and corrupt South Vietnamese government system, province and district chiefs as well as senior ARVN officers had to pay bribes to their patrons, and to demand payments from their underlings, as well as from ordinary citizens who required government licenses, goods, or services. Local administrators often charged peasants for food and construction materials the Americans had provided to the GVN for free distribution, sold licenses and permits to the highest bidder, and diverted a large percentage of the goods with which they had been entrusted to the black market. Many government officials functioned "more as intimidators of the regime's opponents and exploiters of the common people than as defenders of the nation."[12]

Everything was for sale in South Vietnam, including a great many government officials. A person with funds and the right contacts could circumvent the law to obtain a draft exemption, a lenient criminal sentence, or a dozen rocket-propelled grenades. Many American Army units arrived in Vietnam with heavy cotton uniforms and standard-issue leather combat boots. It was easier for American soldiers to buy new, lightweight tropical uniforms and boots on the black market than to wait for the army to distribute them.

The NLF was almost certainly the largest single purchaser of American weapons and ammunition through the black market in the early years of the conflict, and often the sellers were GVN officials. Peasants were hired en masse by the GVN to do construction work for one program or another, but all too often they were paid late, or not paid at all, as payroll funds were embezzled by provincial chiefs and project managers. In the Popular and Regional Forces, the supposed backbone of the GVN's village defense program, unit rosters were loaded with "ghost soldiers." These were men who had paid a fee to a senior officer or provincial official so they wouldn't have to serve at all, or men who'd been killed but remained on the roster so that the official could collect their salaries from the government paymaster. "Corruption guaranteed incompetence in office, high or low," observes Neil Sheehan in his riveting study of the war, *A Bright Shining Lie*. Government officials kept

> *their positions by their facility at forming corrupt alliances with those above them and at creating other corrupt alliances with those below in order to channel money upward. . . . Lines of authority that needed to function if the country was to be governed rationally and that were already weakened by the influence of family ties and religious and factional connections were undermined entirely by those networks within networks of graft. . . . The Saigon regime had, in fact, evolved a system in which no one was permitted to keep his hands clean. For all to be safe, all had to be implicated.*[13]

Some Americans participated in the Saigon officials' various scams, if only by turning a blind eye to flagrant abuses by their Vietnamese counterparts, or by taking payoffs to do so. In March 1965, former army adviser John Paul Vann returned to Vietnam as senior USAID adviser in Hau Nghia Province, just west of Saigon. He was shocked by the gains the VC had achieved in the countryside since he had left in 1963, as well as by the incompetence and venality of the province's senior officials, civilian and military. And Vann had developed a grudging respect for the enemy. As he wrote to General Robert York in May:

> *There is a revolution going on in this country—and the principles, goals, and desires of the other side are much closer to what Americans believe in than those of the GVN [the Saigon Government]. . . . I am convinced that, even though the National Liberation Front is Communist-dominated, that the great majority of the people supporting it are doing so because it is their only hope to change and improve their living conditions and opportunities. If I were a lad of eighteen faced with the same choice—whether to support the GVN or the NLF—and a member of a rural community, I would surely choose the NLF.*[14]

In the summer of 1965, responsibility for coordinating the vast array of American pacification programs fell on the shoulders of Ambassador Henry Cabot Lodge, the patrician Bostonian who'd served for many years as US senator from Massachusetts. This was his second tour of duty as ambassador to South Vietnam. Lodge exuded confidence and sophistication, and he had an abiding interest in the pacification process. He joined a select group of senior American officials in believing the war could never be won unless the government wrested control of the villages from the VC. Unfortunately, Lodge lacked the staff in Saigon, or the pull in Washington, to overcome CIA, USAID, and MACV resistance to surrendering some measure of control of their pacification projects to an overarching organization or agency. Thus, in 1965, and for a considerable period afterward, pacification remained "a patchwork quilt that reflected political turf wars and differing objectives found in the U.S. Embassy, MACV, the CIA, and the various players in Washington."[15]

The main goal of USAID's programs was to raise the standard of living of the peasantry. AID workers distributed livestock and seed and devised innovative irrigation techniques. AID workers supervised the building of schools, hospitals, and ran the ever-expanding refugee program. Thousands of doctors, nurses, and agricultural experts were hired by USAID to serve in Vietnam, and the organization also administered the Chieu Hoi (Open Arms) amnesty program for Vietcong defectors.

The CIA bore primary responsibility for training twenty-something South Vietnamese men to serve in rural development cadres modeled after the communist Armed Propaganda Teams. The CIA-run program had its origins in a cadre training program developed by ARVN major Nguyen Be, a former Vietminh officer who had impressed CIA operatives with his energy, honesty, and pluck. In Binh Dinh Province, he had transformed local young Vietnamese into well-disciplined, anti-communist cadre teams. Be described the teams as the key conduits between the GVN and the peasants. They lived and worked for extended periods within a single village, providing security, working on small construction projects, and providing basic education about politics and village self-defense. Each team consisted of fifty-nine men, forty-one of whom provided village security. The rest of the team was to assist the village in governing itself, to dispense agricultural information, and to promote public health.

Major Be was put in charge of a national cadre training center and ordered to prepare nineteen thousand cadres by the end of 1965. That goal, like that of so many pacification programs at the beginning of the American war, was overly ambitious, and the program soon ran aground. GVN province chiefs strenuously resisted giving the villagers the autonomy they needed to become self-governing, because it diminished their personal power and prestige. Major Be couldn't recruit sufficient numbers of motivated individuals. A great many of the people he did recruit were from the cities, and they found village life uncongenial and dangerous. The ten-week training cycle for the cadres was too short. Perhaps the biggest problem was the unconvincing political message: that the NLF was going to lose the war, and that Saigon was sure to win. Few villagers saw much evidence of that in 1965. What exactly did the government stand for? Was it a national government, in any legitimate sense? To vast numbers of Vietnamese, the answers were: (1) "What the Americans tell it to stand for," and (2) "No." An American expert on propaganda and pacification work put his finger on one cause of the US-GVN failure:

The Viet Cong propagandist breaks [his work] down into the slogan 'live together, eat together, work together.' This means the Viet Cong propagandist is expected to spend all his time with his psychological targets, blending in completely with their whole existence. Too many of the people on our side are just not willing to do this. . . . What's really needed is the personal touch, and that's where the Viet Cong are beating us so badly.[16]

General Westmoreland's MACV, with far more resources than the CIA or USAID, was a major participant in the "other war," even though Westmoreland himself was philosophically against the idea of American combat battalions undertaking pacification operations. MACV provided the trainers and advisers for the Regional and Popular Forces; army civil operations personnel and engineers worked on a variety of projects with the GVN's Ministry of Rural Development, including road and bridge building and expanding the electricity network in various parts of the country. And of course, American maneuver units often *did* engage in the village war when they were not conducting search-and-destroy operations. And that was quite often. Over the course of the war, American infantrymen ran tens of thousands of small-unit patrols around their base camps in search of guerrillas in order to prevent hit-and-run attacks, as well as indirect fire on their bases by mortars, the only form of artillery most VC units had.

Whether they were concerned with training cadres, improving physical structures in villages, or providing services to the ever-growing number of refugees who fled to the cities, the US/GVN pacification programs had one thing in common: a yawning gap between what they were supposed to accomplish and what they actually achieved. Aside from corruption and inefficiency of the GVN's rural administrative apparatus, there was the persistent problem of the resilience of the VC cadres and guerrillas. They never gave up. If the government was able to secure a village, there was a good bet that within a matter of a few months, the enemy would make a concerted effort to take it back via direct attack, or by intimidation or assassination of local GVN officials.

Everyone involved with the other war recognized that building a bond between the rural populace and the GVN depended on the government's ability to provide security over time, but province chiefs and ARVN officers were notorious for redeploying militia and army forces on a whim, thus leaving newly liberated villages vulnerable to attack. All too often, GVN security forces were part of the security problem rather than its solution. William Nighswonger, a former USAID official who published a study of pacification in Vietnam during the early years of the war, wrote that from all parts of Vietnam, USAID representatives "have reported problems from the presence of ARVN forces in populated areas. Some war damage to villages is, of course, unavoidable, but ARVN and American reliance on artillery and air strikes—in the absence of soldiers to protect the people—has been a costly factor in popular support of the government."[17] As an American USAID adviser in Quang Tin Province reported in February 1965, "a high incident rate of stealing, raping, and obtaining free meals had not endeared the populace towards the ARVN or Regional Forces."[18]

Pacification Around Saigon

The seven provinces adjacent to Saigon remained the top priority in the pacification effort as part of the Hop Tac (Victory) program in 1965. Resources were comparatively plentiful in this area, and the GVN was more responsive to the needs of the province chiefs and their American advisers here than elsewhere, for obvious reasons. MACV was heavily involved in the Hop Tac program, the goal of which was to clear the Vietcong out of the strategically vital area around Saigon. Yet like most of the other pacification initiatives, Hop Tac languished for lack of coherent leadership, and ultimately failed to eliminate such VC strongholds as the Iron Triangle and War Zone D. VC-infested areas were frequently attacked and cleared, but the enemy would inevitably retreat to sanctuaries in either Cambodia or deep in the jungles of Vietnam, and come back after the US/GVN maneuver units had left. In Quang Nam Province, the GVN had earmarked thirty enemy-controlled villages for pacification by the end of 1965. Only eight had been secured by that date, and the government's hold on several of those was tenuous.

In one of the many ironies of the allied strategy during the war, the pacification program was continually undermined by conventional military operations of both the Americans and the South Vietnamese. High-powered air and artillery support, some of it indiscriminate, laid waste to hundreds of South Vietnam's 2,600 villages. In August of 1965, the US Air Force announced it had destroyed 5,300 structures in South Vietnam and damaged another 2,400 thus far that year. By year's end, an estimated half a million South Vietnamese peasants had flooded into Saigon, Danang, and other cities to escape the destruction. There, they took up residence in squalid camps without proper sanitation or housing. Small slums of sheet metal and wood shacks sprang up on the outskirts of Vietnam's two largest cities. Gangs of small children wandered these disease-ridden communities begging and scavenging for scraps of food from garbage piles. Cholera was a common problem.

Senior American military and civilian officials recognized that pacification efforts needed to be streamlined and better rationalized, but it was an uphill climb. Robert H. Miller, head of the State Department's Vietnam Working Group, speculated in October 1965 that there were simply too many high-priority projects in place for any of them to work properly. Perhaps, he suggested in a report, the United States was trying to force too many changes on the South Vietnamese too fast? As Miller put it:

> *I can't escape the conviction that the general thrust of our present effort in Vietnam is increasingly in the direction of assuming governmental functions for ourselves and pushing the GVN aside because of its general inadequacy and incompetence. At the same time, our effort is not attacking what remains the central Communist challenge—gaining control of the country through erosion and subversions at the village level. I fear our present course could lead increasingly to something resembling a U.S. occupation of South Vietnam without our getting at the real, long-term Communist challenge.*[19]

In November, Robert McNamara made another one of his many fact-finding trips to Saigon. The report he prepared for the president upon his return was sobering, to say the least. It appeared tinged with a note of pessimism from the usually upbeat secretary of defense. Despite the steady escalation of the bombing, the rapid deployment of American combat forces, and the use of B-52s on communist redoubts in South Vietnam, the communists were stepping up the number and intensity of their operations. The political struggle was particularly concerning: "The Ky 'government of generals' is surviving, but not acquiring wide support or generating actions; pacification is thoroughly stalled, with no guarantee that security anywhere is permanent and an indication that able or willing leadership will emerge in the absence of that permanent security."[20] William Nighswonger, who'd spent several years working on various pacification projects in the Vietnamese countryside, would have agreed entirely. As he summarized the situation in early 1966:

> *The programs and armed forces that have been created in Vietnam are neither adequate in quality nor properly interrelated for effective application in a particular pacification campaign. The Vietnamese armed forces appear to be well trained in weapons techniques but are poorly prepared to behave properly among the peasants. . . . Despite a plethora of worthy concepts, individual program quality and proper integration of all programs into a cumulatively productive pattern are lacking. . . .*
>
> *The steady escalation of money, materials, and manpower inputs without adequate management can only increase the magnitude of American failure and prolong the agony and futile aspirations of the Vietnamese people.*[21]

Those closest to pacification, men like Frank Scotton, a US Information Agency field officer who spent a good part of every year from 1962 to 1972 in the field in Vietnam, knew that the very fact that Americans considered pacification "the other war" was a big problem. Under Westmoreland's strategy, the war was curiously bisected into a "big unit" conflict with regular communist units of the NLF and PAVN run by the Americans, and the pacification war run by the South Vietnamese. "The only player who seemed to understand the one-war concept," wrote Scotton, "with everything having political impact and purpose, was the Viet Nam Communist Party."[22]

Frank Scotton was the archetype "good American" in Vietnam. He grew up in Massachusetts, the son of a soldier who was killed in the Battle of the Bulge in 1944. Scotton was intensely dedicated, resourceful, and seemingly fearless, exchanging fire with the Vietcong several times as he journeyed across the hinterlands on foot or in a jeep. He came to love the Vietnamese people, their culture, and history. Not surprisingly, he became increasingly skeptical of the American way of fighting in Vietnam.

The Americans and the South Vietnamese Talk Past One Another

By the fall of 1965, it was readily apparent that Westmoreland's misconceived military strategy wasn't the only formidable obstacle to success in America's new war. The relationship between the American patrons and their Vietnamese clients was bizarrely dysfunctional. Of course, thousands of individual Americans and South Vietnamese formed close relationships amid the shared hardships of fighting a war. But broadly speaking, the relationship between the allies at senior levels was marred by misunderstanding and mistrust on both sides. Time and experience seemed to make the relationship more rather than less problematic. The cultural differences between the Americans and Vietnamese were so vast as to be virtually unbridgeable. "Americans are active, impatient, and rationalistic," said one ARVN general. "Vietnamese are quiescent, patient, and sentimental."[23] South Vietnam was a largely Confucian society that valued familial duty over rights, the group over the individual, and hierarchy over equality. Thus, there was little social basis among the people for understanding the Western political ideas and institutions the Americans were constantly pushing them to adopt.

Politicians and generals in Saigon found the Americans' condescending attitude deeply offensive. US Army captain Gordon Sullivan understood why. "In 1965 we decided that we had come to win this war, and we wanted the South Vietnamese to stand aside while we did it. . . . Americans had a very low opinion of Vietnamese people."[24] Decisions about the trajectory of the war from early 1965 on were made in Washington, very often with minimal input from Saigon, sometimes with no input whatsoever. Bui Diem, longtime ambassador to the

United States from South Vietnam, recalled in his memoirs that the crucial escalatory steps taken by Washington in early 1965—Operation Rolling Thunder, the landing of the marines, and the decision to expand the American military presence from 23,000 to 175,000 troops—were all presented to his government only after the decisions had already been made. "The fact is that though it was our war and our country that was at stake," recalled Diem, "we were so junior a partner in the effort that our voices carried no weight. Undoubtedly, one reason for this was an inferiority complex we brought to the alliance. Another was our blind confidence in the United States, which suggested that however grave our doubts about a particular policy, in the larger scheme they were probably not consequential."[25]

The torrent of American military and civilian goods that flooded into South Vietnam greatly exacerbated the corruption and nepotism that had plagued South Vietnam since its inception in the mid-1950s. The ordinary citizens of the South were all too aware of the corrosive effect of American consumer goods and money on the moral fiber of their government officials, army officers, and merchants. The behavior of America's allies stood in marked contrast to the Spartan ethos followed by the vast majority of NLF soldiers and cadres. In the eyes of a great many ordinary Vietnamese, Saigon's dependence on the United States, and the corruption that dependence engendered, undermined its claims to legitimacy.

Many senior GVN officials were cognizant of their growing credibility problem in the eyes of the peasantry, and indeed, the world at large. Stanley Karnow, a journalist who spent many years covering the war in the field, recalled that many South Vietnamese generals "repeatedly tried to assert their sovereignty by defying the Americans in disputes that often resembled quarrels between an adolescent and a parent. They would sulk or rebel or maneuver mysteriously, their petulance betraying an uncomfortable sense of dependence and frustration with the growing American intrusion into their affairs."[26] The more the Vietnamese resisted, the more the Americans simply worked around them, marginalizing their role.

What South Vietnam needed, desperately and above all else, was a leader who could command the same kind of respect that millions of Vietnamese felt for Ho Chi Minh—a father figure who understood the traditional Vietnamese mindset and could present an appealing vision of a future Vietnam that did not involve domination by the Americans or the communists. If the series of coups between the assassination of Diem and the ascent of Thieu and Ky to power demonstrated anything, it was that no such leader was in the offing. South Vietnam was a highly unstable state. There were any number of anti-communist political parties that emerged in opposition to Diem in the 1950s, but as journalist Frances FitzGerald writes, they were "fragmentary and generally unstable coalitions formed around one or two intellectuals or civil servants. . . . And none of these parties had a plan, a program, even an ambition to organize in the countryside. . . . The Saigon politicians and intellectuals would continue to tinker with legislatures and constitutions that did not begin to touch upon the lives of the peasants or even the poor of the cities."[27]

The communists cleverly exploited the peculiar pathology of the American–South Vietnamese relationship, highlighting again and again in their propaganda screeds the "neocolonial" attitude of the Americans toward their "puppets" in Saigon. Washington, they said, was determined to exploit the Vietnamese people in support of its own geopolitical objectives. A few years after the war, Truong Nhu Tang, a high-ranking NLF political official, found it hard to understand why the United States would come to the rescue of such corrupt and incompetent men as the political generals of Saigon:

> *The unrestrained irresponsibility and incompetence of the [GVN] generals had led to apathy and disgust among the people at every level. South Vietnam was a society without leadership or direction—and these essentials the Americans could not provide. They could not impose order on chaos. And without a government that could claim at least some tatters of legitimacy and effectiveness, how could the United States dare commit its troops and its all-important prestige?*[28]

How, indeed?

CHAPTER 8

THE AIR WAR AND
THE HO CHI MINH TRAIL

The Johnson administration hoped to accomplish a great deal with Rolling Thunder. The primary strategic objective was to persuade the politburo in Hanoi to cease its support of the insurgency in the South and come to the bargaining table to work out a political solution to the war. If the politburo didn't budge, the war council reckoned, the North Vietnamese would face an increasingly heavy rain of destruction from the skies. Aerial punishment, the thinking went, would bring Hanoi around eventually. Mac Bundy, who saw firsthand the results of the VC's audacious raid on the American air base at Pleiku that triggered the first Rolling Thunder missions, explained the rationale in his usual crisp, precise prose in a memo to LBJ:

> We believe that the best available way of increasing our chances of success in Vietnam is the development and execution of a policy of sustained reprisal against North Vietnam—a policy in which air and naval action against the North is justified by and related to the whole Viet Cong campaign of violence and terror in the South. . . . This reprisal should begin at a low level. Its level of force and pressure should be increased only gradually [and] should be decreased if VC terror visibly decreases. The object would not be to "win" an air war against Hanoi, but rather to influence the course of the struggle in the South. . . . We believe, indeed, that it is of great importance that the level of reprisal be adjusted rapidly and visibly to both upward and downward shifts in the level of

*Viet Cong offenses. We want to keep before Hanoi the carrot of
our desisting as well as the stick of continued pressure. We also
need to conduct the application of force so that there is always a
prospect of worse to come.*[1]

A second objective of Rolling Thunder was tactical: by interdicting the flow
of troops and war matériel from North to South Vietnam, the United States
hoped to make a significant dent in the enemy's ability to wage the ground war
in the South. A third goal was to buck up the sagging morale of the South Vietnamese government and armed forces.

And so it was that American fighter-bombers and bombers took to the air
for the first Rolling Thunder raid on March 2, 1965. In the months before the
campaign began, Johnson and the war council had repeatedly rejected the preferred strategy of the Joint Chiefs of Staff. They wanted to unleash the immense
destructive power of modern combat aircraft against the North's limited indus-
trial base, lines of communication, and infrastructure, and crush its will to continue to fight sooner rather than later. If they did not give up, Air Force Chief of
Staff Curtis LeMay once remarked—only half in jest—the United States would
"bomb them back into the stone age." In an astonishing display of strategic ob-
tuseness, LeMay told an interviewer eleven years after the war was over that
America could have won the war in two weeks of unrestricted bombing. LeMay
was hardly the only senior officer in the American military in the formative years
of the Vietnam War who failed to grasp that sheer destruction would never be
enough to win.

The Joint Chiefs' position on the use of airpower scared Johnson and his
civilian advisers, who feared with good reason that a full-bore air campaign
against the North, even one of short duration, would lead to an outpouring of
sympathy for the communists and major protests throughout the world. More
menacingly, it might well also lead to the intervention of Chinese air and ground
forces. Lyndon Johnson was not about to take that chance. Having said that,
neither the civilian strategists in the Pentagon nor the leading CIA analysts
were convinced that a limited, escalating bombing program would bring Hanoi
to heel. The CIA, in fact, was deeply skeptical about Rolling Thunder's efficacy.
Nonetheless, the war council felt it had to be tried. The political sensitivity of the

air campaign, coupled with a fear that an excessively exuberant strike commander might provoke Chinese intervention, led Johnson to impose stringent restrictions on how the military could wage the campaign, including, but not limited to, these: no bombing within thirty miles of the Chinese border; no bombing within thirty miles of Hanoi, or ten miles of Haiphong.

Most tellingly, Johnson reserved for himself and his closest advisers the selection of targets, the number of sorties per week, and even the weight of the ordnance for every mission. Each Tuesday over lunch in the White House with his chief advisers, the president made the final target selections by weighing the following criteria: military significance; risk to pilots; risk to North Vietnamese civilians; risk of widening the war further. The senior officers in the Pentagon were livid over the micromanagement of the campaign by civilians. They would continue to lobby for lifting the restrictions, with little success in 1965.

The targeting selection process for Rolling Thunder missions was unwieldy, to say the least. Each week, air force and navy field commanders in Vietnam submitted lists of potential targets to the commander in chief, Pacific (CINCPAC) in Hawaii. Admiral Sharp and his staff vetted them, and sent a refined list to the JCS. The JCS passed them along to a cadre of military and civilian analysts in the Pentagon, and then the list went on to the State Department for further pruning. State then returned them to the JCS for a quick review, and then they went on to the White House for review at the Tuesday lunch.

Rolling Thunder unfolded in two phases during 1965. From March to June, the strikes concentrated on factories, ammunition dumps, barracks, and radar sites along the chief lines of communication. Rather than softening North Vietnam's will to press the fighting in the South, the early Rolling Thunder strikes appeared to strengthen its resolve, just as the CIA had predicted. Immediately after the first bombing raid, the North began to escalate its support for the insurgency.

In July, after the secret approval of Westmoreland's plan for an American-led ground war, the primary focus of Rolling Thunder shifted from strategic persuasion to interdicting the flow of supplies to the South. Now trains, truck convoys, major roads and bridges were attacked. During March of 1965, Rolling Thunder sorties—single strikes by single planes—numbered only 585. In August, American pilots flew more than 3,500 sorties.

Hanoi's Preparations

Well before the first Rolling Thunder strikes, Hanoi had invested heavily in its air defense system, and begun to mobilize the entire population of the Democratic Republic of Vietnam behind the war effort. The Vietnamese, said Uncle Ho, would wage "a people's war against the air war of destruction, in which each citizen is a soldier, each village, street, and plan a fortress on the anti-American battlefront. . . . The war may last another five, ten, twenty years or longer, Hanoi and Haiphong may be destroyed, but the Vietnamese people will not be intimidated."[2] The Americans read this pronouncement as propaganda. It was not. Ho Chi Minh's statement was sincere from the first word to the last, as events would prove time and time again over the next several years.

In December 1964, Armed Propaganda Teams of the PAVN had fanned out across every village in North Vietnam to drum up enthusiasm for the campaign, and to enlist volunteers. Moscow supplied a formidable early-warning radar system, followed soon by SA-2 surface-to-air missiles (SAMs)—"flying telephone poles" traveling at a brisk 2,700 miles per hour—that could knock even the most nimble American fighters out of the sky at 30,000 feet. Vietnam's only fighter pilots were recalled home from their training base in China. The PRC was happy to provide fifty MiG-17 interceptor jets for those pilots in the upcoming campaign against the Americans. Although the 17s were hardly state-of-the-art fighter planes, they were perfectly suitable for executing the limited, hit-and-run tactics the Vietnamese pilots had learned in training, and would employ to surprisingly good effect against American jets.

At the end of February 1965, the politburo ordered the old and the very young to evacuate several cities, especially Hanoi. By the time of the first Rolling Thunder strike, the North Vietnamese had emplaced about five thousand anti-aircraft guns of various calibers around its handful of sizable cities and strategic sites, as well as along the chief lines of communication. Chinese anti-aircraft crews formed an indispensable part of Hanoi's defense network, and Chinese advisers worked diligently with their Vietnamese counterparts to ensure American aircraft would be greeted by a wall of flack over North Vietnam's airspace. More than a quarter million Chinese support troops took up tasks in North Vietnam to free up PAVN fighters for the war in the South. By war's end, more than one thousand Chinese troops had been killed defending the skies over North Vietnam.

The North Vietnamese also broke down urban factories producing machine parts, fertilizer, textiles, and ammunition into small units, dispersing them across the countryside. Oil and gas in large tanks at storage yards were emptied into millions of fifty-gallon barrels and distributed widely.

As the bombing slowly escalated week by week, month by month, millions of North Vietnamese citizens went to work building simple, one-person bomb shelters consisting of concrete pipes three feet in diameter, buried five feet into the ground. By 1968, 21 million such shelters would honeycomb the country—more than one per citizen. In the bomb-drenched panhandle of southern North Vietnam, communist engineers constructed hundreds of underground villages. Even farm animals were kept in underground pens and stables. In the city of Thanh Hoa, engineers built a vast subterranean complex replete with shops, schools, markets, and hospitals. By the end of 1965, about half a million North Vietnamese civilians had been assigned to repair crews along the main lines of communication to the South. Male and female crews worked twenty-four hours a day repairing roads, bridges, and rail lines, as well as building redundancy into the transport system to keep men and supplies flowing to the front.

The First Rolling Thunder Mission

The first Rolling Thunder mission consisted of forty F-100 Super Sabres out of Danang, forty-four F-105 Thunderchiefs (aka "Thuds") flying out of Thailand, and twenty B-57 bombers that hailed from Tan Son Nhut Air Base in South Vietnam. Their target was a large ammunition depot at Xom Bang, thirty-five miles north of the DMZ, in North Vietnam's panhandle. The F-100s went in first to soften up the target and attack the AA batteries. Next, the Thuds made their appearance, sweeping down toward the target in several waves to deliver their deadly payloads.

The mission commander, Air Force colonel Robbie Risner, watched in alarm as his F-105 wingman's aircraft took a near-direct hit. Within seconds, pilot Boris Baird was drifting down into the jungle about a mile from the ammo dump. Risner switched his radio on to the emergency channel, only to find it roaring with excited chatter and yelling. There was trouble: the second wave of Thuds had arrived early, before the first wave had completed its bombing run. Too many planes were stacked up over the target. They were being punished by heavy flak. "Risner decided to exert control," according to air-war historian John Morrocco. "His voice boomed over the radio and silenced all but essential communications. Ignoring the deadly ground fire streaming toward him, Risner directed incoming planes into the target, pointing out anti-aircraft positions to avoid."[3] Soon, the B-57s dropped their entire payloads in one pass, and the first Rolling Thunder mission was a part of history.

About 80 percent of the ammo dump had been destroyed, but the intensity of the flak had come as an unwelcome surprise to the American airmen. Before mission's end, enemy gunners had shot six American planes out of the sky. Helicopter rescue crews managed to rescue five of the six pilots, including Baird. Lieutenant Hayden Lockhart Jr. was captured by North Vietnamese militia after a full week of evading his hunters in the woods. He was the first air force officer captured in North Vietnam.

Ironically, during the entire three-and-a-half-year bombing campaign, weather would diminish the effectiveness of air operations as much as the formidable North Vietnamese air defense system. During North Vietnam's rainy season, from October through April, hundreds of missions were either canceled due to torrential rain or low cloud cover, or carried out under less-than-optimum conditions. "Bad weather often precluded the release of ordnance at the preferred 30- to 45-degree angle to minimize aircraft exposure to flak," writes historian Jacob Van Staaveren, "forcing release at a lesser angle [and] allowing maximum exposure to enemy gunners."[4]

On April 3, navy and air force aircraft struck a crucial link in the communists' North–South supply line—the Thanh Hoa Bridge over the Song Ma River, sixty-five miles south of Hanoi. Known as the "Dragon's Jaw" by the Vietnamese, the bridge was one of the most impressive engineering projects in all of North Vietnam. This road and rail bridge was comprised of two reinforced steel spans, resting on a massive concrete pier, and anchored on both banks of the river by forty-foot-thick concrete abutments. It had taken the Vietnamese eight years to build it. Naval aviators scored first, destroying one of the approaches to the bridge. For the first time in a Rolling Thunder operation, North Vietnamese MiG-17s rose up to challenge the air assault. The MiGs damaged several navy F-8 Crusaders before hightailing it back to their base outside Hanoi.

Then it was the air force's turn. Once again, Lieutenant Colonel Risner was leading the charge. His F-105 Thuds honed in on the target, carrying 750-pound conventional bombs and 250-pound "bullpup" air-to-ground missiles. Descending from seventeen thousand feet through thick bursts of flak, Risner scored a direct hit on the bridge with a bullpup. Several other pilots' rockets struck home, but the damage to the target proved to be superficial. As one pilot put it, "Firing Bullpups at the Dragon was about as effective as shooting BB pellets at a Sherman tank."[5] A second wave of attackers swept in at a forty-five-degree angle, but heavy winds blew most of the pilots off course and their ordnance landed harmlessly on the riverbanks. The bridge remained operational.

The next day, Risner was back for another crack at the Dragon's Jaw, along with more than forty other American aircrews. This time four MiG-17s slipped into the battlespace through a thick layer of haze, catching the Americans unaware. Two Thunderchiefs crashed to the earth after being hit by MiG cannon fire. The railroad tracks on the bridge were badly damaged in this day's attack, but the bridge itself remained structurally sound. Vietnamese repair crews worked feverishly to repair the damage, and the trains were soon crossing the bridge, heading south with war matériel for the insurgency once again.

The first two days of attacks on the bridge produced one of Hanoi's most celebrated women war heroes—one of many. Over the course of those air strikes, a militiawoman named Ngo Thi Tuyen showed undaunted courage, repeatedly carrying crates of ammunition to the gunners. At one point, she lugged two one-hundred-pound cases of ammo to a gun position near the riverbank in one trip. She only weighed about one hundred pounds. She also cooked food for the soldiers, dug trenches, and refused to take a break for sleeping, despite being ordered to do so. She told her harrowing story to an interviewer in 1991:

> As a militiawoman, I was in charge of transporting ammunition
> for the regular forces. That very night, the American planes poured
> bombs into the area and twenty-two of my comrades in arms were
> killed. But we had to defend the Dragon's Jaw Bridge at all costs on

that terrible night—and we had to keep the trucks going over it to
the south. I don't know why I was able to carry those two big boxes
of ammunition at that time. More than once, my strength came
from anger and the need to avenge my dead comrades.[6]

Over the next three years, American aircraft flew several thousand sorties against the Thanh Hoa Bridge, but they never managed to inflict enough damage to put it out of action for more than a few days. The Dragon's Jaw became an enduring symbol of Vietnamese resolve. Not until 1972 was it fully destroyed, only to be rebuilt the next year.

Lieutenant Colonel Risner was widely admired by his superiors and subordinates alike for his daring, and for his leadership. "The man was fearless," remarked one pilot. "He exposed himself to flack as if it didn't exist."[7] Shot down on his sixty-fifth combat mission in Vietnam on September 16, 1965, Robbie Risner spent more than seven years in North Vietnamese prisoner-of-war camps, much of it in the infamous "Hanoi Hilton," where he and Navy commander James Stockdale organized and led the resistance movement among American POWs. Risner spent a total of three years in solitary confinement, and was repeatedly subjected to torture. In his memoir about his life as a POW, *The Passing of the Night*, he attributed his survival to an abiding faith in the power of God. "To make it, I prayed by the hour. It was automatic, almost subconscious. I did not ask God to take me out of it. I prayed he would give me the strength to endure it. When it would get so bad I did not think I could stand it, I would ask God to ease it and somehow I would make it. He kept me."[8]

Back to the Drawing Board for the Air Force and the Navy

By the middle of June, the North Vietnamese had downed fifty US aircraft. Three had been lost to MiG cannon fire. The rest had been downed by anti-aircraft guns on the ground. Both the navy and the air force were frantically engaged in revising their conventional attack tactics and developing new radar and weapons systems with a view to improving their lackluster performance over North Vietnam.

On July 24, a Russian-supplied North Vietnamese SA-2 surface-to-air missile found its first victim—an air force F-4 Phantom. Three days later, a half-dozen American planes were lost when they attacked two dummy SAM sites, defended by a formidable array of anti-aircraft guns. The air force responded to the SAM menace with the "Wild Weasel" program, in which specially equipped aircraft capable of locking on to SAM radars and destroying them with Shrike air-to-surface missiles were employed. Vietnamese anti-aircraft gunners quickly learned to turn off their radars to avoid detection and destruction during attacks, and a deadly cat-and-mouse game developed between the gunners and the American pilots. The Wild Weasel pilots didn't knock out their first SAM until three days before LBJ instituted a Christmas 1965 bombing halt. By that point, Johnson had little hope the pause would bring Hanoi to the bargaining table. He was right to be skeptical.

Flying Rolling Thunder missions was a very dangerous business. Aircrews faced a wall of fire from flak and missiles. A great deal of effort went into improving tactics and technology to deal with the SAMs, but heavy flak was the real killer. Some 80 percent of the 991 planes lost over the course of the Rolling Thunder campaign fell as a result of conventional anti-aircraft fire. Veteran pilots who had served in the Army Air Corps in World War II swore the flak was more intense over key targets in North Vietnam than it had been over Germany. Navy pilot Commander John Nichols described what it was like to run the gauntlet of North Vietnamese air defenses in his book *On Yankee Station*. The North Vietnamese gunners

> could fill a five-square-mile column with murderous flak from 3,000 to 20,000 feet. It was awesome, it was spectacular, it was perilously close to beautiful. The light guns, 23- and 37mm, burst with white smoke. The 57mm shells exploded in dark gray and the heavy 85- and 100mm stuff erupted in black clouds. Mix in occasional strings of colored tracer from heavy machine guns

arcing up to perhaps 5,000 feet, and you can imagine all these
varicolored clouds bursting somewhere in that cone of air every
second for several minutes.[9]

Porter Halyburton, a navigator in a navy F-4 squadron flying off the deck of the USS *Independence* recalled the frustrations he shared with his brother airmen in the first year of the Rolling Thunder campaign:

More than half the missions I flew were at night. . . . Most of
the time we were out looking for truck convoys going from north
to south to connect to the Ho Chi Minh Trail. We were not very
good at it. The Vietnamese were masters of camouflage. They put
fresh-cut greenery over the tops of the trucks. They hear you com-
ing and pull off to the side of the road where they looked just like
a clump of bushes. We were very frustrated that our targets were
not very significant. . . . And flying in the North, we were very
constrained. . . . President Johnson said, "You're not going to bomb
an outhouse up there without my permission." The rules said we
couldn't even attack a SAM site unless they launched a missile at
us first. We had to send in somebody as bait to try to get them to fire
a missile so we could attack the SAM sites. That kind of stuff really
infuriated us.[10]

Halyburton was abruptly shot out of the sky on his seventy-fifth combat mission on October 17, 1965, by a Soviet-built SAM. "I saw the flak coming from the right. You don't hear anything, you just see the little black puffs. All of a sudden there was this thud. We took a hit right in the cockpit. . . . I looked down and saw a big piece of metal sticking out of my hand. I pulled it out and then pulled my ejection handle."[11]

Over the next seven years and five months, Halyburton was a POW in a series of grim camps. He was tortured on a regular basis in an effort to extract incriminating, anti-American statements, and forced to attend communist indoctrination classes as well. Like John McCain and so many other captured American airmen, Halyburton was often handcuffed behind his back and then hoisted off the ground by a rope attached to his wrists. "It was like molten metal flowing through your veins. Just indescribable pain," he recalled.[12]

Halyburton, who hailed from Davidson, North Carolina, found great solace and relief when he was placed in a cell with air force pilot Major Fred Cherry, the son of Black farmworkers from Virginia. The North Vietnamese hoped the two men—one white, the other Black, would come to detest each other, but something like the reverse happened. Cherry was in very rough shape. He'd broken his arm and foot when he landed in North Vietnam. When Halyburton first met him, he was suffering terribly from a postsurgical infection:

> *He really couldn't do anything so I had to bathe him and feed him and help him go to the bucket. And I started raising hell with the camp authorities to give him antibiotics. . . . Fred credits me with saving his life. I don't know about that, but I am certain that he turned my life around. When I moved in with him I said to myself, "God, this guy's in a lot worse shape than I am and he's not complaining." I had been out of touch with other people and was beginning to feel pretty sorry for myself. Taking care of Fred gave me a sense of purpose outside my own survival. It was very liberating. It was really the beginning of the idea that we were all in a brotherhood, all part of a big family.*[13]

By the time Porter Halyburton was shot down, American intelligence agencies had already concluded that Rolling Thunder was failing in its major objectives. More bombing was unlikely to do the trick. Nonetheless, the JCS pressed to step up the air assault of the North. Robert McNamara thought otherwise, and as usual, his voice carried much more weight with the president than the military men. As one army general was to say disparagingly, the secretary of defense had become a "field marshal without qualifications."[14] Right after Christmas, he persuaded LBJ to extend a holiday bombing halt well into January, in the hopes that the Soviet ambassador to the United States Anatoly Dobrynin would succeed in convincing the politburo to open negotiations for a political settlement. Dobrynin dispatched a Polish emissary to Hanoi to try to bring the North Vietnamese around, but he failed. Near the end of January 1966, the pope received a letter from Ho Chi Minh denouncing the bombing pause as "a sham peace trick."[15] In April 1966, deeply frustrated by the lack of concrete results, President Johnson lifted some of the stringent restrictions on Rolling Thunder operations, but not enough to satisfy the pilots. The results of an increasingly intense bombing campaign in 1966 and 1967 continued to disappoint Washington.

Rolling Thunder: Not a Happy Story

Today, Rolling Thunder is seen by all serious historians as the most spectacularly expensive failure in the history of aerial warfare. All told, in 1965 the United States flew 55,000 sorties against 158 major targets, and thousands of "targets of opportunity," in North Vietnam. According to official figures, American aircraft destroyed 819 freight cars; 12 locomotives; 800 trucks; 100 ferryboats, with 1,000 other boats destroyed or damaged. US aircraft had dropped 33,000 tons of ordnance, and 171 planes had been lost. McNamara and others took satisfaction in the statistics. They should not have done so.

The campaign suffered from a host of maladies. Command and control of Rolling Thunder was a subject of constant friction and debate between the White House, MACV, and the JCS, all of whom had their own ideas about strategy and targeting. The navy and air force quarreled over command and control from the beginning until the end of the campaign. By the time of the last mission in November 1968, none of the issues that caused that friction had been resolved to anybody's satisfaction. Search and rescue operations were hampered by a lack of trained personnel and suitable helicopters. In June and July 1965, CIA pilots had to step into the breach and rescue twenty-one aviators, while the air force crews rescued only five.

During 1965, Hanoi was able to step up its support for the South considerably. By year's end, Le Duan was more reluctant to come to the bargaining table than he had been before the bombing campaign started. In January 1966, a CIA assessment claimed the North Vietnamese had "achieved sufficient flexibility in the routing of both imports and internal traffic to ease the distribution problems that developed in the first few months of the strikes."[16] According to one reliable source, the total tonnage of supplies flowing from North to South Vietnam in

1965 equaled the total tonnage for the previous five years.[17] Moreover, the relatively slow pace of escalation of the air strikes had given Hanoi time to develop robust defensive measures. And the North Vietnamese had used that time wisely.

Rolling Thunder had mobilized the will of the North Vietnamese people behind the great crusade for unifying the country. "There was an extraordinary fervor then," recalled a North Vietnamese physician a few years after the war. "The Americans thought the more bombs they dropped, the quicker we would fall down to our knees and surrender. But the bombs heightened rather than dampened our spirit."[18]

Politically, the bombing campaign did nothing at all to aid the American-GVN war effort, and much to hurt it. Historian Max Hastings puts it well:

> Rolling Thunder did incomparably more harm to the government of Lyndon Johnson than to that of Le Duan. International and some US domestic opinion recoiled from the mere fact of the bombing and was unimpressed by its moderation. Contrarily, Johnson faced fierce criticism from congressional hawks who wanted him to hit the enemy harder—to go for the jugular. When he sought credit for his humanity by staging a seasonal bombing pause between December 24, 1965, and January 31, 1966, this was greeted by a familiar stony silence from Hanoi, scorn from the airmen, and worldwide indifference.[19]

As with so many other American initiatives in Vietnam, Rolling Thunder was premised on a faulty understanding of the nature of the conflict and the enemy. The insurgency in 1965 was largely self-supporting. In striking the North, the United States was in effect devoting its main military effort to a decidedly secondary target. The PLAF could pretty much feed and arm its own forces at this stage of the war. Its recruiting efforts were well organized and highly successful. The North's military-industrial base—the initial target of Rolling Thunder—was so small that it could be easily dispersed and continue to function. And so it did.

Besides, the amount of tonnage communist forces in the South needed to receive to effectively counter the escalation of the war by the Americans at this stage of the game was quite small. Intelligence analysts estimated that at the end of 1965, the insurgency could function effectively with as little as thirty-four tons of supplies from the North a day. That piddling amount could be delivered in a mere seven large military trucks. There was no way on earth American airpower could prevent that small trickle of supplies from making its way into South Vietnam, even if the president had dropped most of the strictures on the campaign. And Rolling Thunder strategists greatly underestimated the enemy's resolve and resourcefulness. They could not believe that Hanoi could stand up to an American bombing campaign for more than a few months. Had they taken seriously Vietnam's long history of resistance to foreign domination, they might have calculated differently.

Other Air Operations

A new air campaign began over South Vietnam on June 18, 1965, as waves of B-52 strategic bombers took to the skies in Operation Arc Light to obliterate suspected enemy base camps and assembly points. From that date forward, communist infantrymen lived in mortal fear of the Arc Light strikes. Many VC and PAVN veterans recall the strikes to have been the most terrifying aspect of fighting the Americans. Harry Summers, an army infantry officer who served in Vietnam in 1966 and 1967, once found himself perilously close to an Arc Light strike. He told the author in an interview that "the effect was absolutely terrifying. I thought the world was going to end."[20]

While the air war over North Vietnam was the subject of intense media interest, nearly 75 percent of all sorties by American aircraft during the war were flown against ground targets in South Vietnam. AP correspondent Malcolm Browne had the privilege of flying in the back seat of an F-100 Super Sabre during a ground attack on a Vietcong hamlet in the Mekong Delta on October 15, 1965. "The sky was crystal blue except for great masses of fleecy clouds, and the sun blazed through the plastic canopies above us. In a few moments, the whole of the great Delta was spread out below us, flat and drab." Browne and his pilot climbed to fifteen thousand feet and began to circle the hamlet, waiting for the forward air controller to mark the target so they could go in for the kill. Once the target was marked by a small rocket, *one after another, we went in. The dive down seems vertical, and at one point the ground actually seems to rotate over one's head. The hamlet leapt up to meet us, and now I could see flames coming from some of the tiny objects on the ground. "I strafe," Lieutenant Dorr said.*

While we were still what seemed to me a long distance above the ground, our cannon began to fire . . . the whole plane vibrated from the firing, like an electric massager. Streams of shells ripped into the houses below us, and I could see flashes of light where the shells were exploding. Abruptly, Lieutenant Dorr pulled back the stick and we pulled out just above the hamlet, zipping through a column of black smoke. . . . The speed is so great that everything happens in the space of a few seconds. Timing must be perfect. . . . A dive from 15,000 feet almost to sea level in a few seconds produces excruciating pain in the eardrums as the result of the terrific pressure change.[21]

In addition to jets, fixed-wing transports like the C-130 Hercules and C-123 Provider kept remote or surrounded ground forces of soldiers and marines supplied with airdrops. Fixed-wing aircraft such as the AC-47 gunship poured torrents of fire down on suspected enemy positions at night from 7.62 mm miniguns to keep them from overrunning American and South Vietnamese outposts. Cessna A-37 Dragonflies and a number of other single-engine prop planes were used by forward air controllers.

The helicopter, particularly the Bell UH-1 "Huey" Iroquois, became the most prominent symbol of the war for a simple reason. It was indispensable to the American way of war in Southeast Asia. The road network in South Vietnam was underdeveloped, and a great many ground operations were utterly dependent on the helicopter for transport, air support, and reconnaissance. Choppers, said General Harry Kinnard, the commander of the premier airmobile unit in the army, the 1st Cavalry Division, freed war "from the tyranny of terrain."

The Ho Chi Minh Trail

From the late 1950s, when communist revolutionaries in South Vietnam began limited military and terror operations against Saigon, through the summer of 1964, some forty thousand political cadres and PAVN military specialists— individuals, not units—made their way south to strengthen the sinews of the insurgency. Some went by boat, landing surreptitiously in ports, posing as civilians with false papers. Most, however, made their way on foot. They traveled in small groups of thirty to fifty people down an ever-more-extensive network of trails, mountain passes, streambeds, and narrow, serpentine dirt roads in the rugged Truong Son Mountains in Laos and Cambodia, and thence into western South Vietnam, where they joined their comrades in the struggle against Saigon and its American allies.

Spurred by the air strikes on North Vietnam immediately after the Gulf of Tonkin incident, the first PAVN infantry regiments began their trek down the "Truong Son Strategic Supply Route," better known in the West as the Ho Chi Minh Trail, in September 1964. Sources disagree on the exact figures, but a good estimate is that a total of seven full PAVN regiments made it down the Trail to fight on southern battlefields, in addition to twenty independent battalions of sappers, signalmen, and support troops by the end of 1965. The grand total of North Vietnamese troops and political cadres entering South Vietnam in 1965 was probably fifty thousand. Along with the fighting men and women came porters, many pushing reinforced bicycles that could carry as much as five hundred pounds of ammunition and food, who brought down some thirty thousand tons of matériel. Women nurses and teachers came down the Trail as well.

Every person who made the trip from December 1964 onward potentially came under US air attacks as part of the CIA's secret bombing campaign over eastern Laos. After March 1965, they had to contend with strikes from Rolling Thunder as well. Those who took this long, exhausting journey never forgot it. The trip south was an indelible part of the revolutionary experience, and it has been romanticized and mythologized in Vietnam ever since.

In early 1965, it took as long as two and a half months to complete the journey. In Laos, the Trail ran through nearly impenetrable primeval forests that gave way to steep, rocky mountains. The country was so remote and isolated there that neither the French nor the Laotian government had made any effort at all to control it. Thousands who left the friendly confines of North Vietnam never arrived at their destination. Some men and women were vaporized by American bombs, but far, far more were killed by other means. Some got lost in the immensity of the jungle and never found their way out. Others drowned in rapid streams. Some men and women died of exhaustion, but malaria probably took more lives than any other culprit during the first year of the American war.

The PAVN soldiers of Group 559, the unit responsible for constructing and maintaining the Trail, built small staging camps at intervals of about twenty miles so the travelers could rest and replenish their supplies. Many of these forlorn outposts had small cemeteries for those whose lives were lost along the way. Colonel Bui Tin, who would go on to accept the surrender of the last South Vietnamese government in Saigon in 1975, made the journey south in early 1964. He remembered that even before the American bombs rained down on the Trail, there were many ways to die en route:

> Some soldiers lost their way in the jungle and died of starvation. Small groups sleeping alone at night were pounced on by tigers or attacked by bears. On one occasion, I and three of my companions shot and killed a black bear staggering drunkenly down a hill after it had raided a beehive and eaten all the honey. And in the rainy season there were those who, unable to see clearly, stepped on poisonous snakes and were bitten to death. Then there were the stomach upsets and severe attacks of yellow fever to contend with. . . . It was also easy to lose one's footing on a slippery bridge and fall in without hope of rescue. Another hazard was jungle leeches; we encountered hundreds of thousands of them on our march, and they attached themselves not only to one's legs but also to certain vital organs, causing a hemorrhage and threatening one's future family life.[22]

In preparation for their trip, Colonel Tin and the dozen or so comrades who accompanied him spent two months at a special training camp at Xuan Mai,

North Vietnam. Most of the training consisted of climbing steep hills with packs filled with fifty pounds of bricks for as long as twelve hours a day.

A few days after the US Marines landed at Danang in March, Major General Phan Trong Tue, People's Army of Vietnam, was appointed commander of Group 559 and ordered to expand and improve the network. He himself had marched the length of the Trail during the French Indochina War, when he was a political officer of a Vietminh unit, but he'd done it in reverse, from south to north. When the general assumed command in March 1965, trucks were unable to make the trek:

> *My job was to direct the work of transforming the network of paths and dirt roads that wound through the Truong Son Mountains, now used by pedestrians carrying supplies on their backs, to a system of roads passable for big guns and carriages in both the rainy and dry seasons, to step up supplies to the South. I felt extremely enthusiastic when assigned the task of building the historic road along the Truong Son mountain range because by now the enemy had completely blocked our sea route.*[23]

General Tue confirms in his memoirs that his officers were more concerned during the early stages of the American war with the effects of malaria and food shortages than American bombs. At times, he had to send an entire repair crew to the hospital and replace them with new units because the whole complement got sick.

From April 1965 on, a great struggle ensued between the American airmen and General Tue's Group 559. General Vo Bam, the deputy commander of 559, remembered that "the race between us and the enemy became daily more intense. As the enemy struck key portions of the roads, mountain passes and river crossings in an effort to block our routes, we opened new detours. In this way, the supply network developed more and more."[24]

An American historian who has reviewed the unusually candid periodic reports of Group 559 tells us that General Tue and his staff were constantly pushed to do more with less by the Central Military Party Committee in Hanoi, and that Hanoi, in general, was unsympathetic to complaints about the horrendous working conditions and inadequate construction equipment. Women volunteers made up a substantial proportion of the road repair and construction crews that Group 559 deployed along the length of the Trail.

One of the women volunteers, Nguyen Mau Thuy, described her experience as part of a crew of fifteen people on a nine-mile stretch of road: how working on that road came first even in the face of bombs, and when those bombs came their orders were "not to run for cover . . . but to keep working and stand up and shoot the planes." The women would paint their hair ornaments black to prevent "the gleaming metal" from attracting fire from the air. For the same reason, the women could not "even dry our white underwear" and "had to wear damp clothes in the wet jungle."[25]

Nguyen Mau Thuy was among the better-educated women in her unit, and she was selected for an on-the-job training course for defusing unexploded ordnance. As part of this course, she first learned "to destroy the heavy bombs, and then [find] ways to neutralize the magnetic bombs, leaf-shaped bombs, and so on." She described how it took time to work out how to handle each type of bomb, and so for every type "people died before they learned the trick of defusing them." When it came to the 250-pound bombs, they would first "use baby bombs to explode a crater, and then with shovels carefully prod the big bomb into the hole." With magnetic bombs, "we would have to use wooden shovels to dig them out of the soil. We had to get them out of the roads so the trucks and the people who used steel shovels would be safe."[26]

Many accounts of life on the Trail by North Vietnamese veterans mix reflections of the natural beauty of the landscape with the presence of death. A combat engineer recalled that

> sometimes we landed in a valley where a multitude of white butterflies fluttered like a huge ribbon in the air. At another spot, we came upon a herd of elephants. To the twitter of birds and the shrieking of monkeys, we followed the tracks of deer along the stream in the immense wilderness that seemed to have no boundary.
>
> But the enemy did not let go of us even in this dark recess of the Truong Son forests. Our lines were shattered by their carpet

bombings and we were stunned to see whole hamlets razed by the
bombs, only a few charred pillars left standing. At times we were
ourselves caught in a bombing, each of us scrambling to find a
shelter. When we pushed out of the rubble we embraced each other
with tears in our eyes. Our hearts sunk at the sight of several bod-
ies of young women volunteers floating in a stream.[27]

Over the course of 1965, Group 559 built some two hundred miles of paved roads through the mountains for trucks, along with several large, well-camouflaged logistical hubs. General Tue's command grew from six thousand to twenty-five thousand troops during those twelve months. It included police units, engineers, support troops, anti-aircraft gun crews, and multiple battalions of infantry for defense. Truck convoys first appeared in significant numbers in the fall.

Special Forces, Montagnard Strike Units, and the Trail

In the latter half of 1965, some of the most deadly and dramatic encounters in Vietnam occurred when VC and North Vietnamese units struck remote bases in far western South Vietnam, usually occupied by one US Special Forces A-Team of twelve men, and one or two battalions of local mountain tribesmen they trained and led in strategic reconnaissance missions. Perhaps the most dramatic operation of the year occurred in late July and August at Duc Co, close to the Cambodian border in Pleiku Province. The Montagnard force there was supposed to block communist infiltration in their area of operations, but by late July a VC regiment had besieged the base. When the US Special Forces soldiers attempted to lead patrols outside the wire, they invariably came under intense small-arms fire and were forced back inside. To remedy the situation, an ARVN task force of three battalions of Airborne troops was ferried into the base by helicopter. The task force immediately began to conduct sweeps of the area. About two miles east of the Cambodian border, the ARVN troops and their American advisers were ambushed. Major Norman Schwarzkopf, an army brat who would go on to lead coalition forces in the great ground assault of the Persian Gulf War in 1991, was serving as an adviser to one of the Airborne battalions. He describes what happened:

> One minute the jungle was quiet. The next we were getting shot at from every direction. . . . All around, I heard crack-crack-crack-crack, but the jungle was so dense we couldn't see a damn thing. . . . It was an endless, desperate afternoon; we had walked into a major concentration of enemy forces and they were waiting for us. We knew that if we failed to make it back to the Special Forces camp by nightfall, the enemy would maneuver into position to annihilate us that night or the next day. Five or six times that afternoon . . . I had to stop to call in air strikes, then wait to make sure the planes or helicopters accomplished their task.[28]

As the task force withdrew in darkness in the comparative safety of the camp, a portion of the ARVN 3rd Airborne Battalion, along with Captain Mike Trinkle, an adviser, became lost in the jungle. Major Schwarzkopf volunteered to go out, find them, and bring them inside:

> I made my way alone west of the camp across a wide clearing, all the while talking to Trinkle on the radio. It was pitch black, so I fired a little red flare to help the men orient themselves. "I think I saw it," Trinkle said. "Can you pop another?" The enemy was starting to shoot at me, but I did as he asked and moved on quickly. A couple of hundred yards farther into the jungle, I ran across soldiers from Trinkle's unit and pointed them toward the camp. Finally Trinkle and I linked up and I led the way back in.[29]

By that point, the relief force had lost forty men killed and double that number wounded. In the morning, a very brave air force pilot volunteered to fly his C-123 into the camp's airstrip. The plane was shot full of holes by the time it landed, and then shot up again after taking off, but it made it out, and flew all the way to Saigon so the most seriously wounded during the fighting could get the care they needed.

For the next two weeks, an estimated two VC regiments kept Schwarzkopf and the rest of the allied force boxed in, pummeling them with mortar fire and probes. Sustained American air support somehow kept the enemy from mounting a major assault of the base. Major Schwarzkopf was repeatedly surprised to find himself alive each morning. In mid-August, South Vietnamese marines broke the siege by driving the VC back across the border into Cambodia. By the time Schwarzkopf finished his tour as an adviser, he had been hospitalized twice—once for malaria, and once for amoebic dysentery, and he had been wounded in the left arm by machine-gun fire.

Long-Range Reconnaissance Missions

In September 1965, about a month after the Duc Co siege, the American Special Operations Group was ordered to conduct covert, long-range reconnaissance missions along the Ho Chi Minh Trail in Laos. Their objective, as part of Operation Shining Brass, was to monitor the flow of men and matériel moving along the Trail, to call in air strikes on those targets, and to find downed fliers. The Special Operations Group (aka "SOG") had been formed in December 1964 by the Joint Chiefs of Staff to conduct such sensitive missions. SOG was outside the MACV chain of command. Its commanding officer in Vietnam reported directly to the president's Office of the Special Assistant for Counterinsurgency. Consisting of several thousand personnel, SOG was dominated by Army Special Forces, but also had assets from the air force, Navy SEALS, and CIA paramilitary types.

During the fall of 1965, small teams of Americans and Montagnard operators were inserted into Laos by helicopter from such SF camps as Kham Duc, Kontum, and Khe Sanh. Master Sergeant Charles Petry and Sergeant Willie Card, along with five Nung mercenaries, conducted the first Shining Brass mission about fifteen miles inside Laos. The Nungs, a Highlands ethnic group that had migrated from southern China into Indochina centuries earlier, had a well-earned reputation as fierce and reliable guerrilla fighters. Supervising the mission was a Special Forces legend named Larry Thorne, who had worked miracles breaking down the VC's control of several districts in the Mekong Delta with the help of South Vietnamese militia forces.

The mission objective was to find a suspected logistical hub for truck convoys. The team carried no identification and was armed with foreign weapons. After three days of patrolling in triple-canopy jungle, they discovered a large communist ammo dump and called in an air strike, obliterating the dump. Sadly, Larry Thorne's helicopter went down in bad weather, and he was killed. His body wasn't recovered until 1999.

Not all Trail-monitoring missions were officially part of Operation Shining Brass. In December 1965, Army captain John Waghelstein commanded the Special Forces camp at Khe Sanh in the rugged northwest corner of South Vietnam. Waghelstein led an A-Team of Army Special Forces soldiers and three hundred Bru Montagnards. Their mission, recalled the retired Special Forces officer in an interview with the author, was "to protect the local population, interdict enemy supply routes leading to the south, and to provide intelligence information on enemy troop movements."[30] This was the period of bad weather—from late November until early May—as the monsoon winds blew in from the coast and a thick layer of fog covered the district for weeks at a time. "The bad weather required that greater emphasis had to be placed on reconnaissance patrolling, a step up in agent-derived information, and an increased reliance on information given by the local inhabitants to monitor enemy activity near the Laos-Vietnam border," according to a US army study of the operation.[31]

On the night of December 17, a company or so of PAVN troops occupied a small village on the Vietnam side of the border and began to construct anti-aircraft positions. Waghelstein called in air strikes, destroying the inchoate positions. Three nights later, he received reliable intelligence that two regiments of the 324B Division were operating to the west of his camp. Waghelstein sent out a sixty-five-man patrol to screen the border and get a better idea of what was going on. By the night of the twenty-second, the patrol had found ample evidence of a strong enemy presence.

The next morning, Waghelstein learned that a PAVN Armed Propaganda Unit had held a meeting for the local inhabitants at a nearby rubber plantation. He sent a Bru squad out to investigate. It was captured without firing a shot, but one Bru trooper escaped and made it back to the SF camp. Now Waghelstein redirected his recon patrol to ferret out the enemy force and report back on their strength.

At 1030 the following morning, with the entire region blanketed in a thick fog, the SF patrol made contact with a far-superior enemy force. Sporadic firefights broke out, even as the patrol made its way back toward the camp. Later in the day, as the fog lifted, American forward air controllers were able to spot an entire PAVN regiment on the move. For the next several hours American airpower and the 105 mm artillery at Khe Sanh rained down on the enemy unit, killing several hundred North Vietnamese troops. As Waghelstein recalled, "There were pieces of bodies from this regiment spread all over the countryside." A couple of weeks later, said the now-retired army colonel:

> We got a report we were going to get hit. Around dusk, we started taking 120 mm mortar fire. We couldn't fire back with our 105s because the North Vietnamese were too close. We got shelled all night, and all the buildings, including the A–Team's house, went up in flames. We took over a thousand rounds. They didn't do a ground assault, because we had plenty of air support on call nearby. The marine helicopters flew in under fire and took out thirteen guys who were critically wounded.[32]

The SF house and the rest of the camp were soon rebuilt, and Captain Waghelstein and his Bru warriors went back to the business of monitoring the Trail. Waghelstein believes the PAVN might well have tried to overrun his camp were it not for the excellent intelligence he received from the local ARVN commander, an officer who was widely respected by Waghelstein and admired by the local populace. Many other Special Forces commanders in remote outposts in Vietnam were not so lucky.

The Secret CIA War in Laos

On January 19, 1965, several companies of North Vietnamese regulars mounted a powerful assault on a fortified hilltop near the village of Ban Non-Hang in northeastern Laos. The village was defended by a small force of Hmong tribesmen from the Laotian highlands, trained and led by CIA paramilitary officers. The Hmong are thought to have originated in the Yellow River basin of central China, but they were pushed south into the Indochinese highlands by the Han, the dominant ethnic group in modern China. During the Vietnam War, the Hmong were known as a stubbornly independent people whose men were tough and resilient warriors, as well as farmers and opium traders.

Leading the Hmong that January day in a desperate effort to keep the unit from being overrun was a burly CIA paramilitary officer named Tony Poe. The CIA had been training and advising the Hmong, along with Thai volunteers and other hill peoples, in a largely secret, undeclared war in eastern Laos since 1961. Operation Momentum was the brainchild of a quiet, self-effacing Texan named Bill Lair. He had been working for the Agency in one capacity or another in Southeast Asia since 1951. Now, on the verge of the deployment of American combat forces in Vietnam, that war was heating up. The North Vietnamese and their Laotian allies, the Pathet Lao, had been on an offensive since for a month. As Poe shouted instructions to his Hmong soldiers, he fired off two clips of ammo from his M-1 at a cluster of PAVN infantrymen charging his position. He killed several of them. As Poe ran down the hill to inspect their bodies, he himself was shot in the hip with a rifle round and knocked to the ground.

Suddenly, more North Vietnamese bolted forward, determined to reach the apex of the hill. Poe halted their progress abruptly with a grenade. Then he crawled back up the hill to tell his remaining Hmongs to withdraw to the west, toward Thailand, on foot. Then, while still under fire, Poe led a group of walking wounded on a five-mile hike through the jungle to an LZ, where a CIA helicopter flew them to a hospital in Thailand.

By early 1965 Tony Poe had been wounded at least a half-dozen times by gunfire. He was one of those unusual individuals who seemed to enjoy combat, almost relish in it. Poe joined the marines as a teenager and fought with distinction at Iwo Jima, among other Pacific War hellholes. After joining the CIA, he trained Tibetan guerrillas to resist the Chinese security forces in that mountainous country. Tony Poe—born Anthony Poshepny—was an extraordinarily cagey soldier and a great killer—one of the Agency's best. He was also a raging alcoholic who stayed up most nights with his Hmong charges drinking locally made whiskey. Poe would go to great lengths to instill fear in his North Vietnamese adversaries. A CIA colleague recalled after the war that Poe rarely took prisoners. Sometimes he would personally "slit the throats of captured enemy troops."[33] On one occasion, at least, he cut off the heads of several PAVN soldiers and placed them on spikes along a trail. On another, he convinced a helicopter pilot to fly over communist-held ground in Laos so he could drop a few North Vietnamese soldiers' heads down on the enemy positions.

The secret war in Laos was orchestrated by the CIA, but every aspect of the conflict was supervised and directed by a charismatic, immensely self-assured diplomat named William Sullivan. After graduating from Brown, Bill Sullivan enjoyed a meteoric rise through the ranks of the Foreign Service. By the early 1960s, he had become the star protégé of the legendary diplomat and presidential envoy Averell Harriman, who led the American delegation in the negotiations leading to the neutralization of Laos in 1962. Thus, Sullivan had direct and extensive contact with North Vietnamese negotiators in these talks. Harriman had urged Johnson to give the all-important ambassadorship to Laos to Sullivan. The president obliged in December of 1964.

Bill Sullivan not only managed the war in Laos with great dexterity and decisiveness. He was also able to preserve the illusion in the wider world that the United States was adhering to the Geneva neutrality agreement on Laos of 1962. Sullivan's unprecedented command authority derived from a letter written by JFK dictating that the ambassador to Laos must have unprecedented control over intelligence and military operations in that country. Sullivan had to approve all personnel who served in the theater. He set the ground rules for American advisers, and had to preapprove all attacks on communist forces of all sorts. Bill Sullivan frequently took issue with General Westmoreland's views on military strategy, and made no secret of the fact. Westmoreland found Sullivan, who had no personal military experience, to be both arrogant and abrasive. When he talked about Sullivan around MACV headquarters, he referred to him derisively as "the Field Marshal."

How had the secret war in Laos begun? In the late 1950s, President Eisenhower was more worried over developments in Laos than in Vietnam—or anywhere else, for that matter. Laos was a poor country of placid rice farmers with a large population of tribal hill peoples, and governed by an ineffective and mercurial monarch. Communist insurgents in Laos, the Pathet Lao, grew stronger each month, thanks to abundant financial and military support from Hanoi and Moscow. Ike and his foreign policy advisers worried that if Laos fell to the Pathet Lao, it would open the door to a communist revolution in Burma, and even India, to the west.

Ike told John Kennedy right after the latter's election to the presidency that Laos would be the biggest headache he would face in foreign affairs. After considerable debate and reflection, Kennedy decided to refrain from sending American troops into Laos, and to negotiate an agreement with the Russians, the Chinese, the North Vietnamese, and the Laotians to neutralize the country. The settlement of July 1962, however, was a work of fiction. Multiple regiments of PAVN troops remained in the Laotian jungles despite the agreement. North Vietnam continued to infiltrate regular army forces into the country to support the Pathet Lao's operations, and to secure parts of eastern Laos in order to permit the development of the Ho Chi Minh Trail. The CIA presence there also expanded, as Tony Poe and his colleagues began to funnel large amounts of cash, weapons, and war matériel to General Vang Pao's Hmong army of some twenty thousand men.

In early 1963, Vang Pao's forces displayed great tenacity and tactical dexterity in ousting the PAVN from the strategically significant town of Sam Neva. The Hmong forces regularly inflicted punishment on North Vietnamese columns with slashing hit-and-run raids and ambushes. By early 1965, the CIA's clandestine air force had grown considerably. It was flying special reconnaissance teams into eastern Laos and even North Vietnam to monitor the flow of men and supplies down the Trail. An American pilot who worked extensively with the Hmong recalled that these "road watch" teams "counted trucks, counted troops . . . and got hard intelligence. They were effective. The difficult thing was trying to recruit because the mortality rate was pretty high."[34]

Meanwhile, beginning in December 1964, US Navy and Air Force crews flew covert interdiction missions against targets in northeastern Laos in Operation Barrel Roll. In April 1965, the navy and the air force began to attack North Vietnamese infiltration columns and choke points along the Trail in southern Laos as part of Operation Steel Tiger.

In the summer of 1965, Bill Sullivan and Bill Lair saw to it that Vang Pao's

Hmongs were sufficiently equipped and well supported by airpower to mount a counteroffensive against communist forces southeast of the country's capital at Luang Prabang. The fiery Hmong general did not disappoint. His army crushed several PAVN battalions during the first summer of the American war, and his guerrillas were a thorn in North Vietnam's side for several years after that. "Vang Pao was unquestionably a brave and charismatic leader who possessed an unparalleled understanding of the North Vietnamese mindset," writes historian Timothy Castle. "He was a 'soldier's soldier' who quickly impressed many senior U.S. military and civilian officials. . . . The Hmong general provided tremendous inspiration to his people. But, as the war progressed and involved greater levels of modern technology, it was CIA and U.S. military expertise that controlled the planning and direction (with the ambassador's approval) of the secret war in Laos."[35]

There's little question that in 1965, CIA operatives saw themselves and their Hmong and Thai allies in Laos as defenders of an essentially free government against communist predations. Yet as the war there escalated in violence, asserts historian Joshua Kurlantzick, "many American leaders began to see the operation as less about saving Laos and more a means to kill or maim North Vietnamese, and thus help the war effort in Vietnam."[36]

Historians today agree that American bombing had only a marginal effect on the flow of supplies down the Trail, but there is no question the fighting in Laos diverted PAVN resources away from South Vietnam. But not enough to make much of a difference in the trajectory of the Main Event that was unfolding from the Ca Mau Peninsula in the south to the DMZ up north.

CHAPTER 9
DOMESTIC POLITICS AND THE
ANTIWAR MOVEMENT

Washington's decisions to expand the American commitment in Vietnam were shaped to an extraordinary degree by the pressures and demands of domestic politics. So, too, were its debates and decisions on military strategy. Indeed, it would not be going too far to say that *all* the crucial American decisions about Vietnam in late 1964 and the first six months of 1965 were shaped more by the exigencies of domestic political considerations than by the political and military realities of the war in Vietnam as it was then being fought.

President Johnson was well aware of the grave difficulties the United States faced in trying to prevent NLF insurgents and their allies in Hanoi from conquering a feckless, dysfunctional regime in South Vietnam through a combination of political subversion and military operations. The CIA reports at this time were decidedly pessimistic about South Vietnam's prospects, with or without American intervention. The limitations of conventional troops in fighting guerrillas worried the administration, as it should have done. Then there was history. The French had been defeated in their war against the communists, and the government in Paris was swept out of power. Johnson, aware of all this, expanded the American commitment reluctantly, in large measure because he was convinced that the alternative—a negotiated settlement followed by withdrawal—would lead to a vicious backlash against the administration from conservative Democrats and Republicans for "losing" Vietnam and result in humiliating personal and political defeat.

In the spring of 1964, mindful that he faced a presidential election in November, he told his old mentor in the Senate, Richard Russell, that "I don't think it's worth fighting for and I don't think we can get out."[1] Throughout 1964 and early 1965, Johnson deliberately misrepresented his administration's emerging Vietnam strategy for strictly political reasons: he wanted to keep as many options open as possible, and he wanted to get reelected with his own mandate. He presented himself as the candidate with the firm and steady hand, who would keep American boys out of Southeast Asia, even when he was all but certain he would have to commit American boys to fight in South Vietnam, or watch Saigon fall to communist boys.

Throughout the first ten months of 1964, Johnson and the war council never made a decision on Vietnam before weighing its likely effect on the November election. As Mac Bundy told CIA officer Ray Cline in mid-August 1964, "We know we're not going to do a goddamn thing [in Vietnam] while this election is on."[2] No matter how bad things got in Vietnam, observes historian Fredrik Logevall, "there were compelling reasons, most [in the White House] agreed, to hold off launching the new initiatives [Rolling Thunder and US ground troops] as long as possible, until the end of the summer or later. . . . The war needed to be escalated but not yet. Though the ostensible reason for the decision to delay was confidence that the South Vietnamese could . . . continue to 'jog along' for another few months, much more important were continuing American concerns about how an expanded war would play with major constituencies in the United States."[3]

Even in June 1965, just as he was on the verge of approving General West-moreland's plan for taking the fight to the communists with forty-four combat battalions of Americans, Johnson remained worried about domestic politics. "It's going to be difficult for us to very long prosecute effectively a war that far away from home with the divisions that we have here [in the United States]," said Johnson in a phone call to Bob McNamara on June 21, 1965. The president was "very depressed about it, 'cause I see no program from either Defense or State that gives me much hope of doing anything except just prayin' and gasping to hold on during the monsoon [season] and hope they'll quit. I don't believe they [are] ever goin' to quit. . . . [Senator Richard Russell wants us] to get out of there. . . . And I think it would just lose us face in the world, and I shudder to think what all of 'em would say."[4]

Once Johnson had committed the country to a ground war, he used his considerable guile and the awesome power of his office to keep the skeptics within his own party from expressing their reservations publicly. He dissembled to members of Congress and the press on a regular basis to keep dissent muffled. On January 21, 1965, he told a group of congressmen with a straight face that "the war must be fought by the South Vietnamese. We cannot control everything they do and we have to count on their fighting their war."[5]

The trouble with that statement was, of course, that Johnson was *not* counting on the South Vietnamese to fight their war. He had known for months that Americans had to get into the fight, and soon, or all would be lost. When the administration was on the cusp of initiating Operation Rolling Thunder in early February, Mac Bundy reminded his brother Bill that this dramatic escalatory step was not to be presented to Congress or the American people as something new. "Look, get this straight, the President does not want this depicted as a change in policy."[6]

Although those who understood the dynamics of the fighting saw Vietnam as an indigenous insurgency—a long struggle for independence from foreign domination—Johnson and the other members of the war council chose to begin the American war through a campaign against a peripheral target. They launched an air campaign of "graduated pressure" against North Vietnam because they thought the American people much more likely to support a campaign against "aggression from the North" than the counterinsurgency campaign that the situation seemed to require in the eyes of the people who understand the war on the ground best.

Indeed, although Johnson was a politician with enormous powers of persuasion, it did not seem to occur to him that if he couldn't (or wouldn't) provide a cogent rationale justifying the commitment of American forces to fighting a counterinsurgency war in Vietnam—the war that was in fact being fought there—he ought not commit the country to war at all. That domestic political concerns figured more prominently in the Johnson administration's thinking than the concrete conditions that prevailed in the war itself goes far in explaining why things would go so terribly wrong for the United States in the conflict in Vietnam.

American politics also played a crucial role in Hanoi's strategic calculus, as it faced the prospect of going to war against a superpower. Le Duan, in a

May 1965 letter to Nguyen Chi Thanh, the commander of COSVN, showed a keen appreciation of the positive impact of American domestic politics on the communist war effort:

> *Within the US ruling circles, the "doves" and the "hawks" are at loggerheads with one another. . . . Contradictions between the US and its client regimes and those among the different groups of US lackeys . . . also are growing acute. The enemy is being divided. Thus, militarily we are not yet in a position to prevail over the enemy, but politically we can get the upper hand and capitalize on the enemy's inner contradictions to split his ranks and weaken him to the point of disintegration.*[7]

General Giap wrote at length about the nature of the confrontation in the mid-1960s, and a number of his books were widely available in English. Yet one looks in vain for even a hint that members of Johnson's war council took the general's ideas on protracted warfare strategy seriously. Certainly the CIA and military intelligence agencies had read and reported on these books, but there is no evidence that the war council as a whole was particularly interested in the enemy's strategic mindset. Interestingly, Giap often identified politics as the Americans' Achilles' heel. "Our people greatly appreciate the struggle of the American people against the aggressive Viet-Nam War of the Johnson administration," wrote the hero of Dien Bien Phu, "considering it a valuable mark of sympathy and support of our people's just resistance. . . . The U.S. ruling circles have been increasingly opposed by the American people and have been isolated politically to a high degree in the international arena."[8]

Giap and Le Duan took different views on communist military strategy in 1965, but both die-hard revolutionaries were confident that the American people would not support a war waged against the "revolutionary forces" in Vietnam for long. Even before the marines landed in Danang, Hanoi and the NLF had devoted considerable resources to a propaganda campaign aimed not only at the American people, but at the rest of the world. It proved notably more successful than the propaganda campaign waged by the American government in the long run.

And the men who ran the war effort in Hanoi and at COSVN took heart in the knowledge that the most intractable problem the Americans faced in South Vietnam wasn't truly military in nature. It was political and, in their view, utterly impossible to solve. Washington was committing itself to *constructing* a viable, independent South Vietnam. Defeating the insurgency was a prerequisite for achieving that objective, but even if the insurgency by some imaginary circumstance ceased to exist, there remained the daunting task of creating viable institutions, responsive government, and some sense of loyalty among the people for the government in Saigon. Turning South Vietnam around, they knew, was beyond the capabilities of any foreign power, even the mighty United States. Hanoi's knowledge of this reality goes far in explaining its steely confidence as it prepared to face off against the Americans. This was yet another part of the reality of the Vietnam War that Washington didn't grasp until it was too late.

Given the enormous difficulties involved in transforming a country with absolutely no experience with democratic mores and a fractious political class into a republic, it is astonishing how little time, in 1964 and 1965, that American policy makers devoted to the question of whether or not such a transformation was even possible. The blithe assumption on the part of the Washington decision makers seems to have been that South Vietnam would sort itself out once the communist threat was removed. So long as they followed American advice, how could they go wrong? This notion was pure fantasy, the product of arrogance leavened with naiveté.

Justifying a war to the American people, to the people of any democracy, is never easy, nor should it be. Justifying a major war in Vietnam in 1965 was a particularly tricky proposition, even if the Johnson administration had chosen to do so honestly, because the nation was entering a period of enormous social upheaval where one could almost see tectonic shifts in politics and culture sweep across the land. The civil rights struggle was at the epicenter of this upheaval as white liberals and Blacks began to demand that society in the North as well as the South address the heinous injustice and grinding poverty that afflicted the Black community. As the 1960s progressed, the movement became "increasingly ambitious, impatient, and provocative."[9] In the summer of 1964, two hundred young Black and white volunteers descended on Mississippi to organize Black voter registration, provoking ferocious resistance from White southerners. Three young men suddenly disappeared. They had been abducted, beaten, and then murdered by local police. By summer's end in Mississippi, six people were dead, eighty had been beaten, and one thousand had been arrested. Blacks began to attack police in southern towns, and cities in the North experienced riots and burnings. With this sort of a crisis going on in America, many people, even many previously apolitical people, began to question why the United States was diverting its energies and resources to a war in a country eight thousand miles away that many Americans had not even heard of.

By the time Kennedy had been elected five years earlier, there were already subtle indications of an emerging counterculture taking hold in the youth of the middle class. Rock and roll and the beat poets had begun to make their mark. By early 1965, the nonconformist ideas of a nascent counterculture were percolating, already having profound effects on the way people, especially younger people, thought and felt about themselves, about politics, and the entire American way of life. Catalyzed by Vietnam and the civil rights movement, the counterculture grew rapidly as hundreds of thousands of college-age and twenty-something people came together to question the legitimacy of American institutions and mainstream culture. Americans for the first time took serious notice of something new in the youth culture of their country. By 1967, the counterculture would be in full swing, challenging a great deal more than Johnson's Vietnam policies. The movement became a highly volatile force for change, a rebellion against the establishment, which was defined by its members as a system designed for the repression and stultification of the young, the poor, Blacks, and organized labor. The zeitgeist of the movement called on young people to question all authority, and they obliged. Parents, professors, police, business leaders, politicians—all were suspected of being part of the problem rather than the solution. Hippies were perhaps the most visible symbol of the counterculture, embracing as they did an alternative lifestyle based around rock and roll, recreational drugs, especially pot and LSD, and "free love."

But there were other elements of a distinctly more political and militant caste, including the women's rights movement, gay rights, the Native American renaissance, and above all, the civil rights movement. "What gave unity to all these different forms of rebellion," astutely notes journalist Godfrey Hodgson,

> *joining rebels and radicals in a common cause, was their shared*
> *conviction, vague but unshakable, of the unity of what they were*
> *rebelling against. Behind each specific movement of the sixties*
> *there was one underlying Movement, because behind each spe-*
> *cific injustice there was perceived, shadowy but all-powerful, one*
> *System. All voices that shattered the decorum of consensus were*
> *welcome, because the ultimate enemy was consensus itself. . . . The*
> *dream was that the converging rebellions of students, pacifists,*
> *draft resisters, black militants, Mexican farm workers, welfare*
> *mothers, frustrated suburban housewives, reservation Indians,*
> *penitentiary inmates, hippies from the California beaches . . .*
> *and bored workers on the General Motors assembly lines would*
> *all roll together into one millenarian Mississippi of revolution.*[10]

This was the swell of coalescing public sentiment that Johnson sensed and rightly feared. By the summer of 1965, many members of the emerging counterculture joined with both liberals and radicals in the peace movement in the belief that the system's most malign project was the David vs. Goliath struggle in Vietnam. In Southeast Asia, the United States seemed to be using its immense power and resources for evil rather than good. Young men who identified with the counterculture, or with the beat writers in New York and San Francisco who provided its essential texts and much of its style, had no intention of serving their country in an Asian war justified by what they saw as a bogus anti-communist consensus. These young people wished to become the foot soldiers in the *anti*war army.

The Early Antiwar Movement

The earliest public dissent against American involvement in Vietnam occurred well before the Johnson administration had reached a consensus that American forces would have to be deployed to stave off defeat. Pacifists, religious leaders, and the nuclear disarmament community began to speak openly against the war in 1963. In March of that year, fifty-five prominent Americans sent an open letter to the White House urging President Kennedy to listen to the arguments of newspaperman Walter Lippmann, the eminent Senate Majority Leader Mike Mansfield of Montana, and France's president Charles de Gaulle. All three had expressed grave doubts about the success of any sort of military solution to the struggle. The National Committee for a Sane Nuclear Policy, a decidedly liberal organization that focused on limiting the superpower arms race and nuclear proliferation, sponsored an Easter Peace Walk a month later. Speakers there made numerous references to the conflict in Southeast Asia, and the very real danger that it could spiral into World War III. Civil rights leaders and the editors of two prominent liberal magazines, the *New Republic* and the *Nation*, also registered their objections to America's growing involvement in the conflict during 1963 and 1964. The editors of the *New Republic* urged Johnson to refrain from escalation, arguing in late 1964 that the war "cannot be won by the United States. It can only be won by the Vietnamese." At the same time, the *Nation*, a bit further to the left than the *New Republic*, suggested that "The only honorable victory" for the United States in Vietnam was "in finding an honorable way out."[11]

The chief arguments against waging an American war in Vietnam to come into view by 1965 were these: to the counterculture, political radicals, and many in the liberal religious community, the war was an inherently immoral, inhumane enterprise. Americans had no business fighting a war on foreign soil when there was so much injustice and inequality at home.

Academics, politicians, and journalists, particularly those with expertise in international affairs and foreign policy, argued that the United States had no vital interests in Vietnam, and that the war was a wasteful diversion of scarce resources that would have been better deployed to more crucial theaters in the Cold War, such as Western Europe. A third argument put forward by a relatively small number of people with deep knowledge of counterinsurgency, or direct experience in Vietnam, was pragmatic: a civil war like Vietnam simply could not be won by military means, especially the military means of a foreign power. It was a political war requiring political solutions.

Finally, some critics argued that, while saving South Vietnam from communism was a noble enough objective, the government in Saigon was irredeemably corrupt, and therefore not worth saving.

By early 1965, opposition to American involvement in the war "appeared as only the faintest sort of demurring whisper" to the public at large.[12] The event that more than any other spurred the birth of the antiwar *movement*—nicely defined by historian Melvin Small as "an ever-shifting coalition of pacifists, liberals, social democrats, communists and cultural radicals," was surely Operation Rolling Thunder, for within weeks after the warplanes took to the skies, tens of thousands of college students and other dissenters began to organize a host of events to publicize their views on the war, ranging from teach-ins to marches to demonstrations.[13] The specter of American jets laying waste to a poor, agricultural society such as Vietnam's with high explosives and napalm seemed not only morally repugnant but wildly out of proportion. The results of the bombing, visible day after day in the nightly news broadcasts, shocked and horrified millions of Americans, and millions of others around the world. It undercut the idea that the Americans were the freedom-loving guys in the white hats. In early April, 2,500 clergy took out an ad in the *New York Times* with the headline "In the Name of God, Stop It."[14]

Throughout the remainder of 1965, a strong majority of Americans remained supportive of the burgeoning American war effort and their president's conduct of that conflict. This was, it should be remembered, only twenty years after the end of World War II, before Americans were accustomed to questioning the wisdom of their leaders and national institutions in matters of foreign policy. *Real* Americans supported their president when American troops were fighting in a war on foreign shores. But as more and more troops deployed to Vietnam and the casualty lists grew longer, the antiwar movement began to pick up considerable steam, despite the administration's strenuous efforts to play down the importance of what was happening in Vietnam.

At its height in 1969, the movement would have perhaps 6 million participants. It never developed a well-organized leadership, and was continually beset by internecine conflicts about tactics and objectives. From the beginning, observes historian Charles DeBenedetti, the struggle was "animated (but not dominated) by activists from the country's peace movement and was legitimated (but not led) by members of the policy-shaping elite."[15]

Broadly speaking, liberals in the movement sought to pressure and persuade the government to negotiate an end to the fighting and establish a political solution to the problem of governing South Vietnam. Liberals resisted the radicals' inclination to move from protest and debate to resistance, using violence and civil disobedience. They wanted to exclude communists and other far-left elements from participation in large demonstrations and the like on the grounds that the presence of those groups would alienate mainstream Americans and push them in the direction of supporting the war. Liberals also rejected calls from the political left for an immediate American withdrawal from Vietnam. Americans should not let down their allies, and an immediate withdrawal, most liberals felt, was sure to result in a communist victory.

The radical wing of the movement always sought a great deal more than stopping the fighting in Vietnam. Many of the leaders of Students for a Democratic Society (SDS), for example, imagined themselves forming an anti-imperialist movement committed to social justice at home. The hard-core radicals wanted to spark a revolution at home. They saw Vietnam as a symptom of a wider societal sickness, and demanded fundamental change in American attitudes and institutions. Many believed in militant means. They burned draft cards, seized university administration buildings, destroyed ROTC installations on campuses, and battled police in the streets.

A far-left element among the radicals even took to carrying NLF and North Vietnamese flags at some events. Tom Hayden, president of SDS, and Yale professor Staughton Lynd, a pacifist, traveled to Hanoi in late 1965 on a fact-finding mission, and met with DRV foreign minister Pham Van Dong. The activities of the far left led in mid-1965 to the commissioning of a report on the movement by the Senate Subcommittee on Internal Security. The report concluded that "the control of the anti-Vietnam movement has clearly passed from the hands of the moderate elements who may have controlled it at one time, into the hands of Communists and extremist elements who are openly sympathetic to the Viet Cong and openly hostile to the United States."[16] The report, we now know, was dead wrong. It was but one example of a general phenomenon when it came to the great debate beginning to take shape across the length and breadth of the country: the tendency to state suppositions and opinions as fact.

Nonetheless, consorting with the enemy and waving Vietcong flags were viewed as outrageous acts by most Americans and did little to win the movement new friends. But there was very little truly radical activity during 1965. That would come later, as the futility of the war came more clearly into view, and the bitter struggle between "hawks" and "doves" threatened to rip the fabric of the republic in two.

The Demonstrations

The first significant public event to question the legitimacy of the war in Vietnam was spearheaded by liberal faculty members at one of the nation's elite public educational institutions, the University of Michigan. Three days after the marines landed at Danang, twenty-five university faculty members agreed to make a pitch to the administration for a one-day moratorium from classes so students and faculty could study and reflect on the government's policy in Vietnam. The appeal met with resistance from both the governor of Michigan and the administration. The faculty, they said, had no business deciding when a public issue was important enough to halt classes. Professor Marshall Sahlins suggested an alternative—a more dynamic version of the civil rights movement's sit-in. It was called a "teach-in," a heady admixture of speeches, seminars, and peaceful demonstrations. It could happen over a single night so no one would miss classes. The powers that be agreed, and allowed the organizers to use the university's facilities.

The event was to be held between 8:00 p.m. on March 25 and 8:00 a.m on March 26. It was agreed that only those opposed to the war would present, on the grounds that there was plenty of disagreement among dissenters from the government's positions on the nature of the conflict, and how and when the United States should disengage. Besides, the government had ample resources to make its case for fighting the war.

More than three thousand students turned out for the event, many of them carrying Bernard Fall's classic work on the war, *The Two Viet-Nams*, or other tomes on guerrilla warfare and US foreign policy. The mood "was one of seriousness, even earnestness, as students soberly discussed the war" in small groups led by faculty.[17] The main speaker, Arthur Waskow of the Institute for Policy Studies in Washington, didn't see Vietnam as a symptom of a failing system, but an aberration from the normal course of American foreign policy in need of correction.

Waskow called for a political settlement to the conflict. In the middle of his speech a policeman approached the podium. There was a bomb scare. The building had to be evacuated. Waskow finished his speech on the campus green, which was covered in snow. The bomb scare turned out to be a prank, a false alarm.

Carl Oglesby, a thirty-year-old Michigan graduate and a national officer of Students for a Democratic Society, offered a much more radical critique. The United States was a counterrevolutionary force in Vietnam, and elsewhere in the Third World, when it challenged those who would throw off the shackles of colonialism. Ho Chi Minh and his colleagues were leading a truly important, and entirely legitimate, social revolution in Vietnam. The implicit message was that the United States was fighting on the wrong side in the war.

News of the event at Ann Arbor spread fast among politically active faculty and students at other universities across the country. Buoyed by its success, other teach-ins followed that spring at Columbia, the University of Washington, and NYU. The largest and most colorful of the early teach-ins was held at that hotbed of political activism, the University of California at Berkeley. More than twenty thousand people gathered on May 21 and 22 to hear some forty speakers, including the novelist Norman Mailer, Dr. Benjamin Spock, and journalist I. F. Stone, who was justly renowned for his withering assaults on the administration's policies in Southeast Asia.

The Berkeley event was more raucous in tone and radical in substance than the comparatively staid event at Michigan. The Vietnam Day Committee that met in radical Jerry Rubin's apartment to organize the event was "a strange concoction of radical pacifism, student protest, civil rights activism, leftist politics, and cultural bohemianism peculiar to the Bay Area."[18] Staughton Lynd attacked the very foundations of American foreign policy, passionately rejecting the position of more moderate critics like Arthur Waskow. A coalition with liberals, said Lynd boldly, was an impossibility. It was like "a coalition with the Marines."[19] It wasn't just that Vietnam was wrong. The system that produced the rationale for the war was bankrupt. Paul Potter spoke in the same vein. He called the movement he and thousands of others were forming "a new humanism," meant to challenge the callousness of a commercial, consumer society, in which people were too focused on getting ahead instead of helping their brothers and sisters in need. Potter spoke with haunting prescience in describing Vietnam

> *as an incredibly sharp razor, the divider, that has finally sep-*
> *arated thousands and thousands of people from . . . illusions*
> *about the decency and morality and integrity of this country's*
> *purpose internationally. Never again, never again, will the self-*
> *righteous, saccharine moralism of promising a billion dollars of*
> *economic aid [a reference to Johnson's April 1965 offer to Hanoi*
> *to develop the Mekong River] to people while we spend billions*
> *and billions of dollars to destroy them—never again will that*
> *moralism have the power to persuade people of the essential de-*
> *cency of this country's aims.*[20]

More than 120 teach-ins were held by the end of the academic year in June. Yet it should be borne in mind that in 1965, those who held antiwar views in the colleges were a distinct minority. Only 24 percent of college students that year supported the idea of withdrawing from Vietnam—about the same percentage as American adults in general. At Yale and the University of Wisconsin, another elite public university, thousands of students signed petitions *supporting* the White House's policies.

Not long after the Michigan teach-in, an Inter-University Committee for a Public Hearing on Vietnam was formed with a view to organizing a televised national teach-in. The event, to be held on May 15, would take the form of a debate between White House spokesmen and leading critics of the administration's policy. The centerpiece of the event was meant to be a debate between Mac Bundy and Southeast Asia expert George Kahin of Cornell. Bundy, though, had to withdraw when he was ordered to go to the Caribbean by the president.

Perhaps more important than anything said that day was the publication of a document meant to present the administration's considered views on the war just before the national teach-in commenced. The State Department put together a long, detailed white paper presenting a wealth of evidence that the conflict was not so much an indigenous insurgency in the South as a war of aggression by the North against the South. The paper was called, appropriately enough, *Aggression from the North*. The truth, though, was hard to obscure, and for all the intense effort that went into producing the paper, it failed to convince many skeptics or fence-sitters. As several speakers at the event pointed out during the teach-in, if the North Vietnamese were the main source of trouble in South Vietnam, why were almost all Vietcong fighters captured from the South? Why was such a large percentage of their weapons of American origin rather than from North Vietnamese arsenals? And there was in fact a great deal of hard evidence that the NLF forces were largely self-sustaining, as I. F. Stone pointed out in a cogent and elegant rebuttal to the white paper. The aggression from the North thesis, in short, did not hold water. By the end of the summer, even the administration had de-emphasized the "Northern aggression" thesis, replacing it with the argument that the credibility of the United States rested largely on seeing South Vietnam through its crisis.

The administration pressed back against the epicenter of dissent in 1965—the university campuses—sending a team of experts to colleges to explain the truth as the Johnson administration saw it. The "truth team" didn't make much headway, often as not getting into shouting matches with students and faculty, and again, failing to convince many fence-sitters. But during the first year of the American war, the administration's response to its critics, those who were part of the movement and those who were not, was distinctly muted. In private, Johnson fumed that the dissenters were giving false hope to the enemy, but he refrained from calling his critics unpatriotic in public. He refused to call them appeasers, as he might well have done. It may be, as some historians have said, that the president at this early stage of the game was more worried about being pushed into more rapid escalation by the Republican right than he was by liberals and radicals who wanted him to disengage. In any case, Johnson took refuge in the confident statements of Mac Bundy, the erstwhile Harvard dean, who wrote to Johnson in July 1965, with more than a little condescension, that "none of the special solutions or criticisms put forward with zeal by individual reformers in government or in the press is of major importance, and many of them are flatly wrong."[21]

Like so many other ad hoc antiwar organizations, the Inter-University Committee soon disbanded amid conflict between those who saw themselves as loyal citizens who happened to oppose the administration's Vietnam policies, and more radical elements that saw the National Teach-in as altogether too tame an event.

Teach-ins were not the only vehicle for the expression of dissent from the universities. A few days after the Michigan teach-in, two hundred members of the Yale faculty sent an open letter to President Johnson calling on him to stop expanding the war and negotiate. The letter put forward what was becoming a classic liberal critique of US policy in Southeast Asia:

> *American opinion itself is too divided to sustain a long crisis in Vietnam, much less an enlargement of our participation in that war. Among the people we know best, the community of scholars and teachers, there is extensive opposition to escalation. Indeed, a great many thoughtful people throughout the country, the editors of* The New York Times, *other journalists, publicists of national repute and unimpeachable integrity, like Walter Lippmann, share our view. We believe, therefore, that our policies in Vietnam run the additional risk of creating such discontent, frustration, and disunity here at home as to impair the achievement of other goals and our effectiveness in dealing with the problem of Vietnam itself.*[22]

The Demonstrations Begin

While the teach-in movement was educating American college students about Vietnam and American foreign policy, the leadership of Students for a Democratic Society was busy planning the first large-scale demonstration against the war. SDS had been founded in Port Huron, Michigan, in 1962 as an organization dedicated to fomenting grassroots political reform. It had concentrated before 1965 on the problems of poverty and racism. In the national meeting in December 1964, with ominous signs on the horizon that American troops might be sent to Vietnam to fight, it was agreed after much debate to shift attention to halting the slide toward war. The leaders of SDS were under no illusion that a mass demonstration in the nation's capital would have much impact on the White House policies in Southeast Asia. They did believe such an event would energize and mobilize left-wing activism in general. To many in

SDS, particularly its more left-leaning members, protesting Vietnam was not an end in itself, but a means to the end of building a broad national movement for social and political change.

The March on Washington was planned for Easter Sunday, April 17. The organizers estimated it would attract ten thousand people. The advent of Operation Rolling Thunder, followed by the landing of the marines at Danang, ensured that a great many more showed up. In fact, about twenty thousand people gathered in Washington for the march. It was the largest antiwar demonstration to date in the history of the United States. After circling the White House peacefully carrying signs that read "Ballots Not Bombs in Vietnam" and "War on Poverty Not on People," the crowd made its way slowly down the Mall to the Washington Monument. I. F. Stone launched a well-reasoned assault on the strategy of escalation. It was, he said, both wrongheaded and counterproductive. Judy Collins sang the Bob Dylan classic "The Times They Are A-Changin'" to the delight of a crowd that ardently believed they were. Bob Moses, a Black civil rights leader, spoke of the connections between the government's failure to address the problem of the Black community at home and the war in Vietnam. Paul Potter of SDS spoke eloquently (again) about an America corrupted by the excesses of imperialism and capitalism. He envisioned a vast social movement rising up to challenge those who perpetrated those excesses. Once the speeches were finished, the crowd marched toward the steps of the Capitol, singing "We Shall Overcome."

The community of American artists, writers, and intellectuals also spoke out against the war from its earliest days in various ways. In February 1965, Princeton professor Eric Goldman had proposed to the president a "White House Festival of the Arts," a celebration of American creativity with an exhibition of some of the finest contemporary sculpture, painting, musical performances, and readings by such literary lions as Saul Bellow, John Hersey, and the poet Robert Lowell. Two weeks before the June 14 event, Lowell, who had accepted an invitation initially, withdrew from the event in the most public of ways. He sent a letter to President Johnson declining the invitation, and copied the editors of the *New York Times*, who did him the honor of printing it. Lowell said in part:

> *Although I am very enthusiastic about most of your domestic legislation and intentions, I nevertheless can only follow our present*

foreign policy with the greatest dismay and distrust. . . . We are in danger of imperceptibly becoming an explosive and suddenly chauvinistic nation, and we may even be drifting our way to the last nuclear run. I know it is hard for the responsible man to act; it is also painful for the private and irresolute man to dare criticism. At this anguished, delicate, and perhaps determining moment, I feel I am serving you and our country best by not taking part in the White House Festival of the Arts.[23]

Soon thereafter, Robert Silvers, editor of the prestigious *New York Review of Books*, sent a telegram to the White House in support of Lowell, signed by no less than twenty other writers and artists who'd been invited to attend the festival. They declined to attend as well. Johnson, who was deeply insecure about how the creative class viewed him, was apoplectic. The last thing he needed was a cadre of intellectual heavyweights taking him to task on Vietnam, largely on moral grounds. But that was what he got.

The writer John Hersey was not one of those who signed the telegram. He showed up for the festival, only to read from his short masterpiece *Hiroshima*, about the dropping of the atomic bomb. He prefaced his reading with these words:

I read these passages on behalf of a great number of citizens who have become alarmed in recent weeks by the sight of fire begetting fire. Let these words be a reminder. The step from one degree of violence to the next is imperceptibly taken and cannot be easily taken back. The end point of these little steps is horror and oblivion. We cannot for a moment forget the truly terminal dangers, in these times, of miscalculation, of arrogance, or reliance not on moral strength but on mere military power. Wars have a way of getting out of hand.[24]

And then Hersey read several powerfully moving passages from his book about the suffering endured by the Japanese as a result of the bomb. Many in the audience were shocked and embarrassed that Hersey chose to read from such a book on this occasion. Others thought Hersey showed enormous courage. The cultural critic Dwight Macdonald, also in attendance that night, wholeheartedly supported Hersey's bold decision to read about Hiroshima just a few feet from the president of the United States. Macdonald took the opportunity to circulate an antiwar petition among the audience members, and refused to refrain from doing so when actor Charlton Heston took him to task for dishonoring the president in his own house. LBJ was heard to grumble to a reporter near the end of the evening, "Some of them insult me by staying away and some of them insult me by coming."[25]

Throughout the rest of the year, prominent figures in American cultural and intellectual life spoke out against the war in ever-greater numbers. In spring 1966, an organization of American Writers and Artists against the Vietnam War was formed. That organization sponsored a series of "read-ins" by prominent writers, such as the playwright Lillian Hellman and the literary critic Alfred Kazin. Liberal clergy also began to speak out more vociferously against the war. An Interreligious Committee on Vietnam placed ads in prominent newspapers and magazines calling on the president to seek a cease-fire through negotiations. In June, a group of American clergy went to Vietnam. They returned calling on the president to open up a new peace conference in Geneva.

On the day of the White House Festival, SDS closed out its annual convention in Kewadin, Michigan. It had been a contentious event in which those who wanted the organization to concentrate its efforts on Vietnam butted heads with those who wanted the organization to carry on with its traditional grassroots work fighting poverty and racism, and reforms within the universities. No clear consensus emerged. The end result, though, was that SDS passed up a golden opportunity to lead the growing antiwar movement.

A coalition of liberal peace organizations led by the well-known pacifist A. J. Muste tried to step into the breach. The Assembly of Unrepresented People organized a four-day event (August 6–9) in Washington. About two thousand people were in attendance, "a mélange of Quakers, radical pacifists, Maoists, Trotskyists, community organizers . . . and student radicals."[26] After a silent vigil near the White House to commemorate the dropping of the bomb on Hiroshima, the attendees divided up to attend a series of workshops on politics, pacifism, and social reform. A few of the leaders, including Muste and Joan Baez, attended meetings with White House staffers. On the last day, a march from the

Washington Memorial to the Capitol resulted in the arrest of 350 people who refused to leave the area on police orders. It was the first large-scale act of civil disobedience concerning the Vietnam War.

The National Coordinating Committee to End the War in Vietnam (NCC) had been formed in Washington during the August demonstrations. It was a loose coalition of thirty-three different antiwar groups. The NCC sponsored on October 15 and 16 the International Days of Protest, in which some one hundred thousand people participated. It amounted to a great number of smallish demonstrations around the country, and one very large one in New York. There was very little international participation to speak of. Eleven protesters were arrested in Madison, Wisconsin, home of the University of Wisconsin, when they tried to make a citizen's arrest of the commander of a local air force base. In Austin, Texas, two hundred demonstrators, most from the University of Texas at Austin, clashed with the KKK. At Berkeley, demonstration organizers found themselves locked in dispute as to whether or not to block access to the Oakland Army Terminal and invite arrest, or keep things legal by marching down Telegraph Avenue toward the terminal and staging a rally in a parking lot. The radical faction led by Jerry Rubin gave way. There would be no acts of civil disobedience that first day. During the march the next day, near the border between Berkeley and Oakland, the Hells Angels attacked the demonstrators, and the police had to jump in and separate the warring parties.

By far and away the biggest demonstration over the two days was in New York, where twenty thousand demonstrators marched down Fifth Avenue. They were heckled all the way by hundreds of pro-war counterdemonstrators, who threw eggs, tomatoes, and red paint on the protesters. At the Whitehall Armed Forces Induction Center in lower Manhattan that day, three hundred protesters cheered boisterously when a twenty-two-year-old pacifist named David Miller burned his draft card. It was at once a courageous and a reckless act. Only a few weeks earlier, the president had signed a bill stipulating a five-year prison sentence and a $10,000 fine for burning a draft card. Miller served two years in jail for doing so.

On November 6 in Union Square, New York City, five other young men burned their cards, as pro-war spectators chanted, "Burn yourselves, not your cards!" The spectators were referring to a ghastly incident that had unfolded four days earlier, making the national news. A thirty-two-year-old Quaker, Norman Morrison, had set himself alight just fifty yards or so from Robert McNamara's window at the Pentagon.

Throughout the fall, the major journals of liberal opinion continued to hammer away at the administration's expanding war policies. By year's end, the concern that the ideology of anticommunism was distorting the administration's judgments about Vietnam weighed heavily on the mind of J. William Fulbright, chairman of the Senate Foreign Relations Committee. The Arkansas senator, a Rhodes scholar who probably knew more about Asian history and Vietnam than any of his colleagues save Mike Mansfield, a former professor of Asian history, could no longer remain silent in public about his profound doubts. His failure to do so cost him his close friendship with LBJ, who took Fulbright's dissenting views very personally. For his part, Fulbright felt used and manipulated by his erstwhile friend and fellow southerner. He knew better than anyone that the administration had been misrepresenting its policies in Vietnam from the beginning.

Early in 1966, Fulbright turned the hearings of his committee on an official request for $275 million in aid to South Vietnam into a kind of national consciousness-raising event about Vietnam. The hearings were televised. Their purpose, writes historian Thomas Powers, "was primarily educational: he [Fulbright] made no attempt to propose an alternative policy, but he subjected existing policy to a penetrating, sometimes caustic analysis which it had previously escaped."[27]

At the hearings two impressive witnesses, General James Gavin, a war hero noted throughout the military for his strategic insight and bravery—he was the only American general to have made four parachute jumps in combat operations—and George Kennan, the renowned diplomat and author of the containment doctrine, testified that they saw little to be gained, and much to be lost, by fighting an American war in Vietnam. Gavin thought the American investment in Vietnam was alarmingly out of balance. The best course of action would be to stop escalating, and use the enclaves the Americans had established along the Vietnamese coast as bargaining chips in negotiations with the communists. Vietnam itself was simply too remote and strategically marginal for the United States to fight a major war over there. Bombing North Vietnam would only intensify Hanoi's will to carry on the fight, not break it. Sustained fighting against North Vietnam might well bring the Chinese into the war. Vietnam was not worth the candle, said Gavin, who recalled in his testimony that he had told Robert McNamara recently that "You're going to get murdered if you stay there. Your troops, you'll have to keep reinforcing and reinforcing them. You've got to get out."[28]

Kennan wanted the United States to exit Vietnam as soon as possible as well. If the United States attempted to crush North Vietnam, China would probably step in, he said. Moreover, the conflict with the communists in Vietnam was complicating America's relationship with Moscow at precisely the wrong time. There was precious little to be gained "from the spectacle of Americans inflicting grievous injury on the lives of a poor and helpless people, particularly a people of a different race and color."[29]

In questioning administration spokesmen Rusk and McNamara, Fulbright displayed a deep and subtle knowledge of Vietnamese history and politics that neither member of the war council possessed. In fact, Fulbright had done something no member of the war council had done, not even the Ivy League scholar, Professor Bundy. He had spent a great deal of time immersing himself in the best scholarship and journalism about Vietnam over the preceding several months. Vietnam, he argued, was not a war of aggression by northern communists against a sovereign, pro-democratic South. The conflict had begun as "a civil war in which outside parties had become involved."[30]

So, too, Fulbright expressed deep skepticism of Johnson's long-held belief that American prestige and credibility depended on staying the course in Vietnam. Kennan expressed the same skepticism. Compromise was of the essence, said Fulbright, yet he "did not see in the U.S. position any willingness to compromise."[31] Since Vietnam was clearly not a vital interest of the United States in and of itself, surely compromise was called for. Fulbright elaborated on this point. This was not a war, he said,

> that warrants vast escalation, a vast expenditure of money and many thousands of deaths. I think it is not that kind of vital interest. . . . I also think that the great countries, especially this country, is quite strong enough to engage in compromise without losing its standing in the world and without losing its prestige

as a great nation. On the contrary, I think it would be one of the
greatest victories for us in our prestige if we could be ingenious
enough and magnanimous enough to bring about some kind of a
settlement of this particular struggle.[32]

Throughout the hearings the chairman of the Foreign Relations Committee made it clear he was extremely skeptical of the idea that the United States could win the war by military means. He rejected the notion that the exigencies of the Cold War imposed on America the role of world policeman. "In nations, as in individuals," Fulbright would later write, "bellicosity is a mark of weakness and self-doubt rather than of strength and self-assurance."[33]

At one key juncture in the hearings, Fulbright told Rusk that the United States should welcome a settlement in which all Vietnamese, including the NLF, were allowed to participate: "After all, Vietnam is their country. It isn't our country. We do not even have the right the French [had]. We have no historical right. We are obviously invaders from their point of view. We represent the old Western imperialism in their eyes."[34]

No one knows how much the televised hearings of the Foreign Relations Committee affected the public's perception of Johnson's Vietnam policy, though it was clear by their conclusion that most of the members of the committee shared Fulbright's skepticism, even if they were unsure what to do in Vietnam by way of an alternative. Claiborne Pell, the liberal, quintessentially WASP senator from Rhode Island, perhaps said it best. The hearings, said Pell, "made peace a respectable word and showed that disagreement was respectable, too. If such a group of respectable stuffed shirts as the Senate Foreign Relations Committee could question the war, it gave other people courage to question it."[35]

CHAPTER 10

THE BIG FIGHT IN THE CENTRAL HIGHLANDS

In America's war in Vietnam, politics and political warfare were always more important in shaping the trajectory of the conflict than military operations. Most armed clashes were sterile events that had little or no effect at all on the big picture. This is not to say, however, that all the military campaigns and battles were unimportant. Quite the contrary. Several battles had profound effects on the way the key decision makers came to understand the dynamics of the conflict, and revealed to key audiences in Vietnam and elsewhere the peculiar complexities and ironies of the conflict.

Ap Bac was clearly one of those engagements. So was Binh Gia. A third important armed clash, one that loomed much larger in the minds of the key players than those two, was the ferocious encounter between the US Army's elite 1st Cavalry Division and the regular army of North Vietnam in the remote jungles of the Central Highlands in November 1965. It was called the Battle of Ia Drang Valley—the climax of an American campaign to conquer the North Vietnamese in the Central Highlands called Operation Silver Bayonet.

The sheer volume of carnage at this battle, and the fact that it might very well have turned into the worst disaster to befall the US Army since the days of Custer, shocked the American people. There was no denying after the encounter in the valley that the United States was fighting a major ground war against a determined and skillful enemy. Some Americans back home saw the battle as foreshadowing the inevitable defeat of the communists by superior American tactics and firepower. A handful of Americans who were paying close attention to the developments in Vietnam saw something more ominous. It will perhaps come as no surprise to readers of this book that the adversaries came away from the battle with two very different readings on what it meant.

The Central Highlands is the most remote and beautiful region in all of Vietnam. In 1965, it was home to more than two dozen tribes of Montagnards. Ethnically distinct from the lowland Vietnamese, these groups, who together numbered perhaps 1 million in 1965, practiced slash-and-burn agriculture, supplemented by hunting and gathering. The tribespeople of the Highlands, including the Rade, Jarai, Bru, and Hmong, have struggled to remain autonomous from the Vietnamese majority population for centuries. Most mountain people have darker skin than the Vietnamese. Many groups also file their teeth, wear plugs in their earlobes, and tattoo their bodies extensively. "In Montagnard life," explained a Special Forces handbook from the 1960s, "the village rather than the tribe is the important political, social and economic unit. The villager's life is conditioned by the immediate environment; he knows that environment well—but little beyond."[1]

The lowland Vietnamese in the 1960s looked down upon the Highlanders as primitive holdovers from a bygone age. They were largely untouched by modernity, and therefore thought to be *moi*, or "savages." Villages contained as many as one hundred longhouses, each inhabited by an extended family. Efforts to establish administrative control over the Highlands by the French, and later the South Vietnamese, led the indigenous tribes to form a resistance movement called the United Front for the Liberation of Oppressed Races in 1958.

The spine of the Highlands is formed by the Truong Son Mountains, shared by Vietnam, Laos, and Cambodia. East of the mountains looms a large crescent-shaped plateau about two hundred miles long and one hundred miles wide that contains thickly jungled forests, broken here and there by clearings covered in elephant grass, much of it six or seven feet high. Just southwest of the city of Pleiku, scene of the dramatic February 1965 VC attack that triggered Operation Rolling Thunder, lies a gigantic mountain mass called the Chu Pong Massif. Just north of the Chu Pong runs the Ia River—the *Ia Drang* in Vietnamese. In that river valley, the American and North Vietnamese armies would collide in mid-November 1965 in strength.

It would be difficult indeed to overestimate the strategic importance of this region in a war for control over South Vietnam. The army that held the High-

ABOVE: John F. Kennedy deepened the American commitment to Vietnam considerably by sending thousands of advisers to the South Vietnamese army as well as US Marine helicopters and pilots, and by giving tacit consent to a coup against South Vietnamese president Ngo Dinh Diem. That coup was largely orchestrated by the ambassador to South Vietnam, Henry Cabot Lodge. In the summer of 1965, Lodge would return to Vietnam for a second stint as ambassador, where he struggled in vain to integrate American political and military strategy. (*Courtesy of Wikicommons*)

BOTTOM LEFT: A pensive Lyndon Baines Johnson, flanked by two of his closest advisers, Dean Rusk (*left*) and Robert McNamara. Rusk was a man of great integrity who clung tenaciously to the myth that Ho Chi Minh was an agent of communist mischief in Asia. McNamara believed the Vietnam conflict could be won by applying the wisdom of systems analysis and business administration to warfare, but he saw the error of his ways long before he resigned as secretary of defense. (*Courtesy of Wikicommons*)

BOTTOM RIGHT: Ho Chi Minh, the father of the Vietnamese communist revolution, in a photo from the early 1960s before the American war began. The avuncular Ho was deeply venerated by the people of Vietnam for his unstinting loyalty to the cause of independence and his simple, spartan lifestyle. He was also a master political organizer who was willing to do whatever was necessary to achieve dominion over all of Vietnam. (*Courtesy of Wikicommons*)

Above: The cruel face of counterinsurgency warfare: a Vietnamese father carrying the body of his young child looks up at ARVN soldiers on an armored personnel carrier, as if to say, Why? Tens of thousands of Vietnamese civilians would be killed as a direct result of military operations over the long course of the conflict. *(AP Photo)*

LEFT: A Douglas B-66 light bomber accompanied by four F-105 Thunderchiefs on a bombing mission over North Vietnam. This B-66 is rigged out as an electronic countermeasures aircraft. American pilots had to operate under a welter of restrictions imposed by Washington for political reasons. Rolling Thunder rained down more tons of bombs on North Vietnam than had been dropped on Germany in World War II, but historians view the campaign as a spectacular failure. *(Courtesy of Wikicommons)*

LEFT: Le Duan, not Ho Chi Minh or General Vo Nguyen Giap, was the most powerful member of North Vietnam's senior war leaders, though the Americans did not know this during the war. He was the leading advocate for deploying the People's Army of Vietnam—the conventional army of North Vietnam—to meet the awesome challenge of fighting the United States in the South. *(AP Photo)*

RIGHT: Lieutenant Colonel J. R. "Bull" Fisher, the commander of the 2nd Battalion of the 4th Marine Regiment, which sustained heavy casualties during Operation Starlite, the first multibattalion battle between American combat troops and the regular forces of the Vietcong on the Van Tuong peninsula. Fisher is talking on a field telephone near the end of the battle, the strain of the last few days' fighting clearly etched on his face. Like virtually every other marine battalion commander in Vietnam, Fisher had seen combat in the Pacific War. *(AP Photo)*

LEFT: An American Special Forces soldier inside the camp at Plei Me adjusts a 60 mm mortar, with several Jarai mountain tribesmen looking on. Just twenty miles from the Cambodian border in the Central Highlands, the siege at Plei Me (October 19–25, 1965) by North Vietnamese forces led ineluctably to the Battle of Ia Drang a month later. *(AP Photo)*

ABOVE: A Navy F-4 Phantom fighter-bomber aboard the USS *Independence* in July 1965. This aircraft is armed with a belly bomb as well as Sidewinder missiles. The Phantom was also adopted by the US Air Force and served in various roles, including as a fast-forward air control, reconnaissance, and air-superiority fighter. Without question, it was one of the most lethal and effective combat aircraft during the war. *(AP Photo)*

BOTTOM LEFT: A female Vietcong guerrilla, armed with an American M-16. Women played an enormous role in the war against the Americans. In addition to serving in infantry units, they served as porters, cooks, factory workers, and in road repair crews, both in North Vietnam and along the Ho Chi Minh Trail. This is a propaganda photo. *(Courtesy of Wikicommons)*

BOTTOM RIGHT: Major Norman Schwarzkopf helps a wounded South Vietnamese soldier during the siege of Duc Co. Schwarzkopf saw heavy action in Vietnam and went on to command coalition ground forces during the Persian Gulf War of 1990 to 1991. *(AP Photo)*

RIGHT: Senator William Fulbright of Arkansas chats during a break in the early 1966 hearings of the Senate Foreign Relations Committee with witness Robert McNamara. Fulbright's close study of Vietnamese history convinced him the United States was heading toward disaster. The nationally televised hearings he chaired in early 1966 exposed the doubts many highly respected foreign policy experts held about Johnson's Vietnam policy. *(AP Photo)*

BELOW: First Cavalry troopers carry the body of a comrade to a helicopter for evacuation from the Ia Drang battlefield in November 1965. General Westmoreland claimed the battle vindicated his decision to focus American efforts on destroying the enemy's regular forces as opposed to the guerrillas, who controlled more than a third of South Vietnam's twenty-six hundred villages in 1965. He was incorrect. *(AP Photo)*

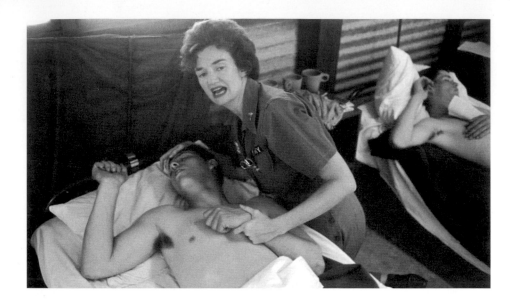

ABOVE: An American army nurse comforts a suffering G.I. Wounded American troops received superb medical care more quickly than their predecessors in earlier conflicts because of the prevalence of medical evacuation helicopters and mobile field hospitals. Army nurses established and staffed public clinics, performed immunizations, taught courses, and visited orphanages. About five thousand women served as nurses in Vietnam; all were volunteers. *(AP Photo)*

BELOW: More than twenty thousand people attended the first major antiwar demonstration on April 17, 1965, making it the largest antiwar protest in American history up to that time. But throughout 1965, most Americans, even most young Americans, supported President Johnson's decision to send American troops to fight in Vietnam. As time went on, support for the war at home dwindled steadily. *(AP Photo)*

lands plateau could strike north into Quang Ngai Province; south toward the approaches to Saigon, or east, along Highway 19, toward the coast in Binh Dinh Province, long a communist stronghold. There were only two major roads in the Central Highlands: Highway 14 ran north to south, connecting the major towns of Kontum, Pleiku, and Ban Me Thuot. Highway 19 threaded its way from the Cambodian border in the west to Qui Nhon on the coast.

A primary mission of American Special Forces in Vietnam, as we said earlier, was to organize and train Montagnard militia and strike forces as part of the Civilian Irregular Defense Group, or as the Americans in the bush used to say, the "sidge forces." By 1964, Army Special Forces had established about thirty CIDG camps in the Highlands, most close to Vietnam's western borders with Cambodia and Laos. Their purpose was to monitor and challenge communist forces that attempted to penetrate the region.

In the late summer of 1965, General Westmoreland strongly suspected Hanoi planned to move to phase three of its protracted war strategy, shifting from guerrilla warfare to conventional conflict. He believed that Hanoi would deploy its regular army to gain control of the big plateau, and then march in force eastward, down Highway 19, effectively cutting South Vietnam in half before the US Army arrived in strength to frustrate that plan. Westmoreland was not far wrong about Hanoi's plan, but he *was* wrong. Le Duan and his colleagues on the Central Military Party Committee had indeed developed and approved such a plan. But after the Americans began to deploy ground combat units in late spring, it had been called off. The campaign was deemed too reckless, given how little was known about the Americans' fighting abilities.

After the PAVN defeat at Duc Co in August, there was a notable lull in communist offensive operations in the Highlands. We can only speculate as to why. Logistical difficulties and understrength infantry units as a result of Duc Co were surely crucial factors. The PAVN had stockpiled ammo and supplies in eastern Cambodia for operations in the Highlands, but these supplies by September were running perilously low. The North Vietnamese maneuver units in the area, we now know, were badly beaten up, primarily by American airpower. Several battalions of PAVN were seriously shorthanded, and half starving, to boot. And so the B3 Front (that is, the communists' Central Highlands headquarters) commander, General Chu Huy Man, ordered his regular forces to spend most of September and early October resting and refitting, and taking on replacements.

By early October, General Man had received orders from Hanoi to resume offensive operations. A mid-1990s Vietnamese history of the campaign describes Man's B3 Front's new objectives as follows: "to destroy a portion of the [South Vietnamese] army, to lure in and destroy a portion of the American forces, to consolidate and expand our liberated zone, to hone and train our troops and our campaign headquarters staff . . . to feel out and gain a better understanding of the American forces and to co-ordinate with . . . the rest of our forces in South Vietnam."[2]

To accomplish his mission, General Man had at his disposal the 33rd and 32nd PAVN regiments, each with roughly 1,500 to 1,800 troops. The 66th Regiment was also assigned to his command, but it was still making its perilous journey down the Trail in early October. It would reach its area of operations in late October. He also had a number of supporting units, including a battalion of heavy (120 mm) mortars and a battalion of heavy (14.5 mm) machine guns, as well as engineers and signal troops.

The opening gambit in the campaign was another classic "lure and ambush" operation, in which the 33rd Regiment's infantry would assault a US Special Forces camp at Plei Me. The 33rd's attack, General Man hoped, would force the ARVN II Corps commander, General Vinh Loc, to send a hastily assembled relief force. That force would have no choice but to come down Provincial Route 5 to get to the Plei Me camp. It was the job of the 32nd Regiment to launch a "maneuver ambush," in which a series of perfectly timed assaults from both sides of a road cut up an enemy column and then destroyed it piecemeal. After that ambush, both PAVN regiments would turn on the camp and annihilate its garrison.

Plei Me at this time was manned by about 450 CIDG troops armed with WWII-era M-1 rifles and BARs, and an A-Team of twelve Army Special Forces soldiers. It was one of fourteen Special Forces–CIDG camps in the remote hinterlands of western II Corps at the time, whipped up in red dust by high winds in the dry season and drenched in mud during the monsoon season, from May to October.

The attack on Plei Me was planned and rehearsed with typical PAVN thoroughness. The area around the camp was reconnoitered without detection for several weeks. A sand table model of the camp was prepared and studied by the officers and noncoms tasked with making the attack. The 32nd Regiment prepared a string of expertly camouflaged bunkers along Route 5 for the ambush, and Montagnard porters working for the North Vietnamese prepositioned supplies and ammo.

October 19 had been just like most days over the previous few weeks for the Plei Me garrison: quiet, and uneventful. But the commanding officer, Captain Harold Moore, was concerned. He'd received several intelligence reports indicating the presence of one or more PAVN regiments in the area. Suddenly, at 1915 hours, small-arms fire started landing within the camp from the southwest. Elements of the 33rd PAVN had stumbled on a small Montagnard patrol outside the wire. The camp went on high alert, as all hands manned their defensive positions.

At 2200, mortar and recoilless rifle fire began to land inside the perimeter, and the killing and maiming began. Within twenty minutes, a listening outpost about a mile to the southwest, manned by twenty Jarai tribesmen, was overrun. Its radio suddenly went dead. At 0030, October 20, about three hundred PAVN assault troops slammed into the triangular-shaped perimeter from the north and northwest. The camp exploded with automatic-weapons fire, and a dozen Montagnard troopers were killed or wounded within the first few minutes. Colonel Vu Sac, commander of the 33rd, then ordered an entire battalion to attack the perimeter from the south around 0100.

By 0110, chaos reigned in and around the camp. As a Special Forces after-action report tells it, "the PAVN were within the defensive wire barriers to the south, on the east near the main gate, and to the north near the corner bunker. They made a determined attempt to overrun the bunker, but the defenders in the vicinity . . . repulsed the attack."[3] American close air support in the form of a C-123 Provider—a flare ship—arrived on station at 0340. Ten minutes later, two A-1E prop plane Skyraiders arrived over the base and began to lay down cannon fire on enemy positions. Between then and 0600 on October 21, 109 strike sorties were flown against the assault forces by US aircraft.

Just after 0500 on the twentieth, Captain Moore requested reinforcements from II Corps Headquarters at Pleiku. General Vinh Loc was hesitant to send a powerful ARVN relief force, suspecting that the PAVN might well be attempting to lure most of his strength out of Pleiku so its forces could seize the crucial town, a provincial capital. True enough, the communists couldn't have held Pleiku for long, given the strength of allied forces in II Corps, but the very act of taking the town would have garnered the PAVN a major propaganda victory. It would have become worldwide news.

Colonel Bill McKean, commander of the 5th Special Forces Group, the top SF commander in Vietnam, didn't hesitate. He conferred with the head of ARVN Special Forces. They agreed to send in reinforcements by helicopter assault as soon as they could be assembled. The relief force consisted of two companies of South Vietnamese Airborne Rangers, about 150 men, and fifteen American Special Forces soldiers. Major Charles "Chargin' Charlie" Beckwith was placed in command.

Beckwith was already well on his way to legendary status in the Special Forces. He was a master practitioner of long-range patrolling and hit-and-run raiding tactics. The Georgia native, who had turned down an offer to play football with the Green Bay Packers, was an intense and driven officer with an explosive temper. He was a great killer, too. Beckwith had fought the communist insurgency in Malaya when he was attached as an exchange officer with the organization many considered to be the best commando unit in the Western world—the British Special Air Service.

The scheme of maneuver called for Beckwith's force to fly from Pleiku to an LZ about three miles from the camp, and then make its way to the fight on foot, evading detection by marauding communist troops. By the evening of October 20, as Beckwith and his staff planned the relief operation, the siege of Plei Me had become the Big Event in Vietnam. By that point, too, General Loc had agreed to send a 1,400-man Armored Task Force to reinforce the camp, provided that American forces assumed responsibility for defending Pleiku city. The 1st Cavalry Division agreed to do so.

The camp garrison was continually shelled throughout the day and night of the twentieth, but no infantry assault was attempted. Beckwith's relief force landed at the designated LZ at 0900 on the twenty-first. The terrain between the LZ and the SF camp was thickly forested. In some places the elephant grass was taller than Beckwith himself, who stood six feet two inches tall. The relief force had to hack its way through the jungle with machetes. By dusk, they had closed in to within four hundred yards of the camp. Fearing that his unit would be shot at by nervous Montagnard troopers if it approached at dusk, Beckwith decided to wait until dawn and then make a run for the camp gate. According to his own account,

> *We evidently caught the enemy by surprise. Once on the road we dashed for the camp and took some light fire. A Vietnamese lieutenant was killed. So, too, was a newspaper photographer who, without permission, had gotten on one of the choppers back in Pleiku and had come with us. . . . Within a half hour everyone was in the camp. The first thing I noticed on going through the gate was the Montagnard tribesmen who had been killed while defending the camp; they were still lying in the wire. I mean everywhere. Dead people. . . . There were about sixty other dead Montagnard soldiers stuffed into body bags and stacked up like cordwood. The smell was terrible.*[4]

That morning, as Beckwith and the Special Forces troops began to reorganize and strengthen the camp defenses. Colonel McKean then ordered Beckwith to mount a reconnaissance patrol outside the perimeter. Beckwith, who guessed that the entire camp was surrounded by at least a full PAVN regiment, objected in no uncertain terms, but McKean insisted he send out the patrol. Beckwith obliged. About two hundred men left the confines of the camp at 1300 hours. Within a few minutes the patrol was pinned down by merciless enemy fire and unable to move forward or backward. By the time they returned to camp under cover of darkness, one American SF officer and twelve Jarai tribesmen had been killed, and another twenty-six men wounded.

After this episode, Beckwith was given top priority for air support missions, and the NVA's 33rd Regiment was pummeled by napalm, 250-pound explosive bombs, heliborne rockets, and machine-gun fire more or less continually throughout the twenty-third and twenty-fourth. Nonetheless, the garrison at Plei Me continued to suffer under a rain of mortar and small-arms fire over those two days and nights. Major Beckwith recalled that *the nights were worse, far worse, than the days. Ropes of green and orange tracers flew into and out of the camp. Overhead, circling C–46 Flareships kept the area illuminated. Multicolored parachutes, which had been used to resupply us, were strewn here and there and gave the camp a raffish appearance. The pounding intensified. Mortars and recoilless rifles fired relentlessly. Amazingly, during these terrible nighttime hours the camp rats, oblivious to the havoc they were a part of, continued to come out and run over the ruins just as if everyone was asleep.*

Bombers came over again on October 24th and began to eat up the NVA. I'd say our side flew seventy-five to one hundred sorties a day. We just walked these air strikes all around the outside of the camp. We used a lot of air, and we broke the enemy's back with it.[5]

The Armored Task Force
Moves Toward Plei Me

While all this was going on, the Armored Task Force of 1,200 men and sixteen tanks finally began its trek down Provincial Route 5 toward the camp, well prepared for the inevitable ambush. It departed Phu My at 1400 on Saturday, the twenty-third, with several tanks and APCs in the vanguard, but it could only go as fast as the infantrymen could clear the flanks as the column proceeded. At 1750, the front of the column entered the 32nd Regiment's ambush kill zone, and began to take very heavy fire from both sides of the road. But the tankers and the infantry were ready for the onslaught. The historian J. P. Harris describes what happened: "There was no panic among the ARVN troops in the main body. The fight was entirely expected. The tanks fired canister from their 76 mm main armament, and both tanks and APCs opened up with their machine guns. Accompanying infantry joined in with their weapons. American F-100 jets then struck the PAVN with cannon fire and napalm, and helicopter gunships attacked it with rockets and more machine gun fire."[6]

Under such pressure, the communist attack withered. Fighting continued for two hours, but the ARVN got the better of the fight, and the 32nd's troops withdrew into the jungle to lick their wounds.

Major Nguyen Truong Luat, ARVN commander of the relief column, was gratified by his unit's performance in combat, but he was a very experienced officer, with an abiding respect for the fighting prowess of his adversaries. He refused to press on to relieve the camp until he had been resupplied and provided with artillery fire so he could move forward under cover of a rolling barrage. The US 1st Cavalry Division command obliged with the artillery support, carving several fire bases in the jungle on Sunday, October 24.

The relief column resumed its march toward the camp on Monday afternoon. It reached its destination at dusk, encountering only desultory small-arms fire. An ugly scene marred the boisterousness of the camp's beleaguered garrison. Charlie Beckwith was furious that it had taken the column so long to arrive. He refused to allow Major Luat and his unit to enter the camp, ordering them to bivouac outside the gates, on the grounds that the camp, which also contained the families of the CIDG troopers, was too crowded. Major Luat was incensed at this slight, and after launching into a tirade in no less than three languages—English, French, and Vietnamese—he threatened to shoot the burly American commander. Several American Special Forces soldiers quietly flipped their safeties off their weapons, and cooler heads prevailed. The Vietnamese major walked away.

The siege of Plei Me was over. Charlie Beckwith deserves credit for getting the emergency rescue force to the scene in a hurry, and reorganizing the rather weak defensive positions within the camp wire. But as Beckwith himself was the first to admit, the crucial weapon in the entire operation had been American airpower. Between October 20 to 29, US aircraft dropped 1.6 million pounds of explosives on suspected enemy positions around the camp. Remarkably, a day after the siege had been lifted, an element of the badly chewed up 33rd PAVN Regiment caught an ARVN patrol a mile or so from the camp by surprise and killed twenty-seven troops. No one could accuse the 33rd Regiment of being quitters. The Americans would find out many other PAVN units were as well over the next month, as the US Army's most mobile and innovative division, the 1st Air Cavalry, took to the skies in the most ambitious search-and-destroy operation of the Vietnam War thus far.

The Cav and Its Helicopters

War, Carl von Clausewitz tells us, is a chameleon, but its essence is timeless. Every era in military history since the Napoleonic Wars seems to produce a new technology, weapon, or strategy that promises to "revolutionize" organized violence. Railroads, the telegraph, and the rifled musket combined to produce the unprecedented carnage of the American Civil War. The tank broke the stalemate of the Western Front in World War I, and the Germans' combined arms "blitzkrieg" doctrine ensured that World War II would be the most destructive war in human experience, defined by rapid movement of armored divisions, covered by airpower and artillery.

In the early 1960s, the helicopter was coming into its own as an instrument of war. It promised to revolutionize ground war by freeing the infantryman from the tyranny of terrain. The US Marines had pioneered the use of helicopters, forming an experimental unit at Quantico, Virginia, even before they had a viable combat helicopter with which to experiment. In Korea, the marines used light, underpowered choppers to evacuate the wounded and occasionally resupply a remote combat outpost. By 1963, the US Army had seized the initiative from the Marine Corps, investing heavily in what it called "airmobile warfare." In Georgia and the Carolinas, mass formations of Bell UH-1 "Hueys," joined by an assortment of both larger and smaller choppers, crisscrossed the skies, converging on mock guerrilla forces. First, gunships, known as "hogs," would prep the landing zone with machine-gun and rocket fire. Then troop transports, known as "slicks," would swoop into predesignated landing zones, where infantrymen would debouch, form up, and commence their hunt for "the enemy." The enemy in these exercises was inevitably a guerrilla force of a company or two of American infantrymen practicing the tactics of the Vietcong.

Meanwhile, larger helicopters, twin-engine Boeing CH-47 Chinooks and Sikorsky CH-54 Flying Cranes with astonishing lift capacities, transported artillery pieces, fortification materials, and water and ammo to temporary combat bases. In the experimental Air Assault Division—soon to be known throughout the world as the 1st Cavalry Division, Airmobile—helicopters did the work of supply trucks, armored reconnaissance units, and ground artillery in conventional divisions.

The commander of the 1st Cav was one of the army's most promising and ambitious officers, a soft-spoken Texan named Major General Harry W. O. Kinnard. He was a proven combat leader with a well-deserved reputation for thinking outside the box. A fine athlete at West Point with an adventurous spirit, Kinnard joined the 101st Airborne Division in World War II. He commanded a battalion of that outfit in the Normandy invasion, dropping behind enemy lines hours before the allies crossed the beaches. Before the war concluded in May 1945, he had been awarded a Distinguished Service Cross, the army's second-highest medal for bravery, as well as a Silver Star. After the war he remained passionately committed to the development of airborne operations, a commitment that earned him the coveted slot of commander of the only airmobile division in the army.

"Airmobility is a state of mind," said Kinnard. "We are leaving behind the trucks and jeeps and seeing how far we can go by aircraft."[7] A historian of the Cav's operations in Vietnam who served as an officer with the division in Southeast Asia describes the process by which this experimental unit became the most capable and feared US Army division in Vietnam: "Ground elements began thinking in terms of air vehicles; commanders and staffs substituted space and distance measurements with time intervals. Aviators became familiar with problems faced daily by ground troops. New concepts in supply and evacuation were developed; techniques in communications and the control of widely dispersed units were perfected. Thousands and thousands of actions were designed to forge the unit into a finely tuned mesh of men and machines."[8]

The more General Westmoreland learned about Harry Kinnard's division, the more he wanted the unit for service in Vietnam. Its capabilities were nothing short of astonishing. It could conduct operations in places where no mechanized or standard American infantry division could go, and Vietnam, with its underdeveloped road network, was chock-full of such places. The Cav could maneuver over far greater areas than any three conventional infantry divisions; it could conduct raids farther behind enemy lines than any World War II officer would have thought possible. It could execute long-range reconnaissance, and screen wide fronts. It could bring a great deal of combat power to bear in a hurry for any ground unit facing annihilation.

On July 1, 1965, the 1st Cavalry Division was officially activated. With prodding from General Westmoreland, Robert McNamara made it clear he wanted the unit to embark for Vietnam as soon as possible, if not sooner. Westmoreland saw the unit as the perfect weapon for the crucial struggle then forming up in the Central Highlands.

Kinnard was given until July 28 to get the division ready to sail to Southeast Asia. A mad scramble followed to flesh out the division's roster of sixteen thousand men. It was a tall order. Kinnard had to beg, borrow, and steal more than three thousand men from other units, including scores of scarce helicopter pilots and mechanics for the unit's four-hundred-plus choppers. The general's job was made all the more difficult by LBJ's refusal to declare Vietnam a national emergency. That meant that more than one thousand soldiers who had trained with the division would not be able to go to Vietnam because their tours of duty were coming to an end too soon to justify their leaving in the first place. "We had to strip out a great many highly trained men at exactly the worst time, namely, just as we were preparing to go to war," Kinnard remarked years later.[9] There were other problems to be overcome at lightning speed. All the helicopters had to have new navigation devices installed, and the infantrymen needed to turn in their heavy M-14 rifles for the lightweight, overly delicate M-16s, and then get used to shooting the new weapons.

It took no less than ten cargo ships, six troop ships, and four escort aircraft carriers to transport the division to Vietnam. A vast new camp for the division about half the size of Manhattan was established on the eastern edge of the Central Highlands near An Khe. Westmoreland would have preferred to base the entire division at Pleiku, in the very heart of the Highlands, but Admiral Sharp at CINPAC vetoed that plan, on the grounds that Pleiku was too remote to defend in case of a major attack. Soon, Camp Radcliff contained the largest heliport in the world. It was nicknamed "the golf course" because it was covered in grass so the Highlands winds couldn't whip up the dirt when the helicopters flew in and out of the place.

General Kinnard had aggressively lobbied to deploy his division in operations against the Ho Chi Minh Trail in Laos. Westmoreland and his superiors ultimately turned down his proposal because it would create a slew of political difficulties. At the end of October, with two regiments of PAVNs recovering from defeat at Plei Me, and perhaps several others in the western Highlands, Kinnard had little trouble convincing the powers that be to unleash one brigade of the 1st Cav against the People's Army of Vietnam there. The Cav's planners described the unit's first big operation as follows:

> [The] concept was to conduct an intensive search for the enemy, looking everywhere—in the villages, in the jungles and along the stream beds. By wide-spread dispersion, made possible by excellent communications and helicopter lift, [elements of the division were] to sweep large areas systematically. Each battalion was to be deployed with supporting artillery and was to further disperse its companies. Vigorous and intensive patrolling from company bases was to be conducted. When contact was first established, a rapid reaction force was to be assembled swiftly and lifted by helicopters to strike the enemy. Rapid air movement of artillery batteries, plus extensive use of tactical air strikes, would provide the fire support. . . . Here was air mobility's acid test. The next few days [from October 27 to November 9] would reveal whether three years of planning and testing would bear the fruits of victory—for a concept and a division.[10]

General Kinnard and his senior officers were chomping at the bit to tear into the enemy. The division had arrived in Vietnam amid much hoopla, yet the first limited operations by elements of the division had been criticized by MACV and the American media for a lack of results. Therefore, it must have been frustrating, not to say embarrassing, when the 1st Brigade's first five days of operations (October 27 to October 31) in Operation Silver Bayonet produced only fleeting contact with small groups of enemy troops. Indeed, as J. P. Harris points out, the Cav's "initial operations amounted to a great deal of frenetic, ill-directed flying about in helicopters, followed by a lot of ineffective thrashing around by ground troops."[11] Broadly speaking, the early search areas were too far north to detect the PAVN 33rd and 32nd Regiments. Harris, having examined in detail the communications between the Cav and the ARVN II Corps intelligence sections, suggests that the latter organization had a very accurate idea of the disposition of the PAVN forces in the region at this point, but Cav officers from Kinnard on down thought the commander of II Corps, General Vinh Loc, and his staff to be incompetent, and took their intelligence reports with a grain of salt. Harris may well be correct. All too often Vietnamese and American officers talked past one another.

Another factor detracted from the Cav's effectiveness in the hunt of late October. Within a day after operations began, a logistical crisis abruptly emerged. The Cav's birds were consuming so much fuel that a serious shortage developed. In fact, the shortage was so acute it appeared for a while that the operation might have to be called off. That didn't happen. The air force stepped into the breach. It began to ferry in five-hundred-gallon collapsible fuel bladders in C-130 transports. That alleviated, but did not solve, the problem. In fact, fuel shortages continued to affect the performance of the division throughout the campaign. Lack of fuel and the tremendous wear and tear on the helicopters meant that only one of the division's three brigades could be deployed in airmobile operations at one time.

All of the 1st Brigade's maneuver units were engaged in reconnaissance operations early on in Silver Bayonet, but it was the division's reconnaissance squadron that made the first significant contact with the enemy. The 1st Squadron of the 9th Cavalry Regiment consisted of three troops—a troop being the cavalry's equivalent of an infantry company. Each troop contained a combination of light Sioux Scout helos, Huey helicopter gunships, and an airborne rifle platoon carried in five or six Huey transports. If the Scouts located enemy forces, the troop commander could use the gunships to mount an aerial attack, land the rifle platoon to engage in combat or ground reconnaissance, or both.

The commander of 1/9 was one of the most widely respected officers in the entire division. Lieutenant Colonel John B. Stockton exemplified the swashbuckling spirit of the old horse cavalry. He had a habit of sidestepping orders or regulations he found wrongheaded, drawing the ire of his superiors. Tall and lean with a handlebar mustache, Stockton looked the part of a cavalry commander. His call sign in Vietnam was "bullwhip 6." Before sailing to Southeast Asia, the colonel sent one of his men to Philadelphia to purchase decidedly nonregulation black Stetson hats for his officers, to be worn on special occasions. Years after the war, troopers in the 1st Cav would have no trouble at all believing John Stockton had been the model for Robert Duvall's famous character in *Apocalypse Now*, Lieutenant Colonel Kilgore.

Just after 0800 on November 1, Stockton's B Troop under Major Robert Zion spotted a dozen or so North Vietnamese infantrymen in an open field about seven miles southwest of Plei Me. At last, the hounds had found some foxes. Zion landed his rifle platoon. They immediately engaged the startled PAVN soldiers. With the help of the gunships, they quickly overwhelmed the enemy force, killing twenty and capturing nineteen. These were men of the 1st Battalion of the 33rd Regiment, which had taken about 40 percent casualties during the Plei Me fight. It soon became clear why they had fought instead of vanishing into the jungle: they were defending a small hospital. Zion's men uncovered a treasure trove of documents revealing the PAVN's march routes and hidden supply dumps in the area. The documents were quickly helicoptered back to the 1st Brigade's base at the Catecka tea plantation. Stockton ordered two more rifle platoons to the scene to secure the area, and the air force used the intelligence gathered at the hospital to target suspected enemy positions.

At 1410, an estimated force of about 150 North Vietnamese troops were marching toward the hospital at a brisk clip. Stockton called in an additional rifle company to bolster his three platoons there. The NVA launched a powerful assault, but was turned back. Heavy fighting continued until dark, when the North Vietnamese withdrew toward the Cambodian border to the west.

The harried 1st Brigade search-and-destroy mission continued over the next day or so, with a handful of fleeting enemy sightings. An LZ was established just a mile east of the Cambodian border—LZ Mary—just to the south of the Drang River. Stockton ordered his ground forces to set up three platoon-size ambush sites in the vicinity of the LZ. Around 1930 hours on November 3, a company from the 8th Battalion of the 66th Regiment approached the southernmost of the ambush sites, where a platoon-size force commanded by Captain Chuck Knowlen was waiting patiently. The battalion stopped about one hundred yards short of the killing zone. It had just completed the arduous journey down the Ho Chi Minh Trail. The men were in high spirits, knowing their new base area was close by. The 1st Cavalry Division's after-action report vividly describes what happened next: "At 2100 hours the NVA unit formed up and moved confidently and noisily along the trail. . . . The [American platoon] allowed the first element to pass through and sprung the trap on the weapons platoon, whose men were carrying machine guns, mortars and recoilless rifles. At 2105 eight Claymore mines set along a 100-meter kill zone belched fire and steel and troopers blazed away with M-16s for two minutes. Simultaneously, Claymores sited both up and down the trail pumped death into the enemy column. There was no return fire."[12]

Nonetheless, Knowlen knew when his force was heavily outnumbered by the dazed North Vietnamese. The decision to trigger the ambush had been a risky one to say the least, and indicative of the pressure placed on all hands in the division to engage and kill enemy forces. Knowlen's platoon hightailed it back to the relative safety of LZ Mary, covered by mortar fire from the LZ. They made it back inside the perimeter just in time to help the company-size force there fend off an attack by no less than two full companies of the 66th Regiment. The mortar fire had given away the location of LZ Mary. Knowlen's "suspicion that he had stamped on a tiger's tail," writes J. P. Harris, "proved valid. . . . The whole episode was symptomatic of the increasing desperation of the senior officers of the 1st Cavalry Division to find and engage substantial numbers of the elusive North Vietnamese."[13]

At 2315, the NVA launched a second assault—this one supported by snipers in the trees above the Americans. The attack came within a whisper of overrunning the entire LZ. Major Zion, in command at Mary, radioed Stockton. He needed reinforcements, and fast. According to "the book," Stockton needed the permission of his superior, General Dick Knowles, to release the brigade's reserve infantry company at Duc Co. But there was no time. Not if Stockton wanted to save his fighters at Mary from being wiped out. And so it was that Lieutenant Colonel John Stockton ordered the first nighttime helicopter assault of a perimeter under heavy fire in military history. Although most of the choppers were hit by small-arms fire on the way in or the way out, they succeeded in landing the infantry company, and the assault was turned back. The 66th Regiment commander launched several more probes in the early morning before withdrawing into the jungle.

The 3rd Brigade Arrives for Silver Bayonet's Main Engagement

After the defense of LZ Mary, the 1st Brigade continued to make sporadic contact with the enemy. On November 6, two companies from the 2nd Battalion, 8th

Cavalry engaged what was probably the 3rd Battalion of the 33rd PAVN Regiment in a firefight that lasted a full afternoon. Twenty-six Americans were killed and fifty-three wounded. NVA casualties were estimated at seventy-seven killed. That fight—more or less a draw—was the last major contact for the 1st Brigade.

In fact, the 1st Brigade's effort to destroy multiple battalions of communists came up rather short. Between November 9 and 12, the brigade withdrew from its base at the tea plantation and was replaced by the 3rd Brigade, under Colonel Tim Brown. For his part, General Kinnard was deeply perturbed that his magnificent division had yet to destroy a large number of enemy soldiers. Westmoreland, surely, was equally displeased. If the 1st Cavalry Division couldn't wipe out a regiment or two with all of its vaunted power and mobility, how would traditional American infantry divisions do against the PAVN?

Now, on November 13, Colonel Brown ordered his most experienced battalion commander, Lieutenant Colonel Hal Moore of the 1/7 Cavalry, to conduct a helicopter assault just to the east of Chu Pong Massif. Division intelligence was all but certain there was at least a full, fresh PAVN regiment there. Intelligence was correct, but it didn't have the full picture. In fact, two battalions of the fresh 66th Regiment were camped on the eastern face of Chu Pong, along with the remnants of the battered 33rd Regiment, which was taking on replacements in preparation for further combat. The communist soldiers were positioned roughly 1,500 feet above the valley floor. The 8th Battalion of the 66th was seven miles to the northeast of Chu Pong. The 32nd was about nine miles to the northwest near the Cambodian border.

Moore, a tall, soft-spoken yet charismatic officer, had been in command of 1/7 for almost eighteen months. He was held in high regard by his men for his loyalty, integrity, and tactical acumen. Like his brigade and division commander, Moore was very eager for a fight—perhaps too eager. He had already been selected for promotion to colonel, so if he was going to lead his battalion in a serious engagement, it would have to happen soon. On the night of the 13th, Moore decided to break with standard operating procedure in the morning and land all four of his companies at one LZ. From that base, he planned to disperse individual companies in pursuit of the enemy. He had one big problem. Because of the torrid pace of the division's operations to date, he could only get sixteen slicks to ferry his unit to the LZ. That meant he could land only about eighty of his 431 troops at one time—each slick could carry only five or six combat infantrymen and their equipment. It would take about half an hour for the birds to pick up another eighty troopers and ferry them to the LZ. His entire force wouldn't be in place for at least three hours, and probably more than that, given the inevitable friction of military operations.

Shortly after first light on November 14, Moore and a few members of his command group flew over the AO and selected an LZ about the size of a football field, just east of the foothills of the Chu Pong. It was an oval-shaped clearing, surrounded by tall trees and high grass. It could accommodate eight Hueys at one time—four on each side of a small grove of trees in the middle of the clearing. Moore had good reason to believe the enemy was very near the site of LZ X-Ray. A communication wire was spotted close to the clearing. Before the assault began that morning, the division's artillery would fire for eight minutes on two other potential clearings in the area as a diversion. Then the big guns would turn their fire on LZ X-Ray for a full twenty minutes before the first wave of troopers touched down.

It was a bright, blue sunny morning at the Plei Me Special Forces camp, where Moore's battalion mounted up for its ride into history. The first lift of Hueys touched down at X-Ray at 1048. Captain John Herren's B Company sent out four patrols in different directions to scout out the area, while the main body of the company secured the LZ. Colonel Moore set up his command post in the grove of trees, next to one of the clearing's many large brown anthills. This one was about the size of a pickup truck.

At 1120, one of the recon patrols from Bravo captured an unarmed PAVN soldier, probably a deserter. He was scared out of his wits by the Americans, and shaking badly. He quickly told a South Vietnamese translator that several battalions of his comrades were up on the big mountain, and their commanders were eager to fight with Americans.

"When you dropped troops into X-Ray," recalled the tactical commander of PAVN forces during the Ia Drang battle, Lieutenant Colonel Nguyen Huu An, "we were ready, we had prepared for you and expected you to come. The only question was when."[14] By 1230, Moore had most of Captain Tony Nadal's Alpha Company on the ground. He ordered Nadal to take the place of Bravo in securing the LZ; then he ordered B Company to push up a fingerlike ridgeline to the northwest of the LZ to see what it could find. Within fifteen minutes, B's platoons were taking light sniper fire. Then the pace of enemy fire escalated rapidly. AK-47 and light machine-gun rounds zipped and whined through the jungle, in the general direction of the American advance.

The leader of 2nd Platoon, B Company, Lieutenant Henry Herrick, an officer with a tendency to be overaggressive, spotted a group of enemy infantrymen directly to his front. He asked Captain Herren if he could give chase. Herren said yes, but he warned his platoon commander not to get too far ahead of the rest of the company. He didn't want the entire platoon to get cut off.

Herrick and his men gave chase, stumbling into a trap. PAVN troops, perhaps a hundred of them, immediately began to envelop the platoon, killing several Americans within a few minutes, and cutting the survivors off from the main body of B Company. Moore immediately called for elements of Nadal's A Company to secure B Company's left flank. It was roughly 1345. Then, recalled Moore, "one full enemy battalion, more than five hundred determined soldiers, [came] boiling down the mountain toward Herrick's trapped 2nd Platoon," as well as toward other elements of B Company.[15]

By his own count, Moore had about 250 of his 430 men on the ground at this point. The colonel's thoughts turned briefly to his famous predecessor in the 7th Cav, George Custer, and his disastrous fight against the Lakota and Cheyenne at Little Big Horn in June of 1876. It was entirely possible he and his troopers could meet the same fate. "We had to move fast if we were going to survive, had to get off that landing zone and hit him before he could hit us. Only if we brought the enemy to battle deep in the trees and brush would we stand even a slim chance of holding on to the clearing and getting the rest of the battalion landed. . . . If the enemy closed the way to the helicopters all of us would die."[16]

Moore had a weapon that Custer lacked: air support. He got on the horn to the brigade's fire support coordinators, who were flying overhead with the battalion's operations officer, Matt Dillon. Moore asked for all the support they could muster—rockets, artillery, and jet strikes—against both the approaches to the LZ from the west and south, as well as against the PAVN actually engaged in assaulting his companies. "Within minutes the air in the valley was filled with smoke and red dust as a blessed river of high-powered destruction rained from the skies," recalled Moore.[17] Unfortunately, the fact that Herrick's platoon was so far to the front prevented close-in support for some time, but the PAVN infantry pouring down the mountain toward the LZ were badly chewed up by the aerial fire.

Alpha Company's 3rd Platoon caught a full company of PAVN infantrymen running across their front, and blasted away at them, killing at least a dozen in the initial salvo. Sergeant First Class Troy Miller saw it happen. "The enemy was well camouflaged and you could barely see them because their khaki uniform and hats of the same color blended in well with the brownish-yellow grass. They all seemed very well disciplined and did not seem to have any fear of dying at all."[18]

Meanwhile, Bravo's other two platoons were ordered to assault toward Herrick's trapped platoon to attempt a rescue. By the time they closed within seventy-five yards of their objective, they had taken too many casualties to continue. Moore ordered them to withdraw. It was around 1430. By then Herrick's platoon had seen three leaders killed in rapid succession by enemy small-arms fire: Herrick himself, and Sergeants Carl Palmer and Robert Stokes. Moore, sensing another big assault was brewing, also ordered newly arrived Charlie Company to man the unprotected south and southwest portions of the LZ perimeter.

The Americans on LZ X-Ray were in serious trouble. "Too thin on the ground to comply with fundamental principles," observes the campaign's most meticulous historian, "the Americans didn't have all-around defense, defense in depth, or any sort of reserve. The north and eastern sides of the landing zone were almost totally undefended. Had the North Vietnamese been able to attack from these directions in real strength . . . much of Moore's battalion might well have faced destruction."[19]

At 1442, eight helos ferried in the remainder of C Company, but Moore had to wave off the next eight choppers carrying elements of D Company because the LZ was sizzling with fire. Just as the new arrivals joined the C Company line on the south and southwest perimeter, Colonel An ordered Major Le Tien Hoa's 7th Battalion of the 66th to launch a two-company assault in their direction. The PAVN assault force drove around A Company's left flank and slammed into the guns of Captain Bob Edwards's C Company from the south. Vicious close-in fighting continued for well over an hour. At 1615, the North Vietnamese retreated after taking very heavy casualties.

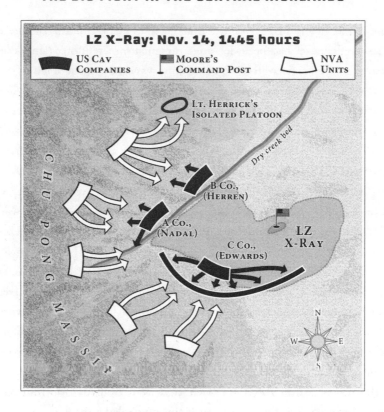

By this point, the lost platoon had suffered eight dead and thirteen wounded, yet it somehow managed to hang on to its small clump of ground. They called in artillery fire close to their tiny, twenty-five-yard-wide perimeter. Specialist Marlin Dorman recalled that the North Vietnamese "tried to crawl up on us. We put our guns flat on the ground and laid . . . fire into them two and three inches high. We fired real low and we stopped them. All this time there were snipers ten to fifteen yards away. If you stuck your head up they shot at it. But we were killing them right and left."[20]

Company D and the battalion's recon platoon had flown into X-Ray around 1520. Finally, Moore had sufficient troops to make a complete perimeter. Colonel Brown also directed Captain Myron Diduryk's D Company, 2/7, to prepare to be lifted into the battle. It would arrive at the scene of the battle at 1700. At 1545, Moore took stock of the situation. "Except for the predicament of . . . the cut-off platoon, I was feeling a good deal better about the situation. We had all our men in; massive firepower had been deployed; a company of reinforcements was on the way; our two-chopper lifeline landing zone was secure; most of our wounded were either evacuated or awaiting evacuation; and we were holding tough."[21]

Just around this time, Moore ordered A and B Companies to make another attempt to rescue the lost platoon. They jumped off from the line of departure at 1620 under a rolling artillery barrage, but they were in trouble from the start. The enemy, writes Moore, "had obviously taken advantage of the temporary American withdrawal [to the assault line of departure] to move well down the slope [of Chu Pong] and draw the circle that much tighter around us. Some were in the trees. Others were dug into the tops and sides of the termite hills. Still others were in hastily dug fighting holes."[22]

B Company suffered thirty casualties while gaining less than one hundred yards. "We stood up and started the assault," remembered Lieutenant Dennis Deal, on the far right flank of the maneuver. We "got out of the trench and the whole world exploded. I don't know how many there were. I couldn't see ninety percent of them, but I sure heard their weapons. We had men dropping all over the place. Finally, the assault line [of 2/7 troopers], which had started out erect, went down to our knees. And then down to the low crawl. One of my men right in front of me absorbed the impact of a rocket-propelled grenade."[23]

Second Platoon of Alpha Company made a bit more progress, but it soon ran into an entrenched machine-gun position and was pinned down. The platoon commander, Lieutenant Walter Marm, tried to knock out the gun with an M72 antitank weapon. It missed. Marm immediately rose and charged across the thirty yards separating the Americans from the North Vietnamese, and tossed a grenade, killing several enemy soldiers. Then he shot several more who tried to flee the scene. Marm was then shot in the face for his trouble. Miraculously, he survived the battle, and was awarded the Medal of Honor for his actions on November 14.

Moore called off the assault at 1740. The fighting had been so intense that afternoon that army medevac choppers refused to take out the wounded. Major Bruce Crandall, commander of the 229th Assault Helicopter Battalion that had flown 2/7 into the battle in the first place, stepped into the breach. He and Captain Ed Freeman, who had won a battlefield commission fighting at Pork Chop

Hill in Korea, volunteered to fly through a gauntlet of fire with ammo and water, which was in desperately short supply on the ground at X-Ray, and to take out the wounded. Crandall, too, would be awarded the Medal of Honor for action this day, but not until 2007.

The first night at X-Ray was relatively calm, considering the ferocious intensity of the previous fighting. The US Army cannon-cockers had a busy night, firing some four thousand rounds of 105 mm shells into suspected enemy assembly areas. At one point the big guns rained down high-explosive shells on a half-mile-long column of enemy troops carrying lights down the eastern face of the mountain, making their approach to their morning fighting positions. The enemy attempted several squad-size probes, sometimes announced by screams and bugle calls, with a view to provoking the Americans to expose the positions of their machine guns. These probes were rebuffed by small-arms fire. No American was killed that first harrowing night. At Camp Holloway, thirty-seven miles to the northeast, the five surgeons of C Company, 15th Medical Battalion, 1st Cavalry Division, toiled without rest, trying to save the lives and limbs of more than one hundred wounded troopers from the vicious fighting at X-Ray.

November 15—the Second Day of the Battle

Rescuing the lost platoon, three hundred yards off the northwest perimeter, remained Colonel Moore's most pressing objective early on the morning of November 15. He ordered Herren's B Company to make the main effort in the center. Alpha and Charlie Companies would be on its flanks. At 0640, each company sent out a recon patrol with instructions to go out two hundred meters to its front. Ten minutes later, C Company's patrol ran into heavy fire. Several men went down. The fire steadily increased. All the patrols began to withdraw back toward the perimeter. Just behind them as they returned came three hundred North Vietnamese infantrymen, charging out of the tall grass from the south, firing their AK-47s.

"We had planned to launch our attack at two a.m.," recalled Lieutenant Colonel Hoang Phuong of the B3 Front. "But because of air strikes and part of the battalion [7th Battalion of the 66th Regiment] getting lost, it was delayed."[24]

Captain Edwards threw a grenade at the human wave of enemy fighters, only to be shot in the back by a rifle round. He asked Moore to send up the battalion's executive officer to take command, Lieutenant John Arrington. No sooner had Arrington arrived on scene than he was wounded as well. Edwards remained in command.

Quickly the attack morphed into a series of hand-to-hand combats as the North Vietnamese tried desperately to break through the American lines. Edwards asked for reinforcement, but Moore, with only a platoon in reserve, was reluctant to commit it so early in the day. It was a good thing he did not do so.

At 0715, Colonel An decided to go for broke. A full PAVN company assaulted D Company in the southeast sector of the perimeter. Then the Vietcong made their first appearance in the battle. This was the H-15 Main Force Battalion, kitted out in black pajamas. Moore then committed his small reserve to the juncture between D's right flank and C's left. Now there were two big firefights going on simultaneously. By that point, writes the historian John Carland, "the enemy fire was so intense that any movement inside the American position was dangerous. Striking from the south, southeast, and northeast in less than a half hour, [Colonel An] had committed a thousand men to a full-scale attempt to overrun X-Ray."[25]

A handful of PAVN soldiers did penetrate the perimeter this time. They charged directly toward 2/7's command post–medical aid station near the big termite hill. Sergeant Major Basil Plumley, Moore's right-hand man, a burly warrior with four combat jumps with the 82nd Airborne in World War II, pulled out his .45 caliber pistol, chambered a round, and exclaimed, "Gentlemen, prepare to defend yourselves!"[26]

Moore called for more reinforcements. Colonel Brown said he would send A Company of the 2nd Battalion, 7th Cavalry as soon as the fire died down enough to send in more slicks.

The VC assault against Delta Company withered badly. Moore had emplaced no less than nine M60 machine guns to defend its seventy-five-yard front. At 0755, he called on his company commanders to indicate their positions by popping smoke grenades, and then the forward air controllers called in all the close air support they could muster: gunships, jets, and artillery. PAVN casualties accumulated rapidly.

Not long after 0800, two F-100 Super Sabres dropped napalm, but it fell short, incinerating several American troopers and causing general mayhem all around. Still, the show had to go on. A Company of 2/7 landed at 0900 without a hitch. Enemy fire began to diminish. By 1000 hours, all firing ceased, as Colonel An withdrew his assault forces. "The firing stopped as quickly as it started," recalled Sergeant John Setelin of Charlie Company. "The enemy dead were stacked up two to three deep in front of us. In the lulls we would kick and shovel dirt up on them to keep the stink and the flies down."[27]

Moore and his company commanders began to reorganize the defenses. The American commander was looking forward to the arrival of the entire 2nd Battalion of the 5th Cavalry, under Lieutenant Colonel Robert Tully. At 0800, Colonel Brown ordered Tully to march into the fight from an LZ about two miles away. Around that time, Moore decided to take Edwards's very battered C Company off the line and put it, or what was left of it, in reserve. After a busy morning of combat, C Company had sustained a total of 102 casualties, including 42 killed in action. It entered the battle with a 153 men.

Tully's 2/5 arrived at X-Ray unscathed around noon. Now there was one fresh battalion and five very weary companies of Americans holding down the fort. The beleaguered troopers of Moore's 1/7 could breathe a bit easier—those, that is, that could still breathe at all. At 1315, Moore attempted for the third time to rescue the lost platoon. Tully led the attack with two of his own companies, as well as Herren's B Company from Moore's battalion, which knew the terrain all too well by this point. It was a textbook infantry assault, with two companies abreast up front, and one behind in reserve. John Herren's Bravo Company was in the front on the left. He described the assault: "We had no contact en route. We put in a very good helicopter rocket strike between us and the cut-off platoon. Shortly thereafter I saw two North Vietnamese running to the right through the woods about three hundred yards away, getting out of the area. Once we got to the platoon we got some sniper fire from the Chu Pong Hill mass on the southwest."[28]

The lead elements of the assault reached the cut-off platoon around 1520. The survivors didn't stand up at first. They stayed in the shallow holes they had dug soon after being cut off. They appeared to be in a collective state of shock. As Lieutenant Dennis Deal was helping the survivors to their feet, he noticed a badly shot-up North Vietnamese soldier propped up against a tree and clearly on the verge of dying. But he continued to try to pull a grenade from his pouch. Recalled Deal, "I was very impressed by that total dedication. . . . He tried, until he finally died, to get that grenade out of his pouch, and we stood there and watched him. He couldn't lift it more than a couple of inches and then it would fall back and he would start trying all over again."[29]

The entire lost platoon slowly made their way back to the American perimeter, along with its rescuers. The dead and the seriously wounded were carried on makeshift litters. Specialist Galen Bungum, one of the cut-off platoon soldiers, stumbled down a hill on the way to X-Ray, only to end up at the base of the hill, looking right into the face of a dead enemy soldier whose eyes were open, staring lifelessly skyward.

While the rescue force was advancing, Moore ordered his other companies to send out patrols to police the battlefield. Moore himself accompanied C Company's policing action. He described the scene in the battalion's after-action report:

> *Dead PAVN, PAVN body fragments and PAVN weapons and equipment were littered in profusion around the edge and forward of the perimeter. Numerous body fragments were seen. There was massive evidence, blood trails, bandages, etc., of many other PAVN being dragged away from the area. Some of the enemy dead were found stacked behind anthills. We found some of his dead with ropes tied around their ankles, and a short, running end free. I saw two of our dead with similar ropes around their ankles. Possibly they had been captured alive and were being dragged off when killed. We found some of our dead's wallets and dog tags on dead PAVN. . . . Two prisoners were taken and evacuated.*[30]

At 1600 on the second day of the battle, Moore and his men enjoyed the sight of eighteen B-52s unleashing their earth-shattering ordnance on the eastern slopes of the Chu Pong. By November 22, B-52 strikes had deposited about five thousand tons of bombs on suspected enemy positions in the Ia Drang

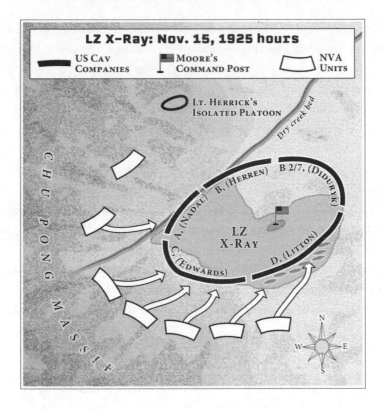

Valley. If the Vietnamese know how many men these strikes killed, they have yet to say.

The night of November 16 was largely uneventful at X-Ray, beyond the steady pounding of American harassment and interdiction artillery fire on suspected enemy assembly points.

November 16—The Third Day of the Battle

The morning of November 16 was another matter. Colonel An remained determined to seize the American-held clearing at the base of the Chu Pong, despite having sustained casualties no Western military commander could have taken without being relieved. At 0422, before the first signs of light, An sent the 7th

Battalion of the 66th Regiment against the southern sector of the American line. Captain Myron Diduryk's D Company bore the brunt of the attack. He recalled that his "left and center platoons were under heavy attack. . . . You could see the bastards come in waves, human waves. We greeted them with a wall of steel."[31] When flares from a C-130 illuminated the battlefield, the enemy would seek cover in the elephant grass, or behind anthills. When the flares burned out, small groups of NVA would rise and charge the lines. Some enemy troops got within five or ten yards of Diduryk's men, but they were all killed with small arms and grenades.

The NVA assault withered. A few minutes later, Diduryk's men turned back another attempt. At 0503, and again at 0630, the enemy attempted to break through Diduryk's B Company. These were considerably less powerful than the first two assaults, and the NVA were beaten back relatively easily. Specialist Pat Selleck remembered the last attack of the morning. "I heard bugles blowing. I saw in the light of the flares waves of the enemy coming down at us off the

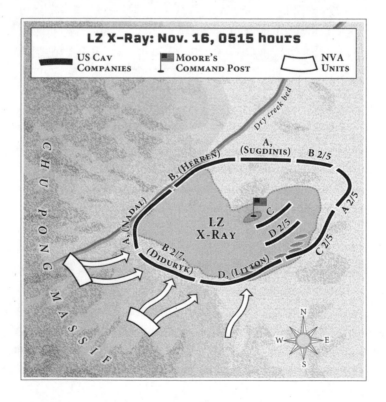

LZ X-Ray: Nov. 16, 0515 hours

mountain in a straight line. . . . They just kept coming down like they didn't care. The line company was shooting them like ducks in a pond."[32]

Diduryk's performance during the morning hours of the sixteenth had been something to behold as he moved men up and down the line, offering guidance and encouragement, and rearranging his defenses. After the battle, Colonel Moore described "the mad Cossack"—Diduryk was born in Ukraine—as the best company commander he'd ever seen in combat in two wars.

At 0655, Moore ordered his men to rise and spray rifle fire into the woods for two minutes straight. In the northeast sector, six PAVN snipers were wounded or killed by this fire. This provoked a charge on the Americans by perhaps forty PAVN, but it was easily turned back. Colonel An had at long last had enough. Those PAVN still in the vicinity of X-Ray were ordered to withdraw back toward the mountain.

The fight at X-Ray, the costliest single engagement for both sides thus far in America's Vietnam War, was over. It was time for mopping up. The Americans had suffered 79 men killed in action and 121 wounded. The NVA body count was 634, but the brigade claimed another 1,215 killed on top of that number—most of them by air strikes of one sort or another. Colonel Moore had every reason to be proud of his men, and of himself. They had prevailed against a much larger infantry force, thanks to Moore's impeccable tactical decision-making under the very worst conditions, to the fighting skill and tenacity of his troopers, and of course, to American airpower. Just before noon, Moore began to withdraw his weary but elated battalion to Camp Holloway. Colonels McDade and Tully would stay the night and depart the following morning.

November 17—LZ Albany

After an uneventful night, Bob Tully's 2/5 marched out of X-Ray for LZ Columbus, three miles to the northeast, at 0900. The battalion arrived in time for a well-deserved hot lunch. A different fate awaited Bob McDade's 2/7. Its destination was LZ Albany, about three miles to the northwest of X-Ray, which was unoccupied by American troops. McDade was an inexperienced battalion commander. He unwisely demurred when he was offered the protection of a rolling artillery barrage as he made his way toward the destination. McDade was afraid the artillery cover would alert the enemy to his presence. Nor did his battalion march toward its objective in tactical formation.

All was well until the battalion was within a few hundred yards of the LZ. There, McDade's recon platoon in the vanguard of the column captured two PAVN deserters. The colonel halted the column in place so that he and his command group could go up to the front and interrogate the prisoners. Many of the soldiers in 2/7, which approached the LZ along a southeast-northwest axis, sat down and went to sleep or began to smoke. They were stretched out over some five hundred yards.

At 1315, just before the first company entered the clearing, the entire 8th Battalion of the 66th PAVN Regiment triggered a perfectly executed L-shaped ambush. Their commander, Lieutenant Colonel Le Xuan Phoi, had been expecting the Americans to arrive at the clearing. First, fire poured out from the base of the "L"—behind the LZ, in the tree line. Then, within a minute or two, mortar rounds began exploding along the length of the column, spraying shrapnel everywhere. PAVN infantry came charging out of the jungle just to the right side of the column, firing their weapons. Scores of American troopers fell dead and wounded within seconds. The North Vietnamese infantry, about three hundred men in all, cut through the column like a scythe in a wheat field. "Within moments," writes an official US Army historian, "platoons and companies ceased to exist as fighting units, and the encounter disintegrated into a frenzied hand-to-hand melee."[33]

The battalion surgeon, Captain William Shucart, was wondering why he smelled Vietnamese cigarettes when the ambush exploded. "Mortars were dropping all around us, then a lot of small-arms fire . . . and then everything just dissolved into confusion."[34] Colonel McDade was pinned down near the head of the column. He could communicate with Colonel Brown, the brigade commander, but he couldn't make any contact at all with his company commanders, as they were in the process of trying to rejoin units that no longer existed. It was complete bedlam. Jack Smith, who later became a correspondent with ABC television, was a member of Charlie Company, which was in the middle of the column. He remembered that "we were being fired at by our own guys. . . . Some were in shock and were blazing away at everything they saw, or imagined that they saw."[35]

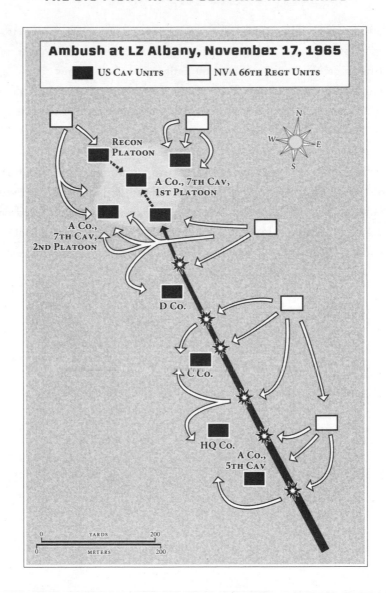

After ten minutes of horrific carnage, the American troopers managed to establish two defensive perimeters, one near the front of the column and one near the back. Between 1345 and 1415, troopers within these perimeters began to pick off PAVN infantry who were walking around cavalierly in the middle of the column, shooting wounded and dying Americans. Around 1415, A-1E

Skyraiders arrived on scene and dropped napalm on about 150 PAVN troops who were forming up to charge the perimeter near the front of the column. At least two dozen NVA tried to run as the ordnance drifted downward, but most were engulfed by fire and killed. There was no time to try to rescue the American soldiers in the middle of the column who still lived. The entire area outside the two perimeters was declared a free-fire zone, and for the next two hours artillery and air support pummeled the battlefield, preventing the enemy from mounting additional assaults. Isolated, small-scale firefights continued until about 1800. Reinforcements in the form of Captain Diduryk's B Company, 2/7, arrived at 1830 and began to help sort out defenses and collect the wounded and dead. Other units arrived early in the morning, but the fighting was over. McDade's battalion had been destroyed. One hundred and fifty-five American soldiers had been killed. Another 121 had been wounded.

PART III

LOOKING BACK

CHAPTER 11
AFTERMATH

Casualties in Operation Silver Bayonet were staggeringly high, by Vietnam War standards. American losses were 304 dead and 524 wounded. US Army figures have it that 3,561 PAVN were killed and 157 captured. A more realistic figure, factoring in the American penchant for casualty inflation, would be 2,000 dead. Half the American dead fell at LZ Albany over the course of a few hours on the bright, sunny afternoon of November 17.

General Westmoreland saw the entire campaign, particularly the fight at X-Ray, as an unambiguous vindication of his attrition strategy, in which American firepower would grind down communist forces until they reached that crucial "crossover point," when Hanoi could no longer afford to replace its losses on the battlefield. Once that point had been reached, he believed, the politburo would see sense and begin negotiations on favorable terms to the Americans and the South Vietnamese. "We'll just go on bleeding them dry until Hanoi wakes up to the fact that they have bled their country to the point of national disaster for generations," said America's senior field commander in late 1967, *still* under the spell of a spectacularly costly misconception.[1]

While the Battle of Ia Drang had vindicated airmobile warfare in a limited, tactical sense—Moore and the Cav had forced the enemy to withdraw from the battlefield—the fighting there did not foil Hanoi's plan to cut South Vietnam in half, as General Kinnard, and many military historians, would argue for decades afterward. We now know that had never been General Man's intention. What's more, the frenetic pace of operations in Pleiku Province placed enormous strains on the 1st Cav's logistical system. In fact, the division required extraordinary help from the air force just to keep *one* of the division's three brigades fighting in high-intensity combat.

Whatever else might be said, killing enemy forces with airmobile assaults was both a very risky and expensive business. The fight at X-Ray had been a very near thing. At several junctures during the first two days of combat, Moore's four-hundred-man battalion might well have been overrun and annihilated. Had the weather been poor enough to constrict air support, such an outcome seems far more likely than not. It is fair to say, too, that the battalion probably would have been overrun even *with* good air support if it had been led by an officer without the extraordinary tactical acumen and coolheadedness of Hal Moore. Colonel Moore made a series of split-second decisions that proved to be right, despite limited information in a highly chaotic situation. And he was clearly a steadying, reassuring force to his men during their extreme trial under fire.

Colonel An, the commander of PAVN forces engaged in the Ia Drang fight, joined his superiors in thinking the PAVN had gotten the better of the Americans in the fighting. "I have seldom attended a battlefield meeting that was so happy and lively" as the gathering of the B3 Front right after the Battle of Ia Drang, wrote the colonel. "Everybody, friends and strangers alike, shook hands to congratulate each other on the victory."[2] Still, he gave the Americans credit. Fighting them was not easy, "as some of our people have claimed. Their firepower was devastating. They had so many aircraft, so many bombs, so much artillery. They were practical people who learned quickly from their experiences, and had game-changing technology. . . . They were clever and ingenious, sometimes capable of completely overturning an unfavorable tactical situation."[3]

Why, though, did the Vietnamese view the campaign as a victory? First, they viewed the fighting through the lens of protracted warfare strategy, not by Western military standards. The B3 Front's forces had fought with great determination and skill against an enemy with far more powerful weapons than their own, and they had inflicted heavy casualties on the Americans. Indeed, they had destroyed an elite American battalion at LZ Albany.

Despite communist propaganda to the contrary, Hanoi's senior leadership never expected its regular forces to defeat American units in set-piece battles in the traditional Western sense of that term. The most plentiful weapon the North Vietnamese had was people, and they were expendable. The regiments that had fought in the Pleiku campaign could be rebuilt and refurbished, and indeed, they were. In light of the Ia Drang fight, Le Duan and the other chief strategists felt reassured that their forces could inflict enough casualties on the Americans to break the will of Washington and the American people to carry on the fight. And that reassurance was indeed a victory of a sort. They had learned a great deal about fighting the Americans during the Pleiku campaign. They hoped to put that knowledge to good use in the future.

The British historian J. P. Harris raises an uncomfortable question that throws a bit of cold water on the idea that Ia Drang was an unequivocal victory for the Americans. Why, he asks, didn't the 1st Cav continue to pursue the enemy after Albany? It would seem to have been the right move in terms of Westmoreland's strategy. It's unclear who called off the fighting, but the records show no indication that anyone in the senior American command even proposed carrying on the fight against General Man's B3 forces. As Harris observes:

> *That the Americans failed to storm the Chu Pong at this stage may be indicative of how much they were shaken—even shocked—by the fury of the PAVN response to their initial probe. It gives a modicum of credence to the Vietnamese Communists' claim that they had won a kind of victory. . . . When the North Vietnamese assaults finally ceased, the Americans merely heaved a collective sigh of relief and withdrew from the battlefield—exactly the sort of seemingly passive response for which they had so often criticized the ARVN.*[4]

Reservations About American Strategy

Although the president and the JCS had formally approved Westmoreland's attrition strategy in late July 1965, a number of important constituencies continued to hold serious reservations about its efficacy throughout the first year of the American war. Maxwell Taylor, Brute Krulak, and Lew Walt continued to favor an enclave, or oil spot, strategy, emphasizing pacification. General Walt was given some latitude as to how to use his own forces in I Corps, but nonetheless, Westmoreland pressed Walt to step up the number of search-and-destroy operations in I Corps at the expense of pacification efforts, both before and after the Battle of Ia Drang Valley, and to complain about the marines' reluctance to do so. As Westmoreland wrote to his superiors on December 8, 1965: "The Marines have become so infatuated with securing real estate and in civic action that their forces have become dispersed and they have been hesitant to conduct offensive operations except along the coastline where amphibious maneuvers could be used with Naval gunfire support which is available. Over the last several months, this matter has been discussed with General Walt and I have written two letters to him emphasizing the importance of having adequate reserves to take the fight to the enemy."[5]

Among the most prominent "on the ground" critics of the declared American strategy for the war in late 1965 was John Paul Vann. The retired army lieutenant colonel, for whom Vietnam had become an all-consuming passion, saw the communist insurgency as a symptom of the leadership crisis in South Vietnam, not its cause. In the summer of 1965, Vann lobbied Ambassador Lodge to hire him to supervise the pacification effort in the South. To that end, he produced in September 1965 a paper titled "Harnessing the Revolution in South Vietnam." He shared the paper with Lodge and Bill Bundy, among others, in which he argued that the government in Saigon was little more than a continuation of the repressive French colonial system with a cadre of venal South Vietnamese generals at the helm. The regime's repressive policies had driven all, or virtually all, of the countries' non-communist progressives into the arms of the NLF, and made it impossible for pacification to gain traction.

Vann pulled no punches. The generals and politicians in Saigon were incapable of pulling themselves together and forming a functional government of any kind, let alone a pro-democratic state. Vann advocated that the United States put aside its worries about appearing to be a colonial power and take charge. It needed to restructure the South Vietnamese government, and train a new class of young indigenous political leaders. The United States needed to cease and desist in its highly destructive search-and-destroy operations. As Vann famously said on another occasion, "This is a political war and it calls for discrimination in killing. The best weapon for killing would be a knife, but I'm afraid we can't do it that way. The worst is an airplane. The next worst is artillery. Barring a knife, the best is a rifle—you know who you are killing."[6]

Vann's proposal was seen as too radical by the higher-ups in Saigon and Washington. It died the old-fashioned bureaucratic way—by being ignored. Meanwhile, the US Army's chief of staff, Harold K. Johnson, certainly had abiding doubts about Westmoreland's ability to wrap his mind fully around the complexities of the battlefield in Vietnam. So doubtful was Johnson, a hero of the Pacific War, that he commissioned in the summer of 1965 a team of army strategists and civilian academics to look at alternative approaches. The study, *A Program for the Pacification and Long-Term Development of South Vietnam* (*PROVN*), wasn't published until March 1966, and then only shared with a very small number of key military and political players, but it expressed strong reservations about the trajectory of the war thus far, and about Westmoreland's governing strategy:

> *The situation in South Vietnam (SVN) has seriously deteriorated. 1966 may well be the last chance to ensure eventual success. "Victory" can only be achieved through bringing the individual Vietnamese, typically a rural peasant, to support willingly the Government of South Vietnam (GVN). The critical actions are those that occur at the village, district and province levels. This is where the war must be fought; this is where that war and the object which lies beyond it [an independent, democratic South Vietnam] must be won. . . . [Next to pacification] all other military aspects of the war are secondary.*[7]

General Westmoreland found the *PROVN* study unconvincing, to say the least, and proceeded to banish it into obscurity by calling for "further study" by his staff. In the months and years to follow, MACV's commander consistently resisted any plan that required the US Army to take on substantial pacification duties. As General John Tillson, one of Westmoreland's senior operations officers, confessed years after the war, "We never did pay attention to the COIN [counterinsurgency] area. My predecessor, Major General Bill DePuy, never hesitated about heavy artillery preparation. He never thought about COIN—he was fighting nothing but a conventional war."[8]

Plenty of officers who had served in Vietnam sensed there was something wrong with the American strategy by the time of the big fight in the Central Highlands. When General Johnson consulted a group of officers of the 1st Division about current strategy in the fall of 1965, he quickly learned the consensus view was, as one colonel put it, "We just didn't think we could do the job the way we were doing it."[9] The junior officers told Johnson flat out that, for the most part, the enemy avoided making contact when the Americans launched big-unit search-and-destroy missions. Constant, intensive, small-unit patrolling was the answer, and it would take a lot of time.

Andrew Krepinevich, a prominent military analyst and former army officer, believes that Westmoreland's approach to Vietnam "was a faithful representation of the Army's attitude on counterinsurgency warfare: give lip service to the classical doctrine [on counterinsurgency] while focusing primary attention on standard operations."[10] He makes a persuasive case for his conclusion. MACV was willing to cede to the ARVN and the Regional and Popular Forces the burden of breaking the stranglehold of the NLF political infrastructure on the villages. Westmoreland would use the US Army to fight the kind of war it had been trained to fight rather than the war it found itself fighting.

The crossover point had always been a flabby, deeply flawed concept. It failed to take account of several pivotal variables, such as the enemy's ability to limit his own casualties by avoiding battle, the limits on American combat operations imposed by Washington, and North Vietnam's demographics at the time. Johnson prohibited American forces from attacking communist formations in Laotian and Cambodian sanctuaries. He ruled out a ground invasion of North Vietnam. Over two hundred thousand North Vietnamese men came of military age each year. Hanoi was willing to take casualties on a scale no Western democracy could sustain in individual battles, but it could also control its rate of losses simply by avoiding big-unit combat, and it did so at various junctures throughout the remainder of the war.

Under these strictures, no army on earth, not even the US Army, was going to bleed the communist forces dry. General Westmoreland also made the optimistic but wrong assumption that there would be many, many multi-battalion clashes between the regular forces of each side after Ia Drang, in which his troops would kill large numbers of enemy troops. It didn't work out that way. Individual battles where the Americans inflicted more than a couple of hundred casualties on communist forces were relatively rare events for the remainder of the American war. The vast majority of small-unit patrols by platoons and companies never made any contact with the enemy. The communist forces in Vietnam could be hard to find. Therefore, they were hard to kill in large numbers.

Over the course of 1965, American troop strength in Vietnam increased from 23,000 to 185,000. In 1964, 147 American soldiers had been killed in Vietnam; in 1965, the figure spiked to 1,369. A cluster of American counterinsurgency and nation-building programs were well underway at the time of the Battle of the Ia Drang, and more were on the drawing board. While General Westmoreland stuck by his strategy at year's end, he knew he had underestimated the strength and tenacity of the enemy, and the difficulty of the job that lay ahead. On November 23, he said he would need considerably more than the additional 100,000 troops the president had approved for phase two of his plan, the 1966 offensive. He wanted an additional 154,000 before the end of 1966. A few days later, the commanding general reported to Washington that even *that* estimate was insufficient. He now estimated he would need a total of 200,000 additional troops in 1966. "It was a drastic step-up, shattering at one blow the scale and force planning that had entered into the President's final decision of July [1965]," remembered Bill Bundy, who was directly involved in the discussions.[11]

The most shocking thing about Westmoreland's strategy for fighting the war was not that it was wrongheaded at the outset, but that neither he nor his superiors in Washington made a serious attempt to revise their approach to the conflict as evidence mounted in 1966 and 1967 that America was losing the war.

The War After 1965

"The incredible thing about Vietnam," quipped the West's leading authority on the war a few weeks after the Battle of Ia Drang Valley, "is that the worst is yet to come."[12] Bernard Fall, the man who first described 1965 as the "Year of the Hawks," was certainly right about that. Nothing much went well for the United States in Vietnam in the years to come, and a great deal went very badly. Fall's brilliant effort to explain the complexities and ambiguities of the Vietnam War to the world came to an abrupt end when he stepped on a "bouncing betty" land mine near Hue, the old imperial capital of Vietnam, on February 21, 1967. At the time, he was accompanying a patrol of US Marines along Highway 1, a road his French countrymen had christened "the street without joy" in the bad old days of the First Indochina War, where it was the scene of countless Vietminh attacks and ambushes on French columns. In one of the war's innumerable ironies, Fall's best-known book about Vietnam at the time was called *Street Without Joy*.

One of the marines who had been in Vietnam at the very beginning of the American war was also there at the very end, albeit in a quite different capacity. "We had marched into Vietnam swaggering, confident, and full of idealism. We believed we were there for a high moral purpose," recalled platoon leader Philip Caputo years after the war.[13] In spring 1975, Caputo found himself back in Vietnam as a war correspondent, covering the final communist drive on Saigon. By that point, Caputo's idealism had faded considerably, and he was no longer swaggering. Nor, it could well be said, were his fellow Americans, and much of the reason was the failed crusade in Vietnam.

In March 1968, a much-disillusioned Lyndon Johnson and a coterie of bipartisan foreign policy "wise men" had come to the realization that, despite its unmatched military power, the United States could not prevail in Vietnam through force of arms. That dramatic conclusion had been prompted by one extraordinarily bold and bloody military operation. Hanoi's January–February 1968 Tet Offensive—named after Vietnam's great New Year holiday—had cost the insurgent forces of the National Liberation Front horrendous casualties. Almost half of the eighty-four thousand troops in the assault forces had been killed, and all the ground they had managed to take had been recaptured within a mere month by the Americans and South Vietnamese.

Yet the very fact that the Vietcong, ably supported by elements of the People's Army of Vietnam, had been able to mount so many simultaneous attacks— all major cities, most provincial capitals, and many military installations had been assaulted pretty much at once—put the lie to General Westmoreland's claims in November 1967 that "the enemy was on the ropes," on the verge of defeat. By that point, the war, and all the bitterness and confusion and shock that came with its strange twists and turns, had polarized American society as no event had since the Civil War a hundred years earlier. Indeed, the country

seemed on the verge of a kind of collective nervous breakdown. There was riot-
ing in many cities, and violence marred many antiwar demonstrations. President
Johnson could no longer appear in public without creating a potentially violent
disturbance. The Secret Service feared for his safety. The war had destroyed his
presidency. In the wake of Tet, Lyndon Johnson declined to run for reelection.

Johnson's successor, Richard M. Nixon, claimed to have a secret plan to bring
peace to Vietnam. He was dissembling, just as Johnson had done when he secretly
committed the United States to a major ground war in 1965. Nixon expanded
the conflict into neighboring Laos and Cambodia and unleashed a massively destructive bombing campaign over the North in a futile effort to soften Hanoi's
bargaining position at the peace talks in Paris. By the time the warring parties put
their signatures to the "Agreement on Ending the War and Restoring the Peace
in Vietnam" on January 27, 1973, more than fifty-eight thousand Americans and
3 million Vietnamese had lost their lives. Much of South Vietnam had been reduced to a wasteland by American bombing and chemical defoliants.

The "peace agreement" of January 1973 led to the withdrawal of all remaining American combat forces from Vietnam within a couple of months, and established a cease-fire between the Vietnamese combatants. Nixon proclaimed
the agreement brought "peace with honor" to the United States. This was largely
self-serving rhetoric, for the peace agreement brought neither peace nor honor.
It was little more than a well-choreographed piece of diplomatic fiction to ensure
a "decent interval" between the withdrawal of the United States and the fall of
South Vietnam. Heavy combat erupted within a matter of hours after the cease-
fire went into effect. What the accords *did* signal was the beginning of the final
phase of the communists' thirty-year struggle to unify all of Vietnam under their
rule. Even with billions of dollars of military and economic aid from the Americans, the hapless South Vietnamese army was no match for the twenty-plus divisions of PAVN troops Hanoi had deployed in its Ho Chi Minh campaign to
conquer the South in early 1975. "The North Vietnamese simply rolled over the
countryside, driving on Saigon," wrote Phil Caputo. "Except for a brief, hopeless
stand made by a single division at the provincial capital of Xuan Loc, the ARVN
offered no significant resistance. The South Vietnamese Army broke into pieces.
It dissolved."[14] So ended the most divisive event in twentieth-century American
history—the nation's first lost war.

CHAPTER 12

REFLECTIONS

"The first, the supreme, the most far-reaching act of judgment that the statesman and commander have to make," famously wrote the great philosopher of war, Carl von Clausewitz, "is to establish . . . the kind of war on which they are embarking; neither mistaking it for, nor trying to turn it into, something that is alien to its nature."[1] From the vantage point of more than fifty years, it's difficult to quarrel with the idea that Lyndon Johnson and the war council gravely misjudged "the kind of war on which they were embarking." When all is said and done, it seems no one on the war council, least of all the president, was able to grasp that the crisis in Vietnam was not *fundamentally* a part of an international communist conspiracy against the West, driven by the machinations of Beijing and Moscow. Rather, it was a complicated, civil conflict between the Vietnamese, in which communist-led revolutionaries with impeccable nationalist credentials were locked in conflict against a Saigon regime with pitifully weak ones. And those credentials were made weaker still by the impending infusion of US military forces and the inevitable takeover of management of the war by Washington from Saigon.

"The perception of Vietnam itself in Washington," astutely observes the British journalist Godfrey Hodgson, "was bizarrely unreal."[2] The war council consistently viewed the conflict through the distorting lens of the Cold War rather than through the prism of Vietnamese history and politics. In the collective understanding of official Washington, Vietnam was not really a place with its own history and unique national characteristics. Rather, it was a remote part of the developing world whose importance rested on the fact that monolithic world communism happened to be on the march there. The Johnson administration, in short, was largely blind to the political as well as the military dynamics of the struggle in Indochina. Little wonder America's war effort was destined to come to grief. "It is depressing," writes Hodgson, to read the documentary record of the American escalation "and see how the written arguments of men with reputations for clarity and intelligence—Robert McNamara, John McNaughton, the Bundy brothers—were dominated by cliché, fixed ideas, unexamined assumptions and a persistent tendency to argue from predetermined conclusions." The only way for the withdrawal option to have gotten a fair hearing, Hodgson believes, as I do, was for the Johnson administration to have lifted the veil of secrecy over the proceedings and conducted a thorough debate in the press and in Congress. But "public debate was the last thing on the president's mind."[3]

Many historians of the war have argued that the "cold war consensus" in domestic politics pushed Johnson and the war council inexorably toward major war, leaving them, in effect, no other viable choice. According to this argument, both major political parties, the elite foreign policy establishment, and the public at large had accepted responsibility for challenging the expansion of communism in Europe by 1947. By the mid-1960s, China had replaced the Soviet Union as the engine of communist revolution, and Vietnam had become the crucial battleground. If the Johnson administration failed to meet the challenge in Indochina, according to this viewpoint, it would face even more difficult challenges elsewhere in Asia, Africa, and Latin America. The balance of forces between the Free World and the communists would shift markedly in the wrong direction. And the Democrats would have taken a pasting in the midterm elections in 1966 for being soft on communism. Therefore, sadly, Johnson had no other live option but to stand firm in Southeast Asia.

The Harvard historian Fredrik Logevall has pretty much demolished this line of argument in his masterful book about American decision-making in the early- and mid-1960s, *Choosing War*. Too many influential people and institutions had put forward compelling arguments for moving along a political track toward disengagement for the Johnson administration to have been "locked in" to pressing ahead with war, he contends, especially since Johnson had been given a broad mandate with his spectacular success in the November 1964 election. The "cold war consensus" was in the process of breaking down as the Johnson administration tried to come to grips with the crisis in Vietnam. Thus, during the crucial decision-making period, Johnson had two viable options: take over the war or disengage. He chose the former, when each and every day, the argument for choosing the latter became more compelling.

One of the most striking things about the Johnson administration's policy-making process regarding Vietnam during 1964 and early 1965 is the reluctance of the leading participants to entertain seriously the option of a political solution to the crisis.[4] The negotiated withdrawal option was repeatedly brought up in high-level policy meetings, only to be dismissed cursorily by the war council as a dead end. It was touched on by Bill Bundy's working group in their work in November 1964, but never given a thorough airing. George Ball raised the option in many meetings during 1964 and early '65, and wrote several forceful memoranda in favor of the negotiated settlement-withdrawal track. Yet as Ball then recognized, and as McNamara later admitted, the other senior advisers listened to his arguments but never really took them to heart. Ball was seen as the dutiful public servant, putting forward the "devil's advocate" position so others could play off against it.

And then there was the interesting case of Johnson's vice president, Hubert Horatio Humphrey of Minnesota. He was deeply troubled by the administration's slow slide toward war. In a memo to the president dated February 17, 1965, he argued that the United States should go in the other direction before it was too late: "1965 is the year of minimum political risk for the Johnson administration. Indeed it is the first year when we can face the Vietnam problem without being preoccupied with the political repercussions from the Republican right. . . . [By escalating the war we] risk creating the impression that we are prisoners of events in Vietnam. This blurs the Administration's leadership role and has spillover effects across the board. It also helps erode confidence and credibility in our policies. . . ."[5] Johnson was so angry with the vice president's dissent from the White House line that he banished him from high-level decision-making about Vietnam for a year, and pressed forward with an aggressive campaign to convince the political solution advocates that their thinking was wrongheaded.

As Logevall points out, South Vietnam's failure to pull together and mount effective resistance against the insurgency after ten years of advice and support gave the United States a very compelling rationale for extricating itself from Vietnam. Saigon's ability to carry on the fight with energy and determination had long been a prerequisite of American support. By late 1964, as we have seen,

Saigon was not only losing the war; it lacked a functional government and a motivated army. As leading Democratic senators and American allies in London and elsewhere were at pains to explain to the administration, a withdrawal from Indochina under these circumstances was highly unlikely to have a *substantial* impact on American credibility. Vietnam was already a lost cause and had never been of more than marginal relevance to Western security interests. Cutting American losses at this time made good sense.

The war council failed to see that. It failed, concludes Logevall, "not because of any tangible foreign-policy concerns or moral attachment to the South Vietnamese, but because of the threat of embarrassment—to the United States, the Democratic Party, and, most of all, to themselves personally. They were willing to sacrifice virtually everything to avoid the stigma of failure. If the morality of a policy is determined in large part by the commensurateness of means to ends, that of the Johnson administration in Vietnam must be judged immoral."[6]

In other words, Lyndon Johnson went to war because he was more afraid of the personal and political consequences of admitting that the United States had been betting on the wrong horse than he was of starting a major land war in Southeast Asia. This, to be sure, is a harsh judgment. It is also a fair one.

The Long Shadow of the War

Vietnam shook the United States to its foundations, exacerbating already deep cleavages in American society between liberals and conservatives, young and old, Black and white. It left the country baffled and ambivalent about its role in the world as defender of democratic institutions and ideas, and widened the credibility gap between the government and the people. It's hard to disagree with historian James Patterson's assertion that "[n]othing did more than the conflict in Vietnam to alter the course of post–World War II society and politics, or unleash the emotions that polarized the nation after 1965."[7] One of the crucial lessons of the war, historians now widely agree, is that it is beyond the capability of the United States to remake other nations in its own image, and morally wrong to try. To use American power to alter fundamentally the politics and history of a nation like Vietnam, about which senior American policy makers were profoundly ignorant, was to invite disaster, and disaster is what befell them.

Chastened by the searing experience of Indochina, American presidents refrained from committing the country to ambitious foreign adventures in the last quarter of the twentieth century, for the most part. Sadly, in the emotionally supercharged wake of the September 11, 2001, terrorist attacks on the Twin Towers and the Pentagon, Washington forgot this hard-won lesson, and tried to create pro-Western states in both Afghanistan and Iraq, countries US policy makers knew even less about than their predecessors knew about Vietnam. Those wars have not had as dramatic an impact on American society as Vietnam, but they, too, were failed crusades, and for many of the same reasons that obtained in Indochina.

The saddest thing about the American war in Vietnam is that it need never have happened. Indeed, it *would not* have happened if the president of the United States, Lyndon Baines Johnson, had been able to shake himself free of a single misconceived belief: that extricating the United States from Vietnam via a political settlement was tantamount to surrender and would lead ineluctably to a rolling barrage of setbacks in the Cold War, to political disaster for the Democratic Party, and to crushing personal humiliation. After leaving office, Johnson told one of his biographers that

> I knew that if we let Communist aggression succeed in taking over South Vietnam, there would follow in this country an endless national debate—a mean and destructive debate— that would shatter my presidency, kill my administration and damage our democracy. I knew that Harry Truman and Dean Acheson had lost their effectiveness from the day the Communists took over China. I believed that the loss of China had played a large role in the rise of Joe McCarthy. And I knew that all these problems, taken together, were chicken shit compared with what might happen if we lost Vietnam.
>
> For this time there would be Robert Kennedy out in front leading the fight against me, telling everyone that I'd betrayed John Kennedy's commitment to South Vietnam. That I was

*a coward. An unmanly man. A man without a spine. . . . In
the distance I could hear the voices of thousands of people. They
were all shouting and running toward me: "Coward! Traitor!
Weakling!"*[8]

President Johnson stuck to his guns even when his own intelligence
agencies, the leaders of the Senate Foreign Relations Committee, a cadre of
counterinsurgency gurus, and America's leading European allies told him that
the war was a political conflict that could not be won by force of arms, particularly
the arms of a Western, foreign army. Instead of weighing seriously the views of
leading members of his own party, and a welter of foreign policy experts who
argued that Johnson had ample political capital to negotiate an end to the war
without seriously damaging American credibility or his own reputation, he railed
against his critics, and punished people like Hubert Humphrey and William
Fulbright who refused "to get on the team."

When George Kennan, the father of the communist containment policy
Johnson so fervently believed in and believed he was implementing, told the
nation in January 1966 that "there is more to be won in the opinion of this
world by a resolute and courageous liquidation of unsound positions than by the
most stubborn pursuit of extravagant or unpromising objectives," Johnson was
unmoved.[9] He persisted in the "stubborn pursuit of . . . unpromising objectives."
When the CIA, Mike Mansfield, Richard Russell, and William Fulbright coun-
seled withdrawal, the president of the United States dismissed their advice out of
hand. When Charles de Gaulle predicted that if the United States went to war
in Vietnam in 1965, it would stumble into a quagmire for a decade that would
completely dishonor the United States, Johnson reminded himself how much he
loathed the imperious French general.

But the imperious French general was right in the end. Of course, Johnson
himself was aware that there was something fundamentally wrong about the
United States fighting in Vietnam. He told Senator Eugene McCarthy in
February 1966, "I know we oughtn't to be there, but I can't get out. I just can't be
the architect of surrender."[10]

Although success in the conflict in Vietnam ultimately hinged on the South
Vietnamese government's ability to gain the loyalty and respect of the people in

the villages, the American ground war was largely devoted to destroying regular communist battalions and regiments, not taking back the villages from the VC for the government. Westmoreland's way of war—the US Army's way of war—did inflict ghastly casualties on the forces of the revolution, but it also destroyed hundreds of villages and drove several million Vietnamese peasants from their ancestral homes to slums outside of Saigon, Danang, and other urban centers. Once the American war machine was in full gear, it began to shred the social fabric of the country it was supposed to be saving.

Since the 1970s, Westmoreland has often been singled out by historians and journalists as both largely responsible for, and a symbol of, American defeat. This seems rather unfair, now that almost half a century has passed since the war's end. The more we come to know about the conflict in Vietnam, the less likely it seems that *any* American general, or *any* particular military strategy, could have prevented the fall of South Vietnam to Hanoi.

Could the United States have waged a well-executed counterinsurgency strategy, given the American people's notorious impatience for concrete results when their troops are fighting and dying? Could the South Vietnamese political and military leaders have somehow escaped their fractiousness and dysfunction? No one knows the answer to either question for sure, and no one ever will. My best guess is the answer to both questions is "No."

The United States made many mistakes in fighting the war in Vietnam. But the mother of them all was deciding to fight with its own ground forces there in the first place. The dangers inherent in that decision, of course, were not lost on quite a few knowledgeable people both inside and outside the administration. Look, for instance, at this remarkably perceptive analysis of April 1965 by Harold P. Ford of the CIA, written just as the US Marines were granted permission to go on offensive operations against the Vietcong for the first time:

> *This troubled essay proceeds from a deep concern that we are becoming progressively divorced from reality in Vietnam, that we are proceeding with far more courage than wisdom—toward unknown ends. . . . There seems to be a congenital American disposition to underestimate Asian enemies. We are doing so now. We cannot afford so precious a luxury. Earlier, dispassionate*

estimates, war games, and the like, told us that [the communists
in Vietnam] would persist in the face of such pressures as we are
now exerting on them. Yet we now seem to expect them to come
running to the conference table, ready to talk. . . . The chances
are considerably better than ever that the United States will in
the end have to disengage from Vietnam, and do so considerably
short of our present objectives.[11]

Of course, neither American strategic blunders nor South Vietnam's deficiencies fully explain the war's astonishing outcome. Hanoi and the NLF emerged victorious in large measure because they instilled hope and commitment in millions of ordinary Vietnamese that the communist-led revolutionary movement was the best route to a united, independent Vietnam, free from domination by foreign powers. The feckless government of South Vietnam inspired few of its own people and even fewer outsiders; the NLF inspired millions, despite the harshly repressive nature of the regime that controlled it in the North. As we saw in chapter 5, Hanoi's strategists never imagined they could force an end to America's involvement through battlefield victories, despite the torrent of screeds that poured out of the communist camp during the war to the contrary. They could not match the Americans' military or economic power. But they believed, correctly, that they were more than a match for the Americans and their allies in the realms of political power, organizational skill, and commitment. Those elements proved far more effective than American military might in a civil conflict among a people who had suffered from a century of colonial exploitation.

In short, the communists in Vietnam possessed a much more coherent grasp of the political and social dimensions of the struggle than their adversaries in Saigon and Washington. It could well be said that the Americans were not so much outfought in Vietnam as outthought. The Americans' strategic assessments of the nature of the war, of their own strengths and weaknesses and those of their adversaries, were markedly inferior to those of Hanoi and the southern insurgency it directed.

The regular North Vietnamese and Vietcong forces may not have beaten the Americans in big-unit battles, but they performed with great courage and skill in tens of thousands of small-unit fights, and by no means did all those clashes result in American victories. Moreover, the people of the revolution as a whole—porters, construction workers, farmers, soldiers, political cadres, and Vietcong agents who worked on US and South Vietnamese army bases—were able to frustrate America's crucial military and political objectives without winning any big battles. By continuously expanding and improving the Ho Chi Minh Trail, and by deploying large numbers of troops in Cambodia and Laos, the North Vietnamese defeated the pivotal American effort to isolate the battlefield. Despite an ambitious and sustained air interdiction campaign by the US Navy and Air Force to cut the Trail, the numbers of troops and tonnage of supplies brought into the South increased virtually every month between 1965 and 1968.

The audacious Tet Offensive of January 31, 1968, in which every major city, town, and many key military installations in South Vietnam came under simultaneous communist attack, was something of a tactical disaster for Hanoi and the NLF. The communists were driven off most of their objectives within a week, and all the rest within a month. But the Tet's *crucial* objective wasn't to gain and hold territory. Rather, it was to inflict a devastating blow on the American public and its government by exposing the bankruptcy of America's strategy. It succeeded.

After Tet, Lyndon Johnson came to a painful and dramatic conclusion. There could be no military victory for the United States in Vietnam. The fighting needed to be gradually turned over to the South Vietnamese. Recognizing that the war had demolished his personal effectiveness as a leader—precisely the result he had feared if he had negotiated a settlement at the beginning of the conflict in 1965—Johnson decided he would not run for reelection. He could not lead effectively, and he knew it. And he knew it was because of Vietnam.

For the United States, Tet "was a long-postponed confrontation with reality," writes the historian Gabriel Kolko. "It had been hypnotized until then by its own illusions, desires, and needs. The belated realization that it had military tactics and technology but no viable military strategy consistent with its domestic and international priorities made Tet the turning point in the [Johnson] administration's calculations."[12]

After 1968, Hanoi declined to engage its regular forces in big battles and reverted almost entirely to small-unit guerrilla action for about two years. It was rebuilding its strength. American ground forces began to withdraw in large numbers in mid-1969. President Richard Nixon expanded the war into Laos and Cambodia with secret bombings and ground force penetrations, killing tens of thousands, but making no significant dent in Hanoi's will to carry on the fight. North Vietnamese leaders Le Duan and Le Duc Tho, two of the toughest negotiators in the annals of diplomatic history, ultimately obtained an agreement guaranteeing the withdrawal of all US forces from Vietnam by March 1973, while North Vietnamese units in South Vietnam were permitted to remain in place. If the South Vietnamese couldn't win with the Americans, they weren't likely to win without them.

In the spring of 1975, more than twenty divisions of PAVN troops invaded South Vietnam and crushed its army in one of the most lopsided campaigns in military history. President Gerald Ford refused to mount an American air offensive to halt Hanoi's rapid conquest of the South. The United States was done fighting in Vietnam. On the morning of April 30, a North Vietnamese tank crashed through the gates of the Presidential Palace in Saigon. Ho Chi Minh's dream of a united Vietnam had at last been realized, thirty-four years after it began in the little cave at Pac Bo, in the jungles of Cao Bang Province.

A few days before the end came, Major Harry G. Summers, a United States Army officer who had seen extensive combat in Vietnam and been wounded there, said to his North Vietnamese counterpart on a small team in Hanoi that was negotiating the final exit of Americans from the country, "You know you never defeated us on the battlefield." Colonel Tu of the People's Army of Vietnam responded, "That may be so, but it is also irrelevant."[13]

And so it was.

ACKNOWLEDGMENTS

In writing *Year of the Hawk*, I have drawn on the interpretive work of a great many historians, journalists, and soldiers. I'd like to single out here a handful of the authors whose work has been indispensable in shaping my thinking about the Vietnam War over the years: Harry G. Summers, Douglas Pike, Stanley Karnow, Michael Herr, George Herring, Neil Sheehan, David L. Anderson, Fredrik Logevall, Lien-Hang T. Nguyen, Vo Nguyen Giap, David Halberstam, Sir Max Hastings.

Thanks to the staff of the Brown and Columbia University libraries for all their help finding research materials. My editor, Colin Harrison, has been a constant source of encouragement and sound editorial judgment. His assistant, Emily Polson, is an organizational wizard who helped me sort out the photos, as well as the peculiar protocols of an editorial process utterly devoid of paper, which was a bit of a challenge for an "old school" author.

My friends and family have been very supportive of my longstanding fascination with the Vietnam War. Thanks to Todd Mennillo and Ursula Brandl; Pat Tracey, Tom Verde, Mark Sutton, Peter Cornillon, and the entire Ho family: Kay, Katarina, Lucas, and John. My agent and friend John F. Thornton is one of the great gentlemen of book publishing. We have worked together now on six works of history, and I depend upon his wise judgment and counsel in life as well as work.

My sincere, long-overdue thanks to Richard Schetman, my old friend and college roommate. More than forty years ago, when we were seniors at Brown, Rich insisted that I read *Dispatches* by Michael Herr. He thought it was an amazing piece of writing, one of the most evocative things he had ever read about war. I shared Rich's admiration for the book, and it kick-started a deep fascination with the American experience in Vietnam that remains with me today. And it was with Rich, too, that I first viewed one of the most extraordinary war movies in history, *Apocalypse Now*. Of course, we know a great deal more about the Vietnam War today than we did in the late 1970s, but both *Dispatches* and *Apocalypse Now* remain two of the absolutely indispensable sources of wisdom about the first war the United States lost.

A very special thanks to my partner Lynn Ho, who works long, long hours as a family medical doctor, but always finds time to help with computer problems, cooks wonderful Asian food, and tries to get me to go the gym. One day soon, I will go!

NOTES

Prologue: Strange Landing, Strange War

1. Quoted in Edward J. Marolda, *The United States Navy and the Vietnam Conflict, Vol. 2: From Military Assistance to Combat, 1959–1965* (Washington, DC: Naval Historical Center, 1986), 526.
2. Bundy memo quoted in Jack Shulimson and Charles M. Johnson, *U.S. Marines in Vietnam: The Landing and the Buildup, 1965* (Washington, DC: USMC, 1977), 7.

Chapter 1: Vietnam's Struggle Against French Colonialism

1. Christopher Goscha, *Vietnam: A New History* (New York: Basic Books, 2016), 21.
2. British visitor quoted in Max Hastings, *Vietnam: An Epic Tragedy, 1945–1975* (New York: Harper, 2018), 4.
3. French commander quoted in Stanley Karnow, *Vietnam: A History* (New York: Penguin, 1997), 119.
4. Ho Chi Minh quoted in James A. Warren, *Giap: The General Who Defeated America in Vietnam* (New York: Palgrave Macmillan, 2013), 36.
5. Revolutionary quoted in Hastings, *Vietnam*, 7.
6. Sophie Quinn-Judge, "Ho Chi Minh: Nationalist Icon" in *Makers of Modern*

Asia, Ramachandra Guha, ed. (Cambridge, MA: Harvard University Press, 2014), 91.

7. Giap quoted in Hastings, *Vietnam*, 13.
8. Fredrik Logevall, *The Origins of the Vietnam War* (New York: Longman, 2001), 16.
9. George Marshall quoted in George C. Herring, *America's Longest War: The United States and Vietnam, 1950–1975*, 4th ed. (Boston: McGraw-Hill, 2002), 13.
10. Ibid., 16.
11. George F. Kennan, "The Sources of Soviet Conduct," *Foreign Affairs*, July 1947, https://www.foreignaffairs.com/articles/russian-federation/1947-07-01/sources-soviet-conduct.
12. Ibid.
13. Full text of NSC-68 is available at https://fas.org/irp/offdocs/nsc-hst/nsc-68-4.htm.
14. Bernard B. Fall, *Street Without Joy: The French Debacle in Indochina* (Mechanicsburg, PA: Stackpole Books, 1961), 30.
15. Tran Do quoted in Hastings, *Vietnam*, 50.
16. NSC memorandum quoted in Warren, *Giap*, 122.

Chapter 2: The Origins of America's War

1. William J. Duiker, *The Communist Road to Power in Vietnam*, 2nd ed. (New York: Routledge, 2018), 213.
2. Fall quoted in George C. Herring, *America's Longest War: The United States and Vietnam, 1950–1975*, 4th ed. (Boston: McGraw-Hill, 2002), 77.
3. Kennedy quoted in Douglas S. Blaufarb, *The Counterinsurgency Era: U.S. Doctrine and Performance—1950 to the Present* (New York: Free Press, 1977), 53.
4. Wheeler quoted in Lawrence Freedman, *Kennedy's Wars: Berlin, Cuba, Laos, and Vietnam* (New York: Oxford University Press, 2000), 335.
5. Mike Gravel, ed., *The Pentagon Papers: The Defense Department History of United States Decision Making on Vietnam: The Senator Gravel Edition* (Boston: Beacon Press, 1971), 642–43.

6. Ball quoted in Fredrik Logevall, *The Origins of the Vietnam War* (Harlow, UK: Pearson, 2001), 45.
7. Official quoted in Freedman, *Kennedy's Wars,* 357.
8. Official quoted in Stanley Karnow, *Vietnam: A History* (New York: Penguin, 1997), 251.
9. Vann quoted in ibid., 278.
10. Neil Sheehan quoted in Clarence R. Wyatt, *Paper Soldiers: The American Press and the Vietnam War* (Chicago: University of Chicago Press, 1995), 100.
11. Neil Sheehan, *A Bright Shining Lie: John Paul Vann and America in Vietnam* (New York: Random House, 1988), 285.
12. Johnson quoted in Karnow, *Vietnam,* 390.

Chapter 3: Washington: The Complicated Politics of Escalation

1. Johnson quoted in Lloyd Gardner, *Pay Any Price: Lyndon Johnson and the Wars for Vietnam* (Chicago: Ivan R. Dee, 1995), 90.
2. Doris Kearns Goodwin, *Lyndon Johnson and the American Dream* (New York: St. Martin's, 1991), 177–78.
3. I have borrowed the term "war council" from the historian Andrew Preston's fine book *The War Council: McGeorge Bundy, the NSC, and Vietnam* (Cambridge, MA: Harvard University Press, 2006). Professor Preston tells me he adopted the term on the suggestion of another historian of the war, Fredrik Logevall.
4. Wicker quoted in Fredrik Logevall, *Choosing War: The Lost Chance for Peace and the Escalation of War in Vietnam* (Berkeley: University of California Press, 1999), 390.
5. Rusk quoted in David Halberstam, *The Best and the Brightest* (New York: Random House, 1972), 381.
6. Memo dated July 1, 1965. Johnson Library, National Security File, Country File, Vietnam, vol. XXXVII.
7. Johnson quoted in John B. Henry II and William Espinosa, "The Tragedy of Dean Rusk," *Foreign Policy,* Autumn 1972, https://www.jstor.org/stable/1147824?seq=1.

8. Warren I. Cohen quoted in Eric Pace, "Dean Rusk, Secretary of State in Vietnam War, Is Dead at 85," *New York Times*, December 22, 1994.

9. Halberstam, *The Best and the Brightest*, 581.

10. Reston quoted in Max Hastings, *Vietnam: An Epic Tragedy, 1945–1975* (New York: Harper, 2018), 147.

11. Bundy quoted in Preston, *The War Council*, 30.

12. Ibid., 37.

13. Kennedy quoted in ibid., 44.

14. Halberstam, *The Best and the Brightest*, 75.

15. Ball quoted in George C. Herring, *America's Longest War: The United States and Vietnam, 1950–1975*, 4th ed. (Boston: McGraw-Hill, 2002), 172.

16. Ball quoted in Preston, *The War Council*, 51.

17. Baker quoted in Halberstam, *The Best and the Brightest*, 435.

18. Ibid., 436.

19. Bradlee quoted in Robert Dallek, *Flawed Giant: Lyndon Johnson and His Times, 1961–1973* (New York: Oxford University Press, 1998), 5.

20. Clifford quoted in Brian VanDeMark, *Road to Disaster: A New History of America's Descent into Vietnam* (New York: Harper Collins, 2018), 206.

21. Bundy quoted in ibid., 207.

22. Halberstam, *The Best and the Brightest*, 457–58.

23. Johnson quoted in Dallek, *Flawed Giant*, 99.

24. Johnson quoted in Halberstam, *The Best and the Brightest*, 137.

25. Johnson quoted in Howard Jones, *Death of a Generation: How the Assassinations of Diem and JFK Prolonged the Vietnam War* (New York: Oxford University Press, 2003), 445.

26. Johnson quoted in Stanley Karnow, *Vietnam: A History* (New York: Penguin, 1997), 337.

27. Bundy memo quoted in David Kaiser, *American Tragedy: Kennedy, Johnson, and the Origins of the Vietnam War* (Cambridge, MA: Belknap Press, 2000), 379.

28. NSC paper quoted in Robert D. Schulzinger, *A Time for War: The United States and Vietnam, 1941–1975* (New York: Oxford University Press, 1997), 168.

29. Logevall, *Choosing War*, 270.

30. Mansfield quoted in VanDeMark, *Road to Disaster*, 41.

31. Brady quoted in "The River Styx," episode 3, in *The Vietnam War: A Film by Ken Burns and Lynn Novick*, 2019.

32. Adviser quoted in Karnow, *Vietnam*, 423.

33. Taylor quoted in Larry Berman, *Planning a Tragedy: The Americanization of the War in Vietnam* (New York: Norton, 1982), 36.

34. Bundy quoted in VanDeMark, *Road to Disaster*, 27.

35. Ibid., 224.

36. Bundy memo quoted in Lloyd C. Gardner and Ted Gittinger, eds., *Vietnam: The Early Decisions* (Austin: University of Texas Press, 1977), 197–98.

37. Ibid., 198.

38. Johnson quoted in Paul Hendrickson, *The Living and the Dead: Robert McNamara and Five Lives of a Lost War* (New York: Knopf, 1996), 149.

39. Johnson cable quoted in Logevall, *Choosing War*, 318.

40. Malcolm Browne, *The New Face of War* (New York: Bobbs-Merrill, 1965), 100–101.

41. Johnson quoted in Herring, *Longest War*, 153.

42. Full text of the Bundy memo can be accessed at https://history.state.gov /historicaldocuments/frus1964-68v02/d84.

43. Johnson cable quoted in Kaiser, *American Tragedy*, 407.

44. Ball memo quoted in Berman, *Planning a Tragedy*, 45.

Chapter 4: Creeping Toward Major War

1. *Lyndon B. Johnson: 1965: Containing the Public Messages, Speeches, and Statements of the President* (Washington, DC: GPO, 1966), 172.

2. Brian VanDeMark, *Into the Quagmire: Lyndon Johnson and the Escalation of the Vietnam War* (New York: Oxford University Press, 1995), 122.

3. Westmoreland quoted in Andrew F. Krepinevich, *The Army and Vietnam* (Baltimore, MD: Johns Hopkins University Press, 1986), 154–55.

4. US pilot quoted in Dana Benner, "The Battle of Dong Xoai," *Vietnam Magazine*, October 2018.

5. Westmoreland quoted in Graham A. Cosmas, *MACV: The Joint Command*

in the Years of Escalation, 1962–1967 (Washington, DC: Center for Military History, United States Army, 2006), 216.

6. Ibid., 236.

7. Thompson quoted in Fredrik Logevall, *Choosing War: The Lost Chance for Peace and the Escalation of War in Vietnam* (Berkeley: University of California Press, 1999), 22.

8. Editorial quoted in ibid., 399.

9. Greene quoted in William Conrad Gibbons, *The U.S. Government and the Vietnam War: Executive and Legislative Roles and Relationships, Part III: January–July 1965* (Princeton, NJ: Princeton University Press, 1989), 173.

Chapter 5: Hanoi Goes for Broke

1. Resolution quoted in William Duiker, *The Communist Road to Power in Vietnam*, 2nd ed. (Boulder, CO: Westview Press, 1996), 240.

2. Lien-Hang T. Nguyen, *Hanoi's War: An International History of the War for Peace in Vietnam* (Chapel Hill: University of North Carolina Press, 2012), 17.

3. Max Hastings, *Vietnam: An Epic Tragedy, 1945–1975* (New York: Harper, 2018), 150.

4. Bui Tin, *Following Ho Chi Minh: Memoirs of a North Vietnamese Colonel* (Honolulu: University of Hawaii Press, 1999), 33.

5. Ibid., 32.

6. Pierre Asselin, *Vietnam's American War: A History* (New York: Cambridge University Press, 2018), 89.

7. Thanh quoted in Robert K. Brigham, "Why the South Won the American War in Vietnam," in Marc Jason Gilbert, ed., *Why the North Won the Vietnam War* (New York: Palgrave, 2002), 109.

8. Westmoreland quoted in Edwin E. Moïse, *The Myths of Tet: The Most Misunderstood Event of the Vietnam War* (Lawrence: University Press of Kansas, 2017), 11.

9. Douglas Pike, *PAVN: People's Army of Vietnam* (Novato, CA: Presidio Press, 1986), 235.

10. Jeffrey Race, *War Comes to Long An: Revolutionary Conflict in a Vietnamese*

Province, expanded and updated (Berkeley: University of California Press, 2010), xvi.

11. Pike, *PAVN*, 216.
12. Ibid., 212.
13. Bui Tin, *Following Ho Chi Minh*, 40.
14. Xuan Vu quoted in David Chanoff and Doan Van Toai, *Vietnam: A Portrait of Its People at War* (London: Tauris, 2009), 79.
15. Malcolm Browne, *The New Face of War* (New York: Bobbs-Merrill, 1965), 33.
16. Trinh Duc quoted in Chanoff and Van Toai, *Vietnam*, 103.
17. Brian VanDeMark, *Road to Disaster: A New History of America's Descent into Vietnam* (New York: Harper Collins, 2018), 312.
18. US Army officer quoted in Hastings, *Vietnam*, 239.
19. Study quoted in ibid., 240.
20. See Andrew F. Krepinevich, *The Army and Vietnam*, 188–92.
21. Huong Van Ba quoted in Chanoff and Van Toai, *Vietnam*, 155.
22. American officer quoted in Michael Lee Lanning and Dan Cragg, *Inside the VC and the NVA: The Real Story of North Vietnam's Armed Forces* (College Station: Texas A&M University Press, 2008), 177.
23. Beckwith quoted in "The River Styx."
24. Webb quoted in Lanning and Cragg, *Inside the VC and the NVA*, 217.
25. Village chief quoted in Jeffrey Race, *War Comes to Long An*, 73.
26. Leaflet quoted in ibid., 96–97.
27. NLF member quoted in James W. Trullinger, *Village at War: An Account of Revolution in Vietnam* (New York: Longman, 1980), 99.
28. Vo Nguyen Giap, *The Military Art of People's War*, edited with an introduction by Russell Stetler (New York: Monthly Review Press, 1970), 169.
29. Ibid., 175–76.
30. Ibid., 259.
31. Samuel B. Griffith, "Introduction" to *Mao Tse-tung on Guerrilla Warfare* (Baltimore, MD: Nautical & Aviation Publishing Company of America, 1991), 7–8.

Chapter 6: Marines at War

1. Philip Caputo, *A Rumor of War* (New York: Ballantine, 1978), 56–57.
2. Jack Shulimson and Charles M. Johnson, *U.S. Marines in Vietnam: The Landing and the Buildup, 1965* (Washington, DC: USMC, 1978), 27.
3. Caputo, *A Rumor of War*, 89–90.
4. Al Gray, interview with the author.
5. Russell H. Stolfi, USMCR, *U.S. Marine Corps Civic Action Effort in Vietnam, March 1965–March 1966* (Washington, DC: USMC, 1968), 36.
6. Krulak letter to Robert McNamara, May 9, 1966, Xerox of original, in author's collection.
7. Neil Sheehan, "U.S. Marines Kill 600 Guerrillas in 2-day Battle," *New York Times*, August 20, 1965.
8. Otto J. Lehrack, *The First Battle: Operation Starlite and the Beginning of the Blood Debt in Vietnam* (New York: Ballantine, 2004), 104.
9. Petty quoted in Otto J. Lehrack, *No Shining Armor: The Marines at War in Vietnam* (Lawrence: University Press of Kansas, 1992), 41.
10. O'Malley citation in Shulimson and Johnson, *U.S. Marines in Vietnam*, 242.
11. Andrew Comer quoted in ibid., 77.
12. Civil affairs officer quoted in ibid., 38.
13. Lewis W. Walt, *Strange War, Strange Strategy: A General's Report on Vietnam* (New York: Funk & Wagnalls, 1970), 107.
14. Marine quoted in Otto J. Lehrack, *Road of 10,000 Pains: The Destruction of the 2nd NVA Division by the U.S. Marines, 1967* (Minneapolis: Zenith Press, 2010), 33.
15. US Army adviser quoted in Shulimson and Johnson, *U.S. Marines in Vietnam*, 103.
16. Ibid., 199.
17. Walt, *Strange War, Strange Strategy*, 113.

Chapter 7: The Big Buildup and the "Other War"

1. Bui Diem with David Chanoff, *In the Jaws of History* (Boston: Houghton Mifflin, 1987), 153–54.

2. Ross quoted in Al Santoli, *Everything We Had: An Oral History of the Vietnam War by 33 American Soldiers Who Fought It* (New York: Random House, 1981), 50.

3. Al Conetto, *The Hump: The 1st Battalion, 503rd Airborne Infantry, in the First Major Battle of the Vietnam War* (Jefferson, NC: MacFarland, 2015), 41.

4. Waller quoted in ibid., 48.

5. Harris quoted in ibid., 49.

6. Hutchens quoted in ibid., 66.

7. Al Conetto, "In the Beginning There Was the Hump" in *Vietnam* 27, no. 6 (June 2015): 30.

8. Bundy quoted in William C. Gibbons, *The U.S. Government and the Vietnam War: Executive and Legislative Roles and Relationships, Part IV: July 1965–January 1968* (Princeton, NJ: Princeton University Press, 1995), 73.

9. Malcolm Browne, *The New Face of War* (New York: Bobbs-Merrill, 1965), 91–92.

10. Quoted in Race, *War Comes to Long An: Revolutionary Conflict in a Vietnamese Province*, expanded and updated (Berkeley: University of California Press, 2010), xvi.

11. Eric Bergerud, "The Village War in Vietnam, 1965–1973" in *The Columbia History of the Vietnam War*, David L. Anderson, ed. (New York: Columbia University Press, 2011), 270.

12. Marc Jason Gilbert, "The Cost of Losing the 'Other War' in Vietnam" in *Why the North Won the Vietnam War*, Marc Jason Gilbert, ed. (New York: Palgrave, 2002), 164.

13. Neil Sheehan, *A Bright Shining Lie: John Paul Vann and America in Vietnam* (New York: Random House, 1988), 515.

14. Ibid., 524.

15. Bergerud, "The Village War in Vietnam," 279.

16. Browne, *The New Face of War*, 237–38.

17. William A. Nighswonger, *Rural Pacification in Vietnam, 1962–1965* (New York: Praeger, 1966), 145.

18. Ibid., 145.

19. Miller quoted in William Conrad Gibbons, *The U.S. Government and the*

Vietnam War: Executive and Legislative Roles and Relationships, Part IV: July 1965–January 1968 (Princeton, NJ: Princeton University Press, 1989), 65–66.

20. McNamara quoted in ibid., 107.
21. Nighswonger, *Rural Pacification in Vietnam*, 147, 227, 232.
22. Scotton quoted in Max Hastings, *Vietnam: An Epic Tragedy, 1945–1975* (New York: Harper, 2018), 248.
23. ARVN general quoted in ibid., 320.
24. Sullivan quoted in ibid., 268.
25. Bui Diem, *In the Jaws of History*, 156.
26. Stanley Karnow, *Vietnam: A History* (New York: Penguin, 1997), 459.
27. Frances FitzGerald, *Fire in the Lake: The Vietnamese and the Americans in Vietnam* (Boston: Little, Brown, 1972), 239–40.
28. Truong Nhu Tang, A Vietcong Memoir: An Inside Account of the Vietnam War and Its Aftermath (New York: Vintage, 1986), 59.

Chapter 8: The Air War and the Ho Chi Minh Trail

1. Bundy memo in Glenn W. LaFantasie et al., eds., *Foreign Relations of the United States 1964–1968, vol. II, Vietnam, January–June 1965* (Washington, DC: Government Printing Office, 1996), 175.
2. Ho Chi Minh quoted in John Morrocco, *Thunder from Above: The Vietnam Experience* (Boston: Boston Publishing Company, 1984), 96.
3. Ibid., 52.
4. Jacob Van Staaveren, *Gradual Failure: The Air War Over North Vietnam, 1965–1966* (Washington, DC: US Air Force, 2002), 72.
5. Pilot quoted in John Clark Pratt, ed., *Vietnam Voices: Perspectives on the War Years, 1941–1975* (Athens: University of Georgia Press, 1999), 196.
6. Ngo Thi Tuyen quoted in Karen Gottschang Turner, *Even the Women Must Fight: Memories of War from North Vietnam* (New York: Wiley, 1998), 59.
7. American pilot quoted in Morrocco, *Thunder from Above*, 58.
8. Robinson Risner, *The Passing of the Night: My Seven Years as a Prisoner of the North Vietnamese* (New York: Random House, 1992), 158.

9. John B. Nichols and Barrett Tillman, *On Yankee Station: The Naval Air War over Vietnam* (Annapolis, MD: Naval Institute Press, 2013), 52.

10. Halyburton quoted in Christian G. Appy, ed., *Vietnam: The Definitive Oral History, Told from All Sides* (London: Ebury Press, 2006), 222–23.

11. Ibid., 223.

12. Ibid., 225.

13. Ibid., 224.

14. Army general quoted in Brian VanDeMark, *Road to Disaster: A New History of America's Descent into Vietnam* (New York: Harper Collins, 2018), 305.

15. Ho Chi Minh's letter to the pope quoted in Mark Clodfelter, *The Limits of Air Power: The American Bombing of North Vietnam* (Lincoln, NE: Bison Books, 2006), 91.

16. CIA Report, "Impact of Operation Rolling Thunder on North Vietnam," January 14, 1966, Xerox of original in author's collection.

17. VanDeMark, *Road to Disaster*, 343.

18. Physician quoted in Stanley Karnow, *Vietnam: A History* (New York: Penguin, 1997), 450.

19. Max Hastings, *Vietnam: An Epic Tragedy, 1945–1975* (New York: Harper, 2018), 334.

20. Summers interview with the author, August 12, 1992.

21. Malcolm Browne, *The New Face of War* (New York: Bobbs-Merrill, 1965), 123–24.

22. Bui Tin, *Following Ho Chi Minh: Memoirs of a North Vietnamese Colonel* (Honolulu: University of Hawaii Press, 1999), 47.

23. Phan Trong Tue quoted in Karen Gottschang Turner, *Even the Women Must Fight*, 102.

24. Vo Bam quoted in *Vietnam Courier*, North Vietnamese propaganda document, May 1984, author's file.

25. Nguyen Mau Thuy quoted in Turner, *Even the Women Must Fight*, 96.

26. Ibid., 97–98.

27. Combat engineer quoted in ibid., 100.

28. H. Norman Schwarzkopf, *It Doesn't Take a Hero* (New York: Bantam, 1993), 132–33.

29. Ibid., 134.

30. John Waghelstein, author interview.

31. Army study quoted in Albert Garland, *Infantry in Vietnam* (Nashville, TN: Battery Press, 1967), 203.

32. John Waghelstein, author interview.

33. CIA officer quoted in Joshua Kurlantzick, *A Great Place to Have a War: America in Laos and the Birth of a Military CIA* (New York: Simon & Schuster, 2018), 262.

34. American pilot quoted in Timothy N. Castle, *At War in the Shadow of Vietnam: U.S. Military Aid to the Royal Lao Government, 1955–1975* (New York: Columbia University Press, 1993), 82.

35. Ibid., 81.

36. Kurlantzick, *A Great Place to Have a War*, 19.

Chapter 9: Domestic Politics and the Antiwar Movement

1. Johnson quoted in Fredrik Logevall, *Choosing War: The Lost Chance for Peace and the Escalation of War in Vietnam* (Berkeley: University of California Press, 1999), 145.

2. Bundy quoted in ibid., 217.

3. Ibid., 147.

4. Johnson quoted in Michael H. Hunt, ed., *A Vietnam War Reader: A Documentary History from American and Vietnamese Perspectives* (Chapel Hill: University of North Carolina Press, 2010), 76.

5. Johnson quoted in Logevall, *Choosing War*, 315.

6. Bundy quoted in ibid., 331.

7. Le Duan letter quoted in Hunt, *A Vietnam War Reader*, 74.

8. Vo Nguyen Giap, *Big Victory, Great Task: North Viet-Nam's Minister of Defense Assesses the Course of the War* (New York: Praeger, 1968), 56.

9. Charles DeBenedetti, *An American Ordeal: The Antiwar Movement of the Vietnam Era* (Syracuse, NY: Syracuse University Press, 1990), 65.

10. Godfrey Hodgson, *America in Our Time: From World War II to Nixon— What Happened and Why* (New York: Doubleday, 1976), 309.

11. *The Nation* editorial quoted in DeBenedetti, *An American Ordeal*, 102.

12. Thomas Powers, *The War at Home: Vietnam and the American People, 1964–1968* (New York: Grossman, 1973), 48.

13. Melvin Small, *Antiwarriors: The Vietnam War and the Battle for America's Hearts and Minds* (Lanham, MD: SR Books, 2004), 3.

14. *New York Times* headline quoted in ibid., 20.

15. DeBenedetti, *An American Ordeal*, 101.

16. Senate report quoted in ibid., 117.

17. Powers, *The War at Home*, 55.

18. DeBenedetti, *An American Ordeal*, 115.

19. Lynd quoted in Powers, *The War at Home*, 63.

20. Potter speech quoted in Xerox of a University of California, Berkeley, Teach-In pamphlet edited by Louis Menashe, Folkways Records, 1966, author's collection.

21. Bundy quoted in DeBenedetti, *An American Ordeal*, 105.

22. Yale faculty letter quoted in William Conrad Gibbons, *The U.S. Government and the Vietnam War: Executive and Legislative Roles and Relationships, Part III: January–July 1965* (Princeton, NJ: Princeton University Press, 1989), 267.

23. Robert Lowell letter quoted in Dwight Macdonald, "A Day at the White House," *New York Review of Books*, July 15, 1965, 19.

24. Hersey quoted in ibid., 21.

25. Johnson quoted in Powers, *The War at Home*, 66.

26. DeBenedetti, *An American Ordeal*, 121.

27. Powers, *The War at Home*, 109.

28. Gavin quoted in Gibbons, *The U.S. Government and the Vietnam War, Part IV: July 1965–January 1968*, 240.

29. Kennan quoted in Powers, *The War at Home*, 111.

30. Fulbright quoted in Gibbons, *The U.S. Government and the Vietnam War, Part IV: July 1965–January 1968*, 247.

31. Ibid.

32. Ibid.

33. J. William Fulbright, *The Arrogance of Power* (New York: Random House, 1967), 199.

34. Fulbright quoted in Powers, *The War at Home*, 114.

35. Pell quoted in Gibbons, *The U.S. Government and the Vietnam War, Part IV: July 1965–January 1968*, 249.

Chapter 10: The Big Fight in the Central Highlands

1. US Special Forces handbook quoted in J. P. Harris, *Vietnam's High Ground: Armed Struggle for the Central Highlands, 1954–1965* (Lawrence: University Press of Kansas, 2016), 4.

2. Vietnamese history book quoted in ibid., 305.

3. US Special Forces after-action report quoted in ibid., 313.

4. Charlie A. Beckwith, *Delta Force: A Memoir by the Founder of the U.S. Military's Most Secretive Special-Operations Unit*, reprint ed. (New York: Morrow, 2013), 67.

5. Ibid., 70.

6. Harris, *Vietnam's High Ground*, 330.

7. Kinnard quoted in J. D. Coleman, *Pleiku: The Dawn of Helicopter Warfare in Vietnam* (New York: St. Martins, 1988), 20–21.

8. Ibid., 19.

9. Kinnard quoted in ibid., 35.

10. After-action report quoted in Harris, *Vietnam's High Ground*, 354.

11. Harris, *Vietnam's High Ground*, 344.

12. After-action report quoted in ibid., 355.

13. Ibid., 357–58.

14. Colonel An quoted in Lt. Gen. Harold G. Moore and Joseph L. Galloway, *We Were Soldiers Once . . . And Young: Ia Drang—the Battle That Changed the War in Vietnam* (New York: Random House, 1992), 62.

15. Ibid., 72.

16. Ibid., 64.

17. Ibid., 75.

18. Miller quoted in ibid., 79.

19. Harris, *Vietnam's High Ground*, 383.

20. Dorman quoted in Moore, *We Were Soldiers Once*, 118.

21. Ibid., 118.
22. Ibid., 121.
23. Deal quoted in ibid., 122.
24. Hoang quoted in ibid., 145.
25. John M. Carland, *Stemming the Tide: May 1965 to October 1966* (Washington, DC: Center of Military History, US Army, 2000), 129.
26. Plumley quoted in Moore, *We Were Soldiers Once*, 155.
27. Setelin quoted in ibid., 164.
28. Herren quoted in ibid., 171.
29. Deal quoted in ibid., 176.
30. After-action report quoted in ibid., 172.
31. Diduryk quoted in ibid., 186.
32. Selleck quoted in ibid.,190.
33. Carland, *Stemming the Tide*, 138.
34. Shucart quoted in Moore, *We Were Soldiers Once*, 238.
35. Smith quoted in Carland, *Stemming the Tide*, 138.

Chapter 11: Aftermath

1. Westmoreland quoted in Edwin H. Simmons, "Marine Corps Operations in Vietnam, 1967" in *The Marines in Vietnam, 1954–1973: An Anthology and Annotated Bibliography* (Washington, DC: US Marine Corps, 1974), 71.
2. An quoted in Max Hastings, *Vietnam: An Epic Tragedy, 1945–1975* (New York: Harper, 2018), 285–86.
3. Ibid., 285.
4. J. P. Harris, *Vietnam's High Ground: Armed Struggle for the Central Highlands, 1954–1965* (Lawrence: University Press of Kansas, 2016), 399.
5. Westmoreland letter quoted in John A. Nagl, *Learning to Eat Soup with a Knife: Counterinsurgency Lessons from Malaya and Vietnam* (Chicago: University of Chicago Press, 2002), 157.
6. Vann quoted in Neil Sheehan, *A Bright Shining Lie: John Paul Vann and America in Vietnam* (New York: Random House, 1988), 317.
7. *The Pentagon Papers*, Gravel Edition, vol. III (Boston: Beacon Press, 1975), 576.

8. Tillson quoted in Nagl, *Learning to Eat Soup with a Knife*, 161.
9. Colonel quoted in William Conrad Gibbons, *The U.S. Government and the Vietnam War: Executive and Legislative Roles and Relationships, Part IV: July 1965–January 1968* (Princeton, NJ: Princeton University Press, 1989), 102.
10. Andrew Krepinevich, *The Army and Vietnam* (Baltimore: Johns Hopkins University Press, 1986), 154.
11. Bundy quoted in Gibbons, *The U.S. Government and the Vietnam War, Part IV*, 106.
12. Fall quoted in Dorothy Fall, *Bernard Fall: Memories of a Soldier-Scholar* (Washington, DC: Potomac, 2006), 219.
13. Philip Caputo, *A Rumor of War* (New York: Ballantine, 1977), 345.
14. Ibid., 324.

Chapter 12: Reflections

1. Carl von Clausewitz, *On War*, edited and translated by Michael Howard and Peter Paret (Princeton, NJ: Princeton University Press, 1984), 88.
2. Godfrey Hodgson, *America in Our Time: From World War II to Nixon—What Happened and Why* (New York: Doubleday, 1976), 238.
3. Ibid., 242.
4. This point has been made very persuasively by Fredrik Logevall in *Choosing War: The Lost Chance for Peace and the Escalation of War in Vietnam* (Berkeley: University of California Press, 1999).
5. Humphrey memo quoted in Fredrik Logevall, *The Origins of the Vietnam War* (Harlow, UK: Longman, 2002), 126–27.
6. Logevall, *Choosing War*, 411–12.
7. James T. Patterson, *Grand Expectations: The United States, 1945–1974* (New York: Oxford University Press, 1996), 600.
8. Johnson quoted in Gibbons, *The U.S. Government and the Vietnam War, Part II*, 393.
9. Kennan quoted in John Lewis Gaddis, *George F. Kennan: An American Life* (New York: Penguin, 2011), 593.
10. Johnson quoted in David Coleman and Marc Selverstone, *Lyndon B.*

Johnson and the Vietnam War, Miller Center, University of Virginia, 2014, https://prde.upress.virginia.edu/content/Vietnam.

11. Ford memo quoted in Gibbons, *The U.S. Government and the Vietnam War, Part IV*, 21.

12. Gabriel Kolko, *Anatomy of a War: Vietnam, the United States, and the Modern Historical Experience* (New York: The New Press, 1994), 335.

13. Harry G. Summers, *On Strategy: The Vietnam War in Context* (Carlisle Barracks, PA: US Army War College, 1981), 2.

SELECTED BIBLIOGRAPHY

Addington, Larry H. *America's War in Vietnam: A Short Narrative History*. Bloomington: Indiana University Press, 2000.

Anderson, David. *The Columbia Guide to the Vietnam War*. New York: Columbia University Press, 2002.

Appy, Christian G. *Patriots: The Vietnam War Remembered from All Sides*. New York: Penguin Books, 2004.

——————. *Working-Class War: American Combat Soldiers and Vietnam*. Chapel Hill: University of North Carolina Press, 1993.

Asselin, Pierre. *Hanoi's Road to the Vietnam War, 1954–1965*. Berkeley: University of California Press, 2013.

——————. *Vietnam's American War: A History*. New York: Cambridge University Press, 2018.

Bergerud, Eric M. *Red Thunder, Tropic Lightning: The World of a Combat Division in Vietnam*. Boulder, CO: Westview Press, 1993.

Berman, Larry. *Planning a Tragedy: The Americanization of the War in Vietnam*. New York: Norton, 1982.

Braestrup, Peter. *Vietnam as History: Ten Years After the Paris Peace Accords*. Washington, DC: University Press of America, 1984.

Carland, John M. *Combat Operations: Stemming the Tide, May 1965 to October 1966*. Washington, DC: Center of Military History, US Army, 2000.

Caro, Robert A. *The Years of Lyndon Johnson: The Passage of Power*. New York: Alfred A. Knopf, 2012.

Causes, Origins, and Lessons of the Vietnam War: Hearings, Ninety-Second Congress, Second Session, May 9, 10, and 11, 1972. Washington, DC: US. Government Printing Office, 1973.

Clausewitz, Carl von. *On War,* revised ed., edited and translated by Michael Howard and Peter Paret. Princeton, NJ: Princeton University Press, 1984.

Cosmas, Graham A. *MACV: The Joint Command in the Years of Escalation, 1962–1967.* Washington, DC: Center of Military History, US Army, 2006.

Dallek, Robert. *Flawed Giant: Lyndon Johnson and His Times, 1961–1973.* New York: Oxford University Press, 1998.

DeBenedetti, Charles, and Charles Chatfield. *An American Ordeal: The Antiwar Movement of the Vietnam Era.* Syracuse, NY: Syracuse University Press, 1990.

Diem, Bui, and David Chanoff. *In the Jaws of History.* Bloomington: Indiana University Press, 1999.

Dougan, Clark. *The American Experience in Vietnam: Reflections of an Era.* New York: Zenith Press, 2014.

Doyle, Edward. *The North.* Boston: Boston Publishing Co., 1986.

Doyle, Edward, and Samuel Lipsman. *America Takes Over, 1965–67.* Boston: Boston Publishing Co., 1982.

Duiker, William J. *The Communist Road to Power in Vietnam*, 2nd ed. Boulder, CO: Westview Press, 1996.

Elliott, David W. P. *The Vietnamese War: Revolution and Social Change in the Mekong Delta, 1930–1975.* Armonk, NY: M. E. Sharpe, 2003.

Ellsberg, Daniel. *Secrets: A Memoir of Vietnam and the Pentagon Papers.* New York: Penguin, 2003.

Fall, Bernard B. *The Two Viet-Nams: A Political and Military Analysis.* New York: Da Capo Press, 2002.

FitzGerald, Frances. *Fire in the Lake: The Vietnamese and the Americans in Vietnam.* Boston: Little Brown, 2002.

Foreign Relations of the United States, 1964–1968, Vol. II, Vietnam, January–June 1965 (Washington, DC: Government Printing Office, 1996).

Fulbright, J. William. *The Arrogance of Power.* New York: Random House, 1967.

Gardner, Lloyd C. *Pay Any Price: Lyndon Johnson and the Wars for Vietnam.* Chicago: I. R. Dee, 1995.

Gibbons, William Conrad. *The U.S. Government and the Vietnam War: Executive and Legislative Roles and Relationships, Part III: January–July 1965.* Princeton, NJ: Princeton University Press, 1989.

———. *The U.S. Government and the Vietnam War: Executive and Legislative Roles and Relationships, Part IV: July 1965–January 1968.* Princeton, NJ: Princeton University Press, 1995.

Gilbert, Marc Jason, ed. *Why the North Won the Vietnam War.* New York: Palgrave, 2002.

Goodwin, Doris Kearns. *Lyndon Johnson and the American Dream.* New York: St. Martin's Press, 1991.

Goulden, Joseph C. *Truth Is the First Casualty: The Gulf of Tonkin Affair: Illusion and Reality.* Chicago: Rand McNally, 1969.

Halberstam, David. *The Best and the Brightest.* New York: Random House, 1972.

Hendrickson, Paul. *The Living and the Dead: Robert McNamara and Five Lives of a Lost War.* New York: Alfred A. Knopf, 1996.

Herr, Michael. *Dispatches.* New York: Alfred A. Knopf, 1977.

Herring, George C. *America's Longest War: The United States and Vietnam, 1950–1975,* 4th ed. Boston: McGraw-Hill, 2002.

Hoopes, Townsend. *The Limits of Intervention: An Inside Account of How the Johnson Policy of Escalation in Vietnam Was Reversed.* New York: D. McKay, 1969.

Hunt, Michael H., ed. *A Vietnam War Reader: A Documentary History from American and Vietnamese Perspectives.* Chapel Hill: University of North Carolina Press, 2010.

Hunt, Richard A. *Pacification: The American Struggle for Vietnam's Hearts and Minds.* Boulder, CO: Westview Press, 1995.

Isaacs, Arnold R. *Vietnam Shadows: The War, Its Ghosts, and Its Legacy.* Baltimore: Johns Hopkins University Press, 2000.

Jones, Howard. *Death of a Generation: How the Assassinations of Diem and JFK Prolonged the Vietnam War.* New York: Oxford University Press, 2003.

Kaiser, David E. *American Tragedy: Kennedy, Johnson, and the Origins of the Vietnam War*. Cambridge, MA: Belknap Press, 2000.

Karnow, Stanley. "Giap Remembers." *New York Times Magazine*, June 24, 1990, pp. 22–62.

———. *Vietnam: A History*. New York: Viking, 1983.

Kolko, Gabriel. *Anatomy of a War: Vietnam, the United States, and the Modern Historical Experience*. New York: The New Press, 1994.

Komer, R. W. *Bureaucracy at War: U.S. Performance in the Vietnam Conflict*. Boulder, CO: Westview Press, 1986.

Lawrence, Mark Atwood. *The Vietnam War: A Concise International History*. New York: Oxford University Press, 2008.

Lehrack, Otto J. *The First Battle: Operation Starlite and the Beginning of Blood Debt in Vietnam*. New York: Ballantine, 2004.

Lewy, Guenter. *America in Vietnam*. New York: Oxford University Press, 1978.

Logevall, Fredrik. *Choosing War: The Lost Chance for Peace and the Escalation of War in Vietnam*. Berkeley: University of California Press, 1999.

———. *Embers of War: The Fall of an Empire and the Making of America's Vietnam*. New York: Random House, 2012.

———. *The Origins of the Vietnam War*. Harlow, UK: Pearson, 2001.

Mao Tse-tung. *On Guerrilla Warfare*. Translated by Samuel B. Griffith II. 1961; Urbana: University of Illinois Press, 2000.

McMahon, Robert J. *Major Problems in the History of the Vietnam War: Documents and Essays*. Lexington, MA: D. C. Heath, 1990.

McNamara, Robert S., and Brian VanDeMark. *In Retrospect: The Tragedy and Lessons of Vietnam*. New York: Times Books, 1995.

Military History Institute of Vietnam. *The Official History of the People's Army of Vietnam, 1954–1975*. Translated by Merle Pribbenow. Lawrence: University Press of Kansas, 2002.

Nagl, John A. *Learning to Eat Soup with a Knife: Counterinsurgency Lessons from Malaya and Vietnam*. Chicago: University of Chicago Press, 2005.

Neu, Charles E. *After Vietnam: Legacies of a Lost War*. Baltimore: John Hopkins University Press, 2000.

Nguyen, Lien-Hang T. *Hanoi's War: An International History of the War for Peace in Vietnam.* Chapel Hill: University of North Carolina Press, 2012.

O'Nan, Stewart. *The Vietnam Reader: The Definitive Collection of American Fiction and Nonfiction on the War.* New York: Anchor Books, 1998.

Palmer, Bruce. *The 25-Year War: America's Military Role in Vietnam.* Lexington: University Press of Kentucky, 1984.

The People of Vietnam Will Triumph!: The U.S. Aggressors Will Be Defeated! Peking: Foreign Languages Press, 1967.

Pike, Douglas. *PAVN: People's Army of Vietnam.* Novato, CA: Presidio Press, 1986.

————. *Viet Cong: The Organization and Techniques of the National Liberation Front of South Vietnam.* Cambridge, MA: MIT Press, 1966.

————. *War, Peace, and the Viet Cong.* Cambridge, MA: MIT Press, 1969.

Porter, Gareth. *A Peace Denied: The United States, Vietnam, and the Paris Agreement.* Bloomington: Indiana University Press, 1975.

Powers, Thomas. *The War at Home: Vietnam and the American People, 1964–1968.* Boston: G. K. Hall, 1984.

Prados, John. *The Blood Road: The Ho Chi Minh Trail and the Vietnam War.* New York: Wiley, 1999.

Preston, Andrew. *The War Council: McGeorge Bundy, the NSC, and Vietnam.* Cambridge, MA: Harvard University Press, 2006.

Raskin, Marcus G., and Bernard B. Fall. *The Viet-Nam Reader: Articles and Documents on American Foreign Policy and the Viet-Nam Crisis.* New York: Random House, 1965.

Record, Jeffrey. *The Wrong War: Why We Lost in Vietnam.* Annapolis, MD: Naval Institute Press, 1998.

Rotter, Andrew Jon. *Light at the End of the Tunnel: A Vietnam War Anthology,* rev. ed. Wilmington, DE: SR Books, 1999.

Santoli, Al. *Everything We Had: An Oral History of the Vietnam War.* New York: Random House, 1981.

Schulzinger, Robert D. *A Time for War: The United States and Vietnam, 1941–1975.* New York: Oxford University Press, 1997.

Shaplen, Robert. *The Lost Revolution: The United States in Vietnam, 1946–1966.* New York: Harper & Row, 1966.

———. *The Road from War: Vietnam, 1965–1970*. New York: Harper, 1970.

Sharp, Ulysses S. Grant. *Strategy for Defeat: Vietnam In Retrospect*. San Rafael, CA: Presidio Press, 1979.

Shulimson, Jack, and Charles Johnson. *U.S. Marines in Vietnam: The Landing and the Buildup, 1965*. Washington, DC: US Marine Corps, 1978.

Sorley, Lewis. *A Better War: The Unexamined Victories and Final Tragedy of America's Last Years in Vietnam*. New York: Harcourt, 1999.

———. *Westmoreland: The General Who Lost Vietnam*. New York: Mariner Books, 2012.

Spector, Ronald H. *After Tet: The Bloodiest Year in Vietnam*. New York: Free Press, 1993.

Summers, Harry G. *Historical Atlas of the Vietnam War*. Boston: Houghton Mifflin Co., 1995.

———. *On Strategy: A Critical Analysis of the Vietnam War*. Novato, CA: Presidio Press, 1982.

Tin, Bui. *Following Ho Chi Minh: Memoirs of a North Vietnamese Colonel*. Judy Stowe and Van Do, translators. Honolulu: University of Hawaii Press, 1995.

Turley, William S. *The Second Indochina War: A Concise Political and Military History*, 2nd ed. Lanham, MD: Rowman & Littlefield, 2009.

VanDeMark, Brian. *Into the Quagmire: Lyndon Johnson and the Escalation of the Vietnam War*. New York: Oxford University Press, 1995.

———. *Road to Disaster: A New History of America's Descent into Vietnam*. New York: Custom House, 2018.

Warren, James A. *Giap: The General Who Defeated America in Vietnam*. New York: Palgrave Macmillan, 2013.

Werner, Jayne Susan, and David Hunt. *The American War in Vietnam*. Ithaca, NY: Southeast Asia Program, Cornell University, 1993.

Westmoreland, William C. *A Soldier Reports*. Garden City, NY: Doubleday, 1976.

Williams, William Appleman. *America in Vietnam: A Documentary History*. Garden City, NY: Anchor Press, 1985.

Wirtz, James J. *The Tet Offensive: Intelligence Failure in War*. Ithaca, NY: Cornell University Press, 1991.

INDEX

Page references in italics indicate illustrations. "VC" refers to Vietcong, "JFK" refers to John Kennedy, and "LBJ" refers to Lyndon Johnson.

ABOUT THE AUTHOR

James A. Warren is a historian and foreign policy analyst. A regular contributor to the *Daily Beast*, he is the author of *God, War, and Providence: The Epic Struggle of Roger Williams and the Narragansett Indians against the Puritans of New England*; *American Spartans: The U.S. Marines: A Combat History from Iwo Jima to Iraq*, and *The Lions of Iwo Jima: The Story of Combat Team 28 and the Bloodiest Battle in Marine Corps History* (with Major General Fred Haynes, USMC-RET), among other books. For many years Warren was an acquisitions editor at Columbia University Press, and more recently a visiting scholar in American Studies at Brown University. He lives in Saunderstown, Rhode Island.